Printer's Devils

T0282962

Caitlin Press Inc.
3375 Ponderosa Way
Qualicum Beach, BC V9K 2J8
www.caitlinpress.com

Text and cover design by Vici Johnstone
Cover photo by Ron Verzuh; original artwork by Steven Skolka and Tyler Toews of Canadian Murals
Edited by Catherine Edwards
Printed in Canada

Caitlin Press Inc. acknowledges financial support from the Government of Canada and the Canada Council for the Arts, and the Province of British Columbia through the British Columbia Arts Council and the Book Publisher's Tax Credit.

Printer's devils : how a feisty pioneer newspaper shaped the history of British Columbia,
    1895-1925 / Ron Verzuh.
Names: Verzuh, Ron, 1948- author.
Description: Includes bibliographical references and index.
Identifiers: Canadiana 20220440565 | ISBN 9781773861036 (softcover)
Subjects: LCSH: Trail Creek news. | LCSH: Trail news. | LCSH: Canadian newspapers—British Columbia—
    Trail—History. | LCSH: Newspaper publishing—British Columbia—Trail—History. | LCSH: Journalism—
    British Columbia—Trail—History. | LCSH: Trail (B.C.)—History.
Classification: LCC PN4919.T733 T738 2023 | DDC 079.711/62—dc23

PRINTER'S DEVILS

How a Feisty Pioneer Newspaper
Shaped the History of British Columbia,
1895–1925

RON VERZUH

Caitlin Press 2023

Note on the Title

The *Oxford English Dictionary* defines a printer's devil as an errand boy in a printing office. Other sources expand the definition to mean a pesky gremlin who plays pranks, misspells words or even removes them when the printer isn't looking.

Note on Historical Context

Printer's Devils is a history of a certain time and place. It tries to reflect what readers of the newspaper saw in most editions of the weekly and how the editors reflected the prejudiced views of the day. I have attempted to show how the newspaper encouraged nativist bias against ethnic minorities, particularly Black and Asian people, but also against the Indigenous population and the Doukhobors, the immigrant Russian religious sect.

I have looked at the thirty-year history of the *Trail News* through a white person's lens and have used quotations from the paper to reveal an inherent racism. The editors followed the trends of their day and painted everyone but white people with a bias that would be intolerable today. Wherever possible, that bias is exposed and given historical context without resorting to euphemisms or extracting offensive language.

In the interests of explaining how Trail's working-class community were coaxed to see the ethnic community in a pejorative light, I have left the quotations about the "other" intact unless it was possible to make adjustments where the use of negative terms was superfluous or failed to reveal anything substantive about the paper's editorial policy.

A second note on context involves how the editors treated stories about women and girls. Again, their editorial opinions would be anathema to readers today. Women were often depicted as inferior to men and were objects of humour and derision. The editors saw their social role as protecting women from the evils of the times.

A final point: these editors were businessmen first. Their interest was in appealing to a merchant class that supported the paper and a readership that likely shared their views. They were part of a society that viewed anyone other than themselves as lesser beings. I do not support these racist and sexist views and I hope *Printer's Devils* helps readers reject it.

To my great-granddaughters Calliope and Diane with love and hope for the future

CONTENTS

"Reading this book is like listening to Ron tell a story—it makes you want to lean in and pay close attention. This highly detailed examination of the *News* over a 30-year period combines stories of the mundane (such as barn painting, recipes and home remedies for your ailments) alongside events of international importance and entertaining editorials on almost every topic. In our fast-paced world of instant communication and information overload, it provides a welcome visit to the past, where the weekly or daily paper was the sole means of connection with the world beyond your front door and local community."

—Takaia Larsen, Selkirk College, author of *Sowing the Seeds*

"From politics to enterprise, social standards and entertainment, *Printer's Devils* reflects the issues of the day—overt boosterism, rivalries with other towns and newspapers, and political views that consistently favour business interests and conservatism are routine. In contrast, they pilloried the Chinese people and Doukhobors, the labour movement and its leaders, anything socialist and women's suffrage. The book reminds us that history does indeed repeat, as with the anti-vaccination movements around the 1918 flu epidemic and subsequent smallpox episodes. It also confirms how much local interest we have lost with the transition from community-based news publications to the current consumption of media."

—Joey Hartman, BC Labour Heritage Centre

MAP

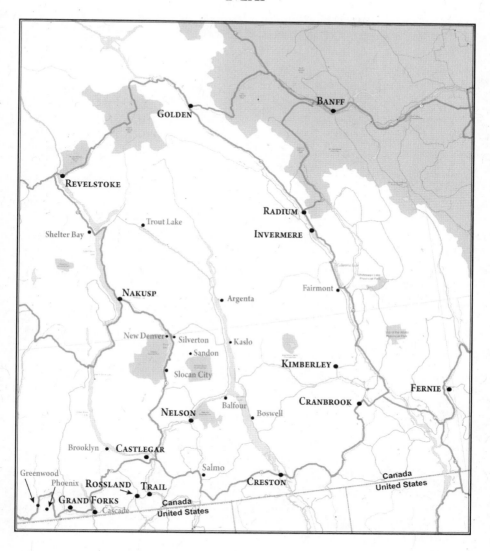

Banff

Golden

Revelstoke

Trout Lake

Radium

Invermere

Shelter Bay

Nakusp

Argenta

Fairmont

New Denver • Silverton • Kaslo
• Sandon

Kimberley

Slocan City

Balfour

Fernie

Boswell

Cranbrook

Nelson

Brooklyn • Castlegar

Salmo

Greenwood

Canada
United States

Phoenix Rossland Trail

Creston

Grand Forks

Cascade

Canada
United States

Canada
United States

Preface

"What's the Greek word for the number five?" Dad shouted from his worn-out old easy chair, his newspaper quarter-folded for a full view of the crossword puzzle. "I don't know," I shouted, to breach the hearing-aid barrier. "Maybe check your crossword dictionary?" Doing his local newspaper crossword was among Dad's favourite pastimes, but not just any crossword. It had to be his local newspaper's crossword. "It's the best," he would often say.

Actually, Dad had to wait to get his first crossword puzzle until the weekly newspaper in his hometown of Trail, British Columbia, finally became the *Trail Daily Times*. The *Times* would grow to be among the oldest continuously published newspapers in the province. But as we'll see, it was the *Times*'s parents, the *Trail Creek News* and then *Trail News*, that informed Dad's family and the rest of the isolated city as it entered the century that then prime minister Sir Wilfrid Laurier claimed would belong to Canada. The *News* served as their compass.

My grandfather was among the Croatian (Austro-Hungarian) immigrants that came north from the Montana mines and smelters to settle in the Trail area. He first arrived in North America in 1893. Seven years later, he migrated from his job as a labourer at the United S&R Company smelter in East Helena, Montana, to the West Kootenay, first to the Boundary Country at Grand Forks. The family would later settle in Trail, where Grandpa and three sons, Frank, Nick and Mike,

Trail Creek and smelter, ca. 1899. Courtesy Columbia Basin Institute of Regional History

Trail townsite, ca. 1897. Courtesy Moyie High House Museum

found work at the smelter.

Grandpa's time with the smelter ended after five years, and he eventually died of a lung ailment perhaps associated with the smelter workplaces at East Helena and Trail. Before succumbing, Grandpa was co-owner of the Victoria Hotel in Trail and later bought land in the area to plant an orchard. The weekly reported it all, including a front-page obituary. By then, Dad was working "up the Hill" and would log thirty-six years there. His older brother Frank was there for forty-four years. Their brother Nick died at twenty-six in an industrial accident in the 1920s.

Growing up in the Gulch, an immigrant enclave, the Verzuh kids would have had glimpses of the weekly newspaper that informed the small industrial community and guided the decisions of the smelter city's citizens. There were also other local newspapers, such as the three daily papers that were once published in Rossland: the *Evening Record*, the mining city's oldest, the *Miner*, and for a few years, the *Evening World*, a union-funded daily. But the *Trail News* was Trail's main source of local news, and it remained so until 1925 when it changed its frequency and became the *Trail Daily Bulletin* and later the *Trail Daily Times*.

Dad, his brothers and sisters, and the rest of the population of Trail, founded in 1901, learned about their city council's decisions, the guest evangelists at local churches, the latest offerings at the Star, Liberty and People's Preference Theatres, and the editor's opinion, usually pro-business and always supportive of the city's largest employer, the Consolidated Mining and Smelting Company of Canada (CM&S).

Back then, the weekly, all four pages of it at first, offered Trailites everything from bad poetry and a few complaining letters to announcements of a new sewing shop or the arrival of Victor, the world-famous accordionist. Grandma couldn't read English, so she couldn't take advantage of the recipes that appeared in the Home-makers' Corner. Opinion columns from far-off commentators, usually American, were lost on my illiterate grandfather; so were the sharp-penned critiques from the editor's desk. And there was no extra money to buy the miracle cures that appeared in weekly advertisements for Tanlac, Adlerika, Vick's VapoRub, and many more.

Like the citizens of any other small town, Trailites got their weekly dose of news, gossip, and entertainment from the local paper. In fact, the Trail paper was essential reading in some homes, for few of them subscribed to the big coastal papers, the *Vancouver Sun*, *Province* or *Daily World*. Dad probably glimpsed a page of the *News* in the lunch box of one of Grandma's immigrant boarders.

Like the rest of town, the Verzuh men were sports minded. Dad was interested in hunting, fishing, hockey, curling, lacrosse, boxing and wrestling, and the *News* covered them all. When the First World War began, news of smelter workers enlisting was prominently displayed. The death of a local man on the battlefield was reported, as were acts of bravery in the fight against "the Hun." Wartime propaganda filled the editorial page, and the promotion of food, fuel and beer restrictions made for regular reading. Deaths at the smelter appeared all too regularly as well.

Policies like the Prohibition Act, Alien Labour Act or Idler's Act were presented, explained, and supported or opposed by strong editorial opinion. Changes in labour laws were followed, as were CM&S rulings on wage increases and benefits. Local 105 of the Western Federation of Miners (WFM), predecessor to the International Union of Mine, Mill and Smelter Workers (Mine-Mill), was accorded a minimum of space, often buried in the "In and Around Trail" column. When the Mine-Mill local went on strike in 1917, the *News* provided coverage amidst editorials that promoted anti-union views.

Dad and his brothers and sisters were enticed by *News* advertisements to attend the local cinema to see silent films featuring screen stars like William S. Hart, Douglas Fairbanks or Charlie Chaplin. These actors were joined by Fatty Arbuckle, Lillian Gish, Mary Pickford and Pola Negri. Mutt and Jeff cartoons were a favourite of the Verzuhs as was the unionized live orchestra. They also saw promotions for the latest dance crazes and craved tickets to hear a local band playing at Swartz Hall.

In addition to a source of entertainment, the *News* offered new ideas and opinions tailored to local tastes, be it about a court case, school board decision or a meeting of the Board of Trade. The *News*, and later the *Times*, were how residents learned about their community, and it shaped how they looked at the outside world. They learned about anarchism and socialism, always from a negative perspective. They learned that capitalism was good and communism was bad. They learned that unions made workers go on strike just to serve the leadership's selfish ends and that a vote for a Conservative politician was a vote for a stable community and a more secure livelihood.

In short, denizens of the smelter city grew up infused with the news, sports and entertainment choices, editorial opinions, snippets of humour and the vision of their town that the six editors who ran the *News* from 1895 to 1925 shaped in them. They grew up knowing every move of their fellow citizens, whether it was a stagecoach trip to Rossland or a motoring adventure to Nelson, a sojourn in the US or an unwanted stay in the local jail.

Printer's Devils is the story of that weekly newspaper and the town it served. Hopefully, it will be a pathway into the pre- and post-First World War generation through the lens of those six country newspaper editors. All but one was American. All were men, quite conservative in political outlook and often anti-union. All were against the Russian Revolution as it fully embraced communism and transformed Russia into the Soviet Union.

As we'll see, all the editors were struggling businessmen who were dependent on advertising from other businesses. They knew it was in their interest to promote the town and saw it as their role to help wean it from rough mining camp to prosperous Interior city. Along the way, we visit the cultures, institutions, politics, and social lives of a working-class community not much different from other such communities in single-industry towns anywhere.

In a way, *Printer's Devils* is a celebration of a long-dead weekly newspaper that served a bygone era. Nowadays, Trailites are likely to get their news and entertainment from Facebook, Twitter, Instagram or TikTok. Still, there was nothing quite like reading the weekly newspaper's account of the drunken brawl on a Saturday night at the Legion Hall, finding out that a couple had eloped or cheering a young athlete on his or her way to the big leagues.

Printer's Devils is a look back at one weekly newspaper in one Canadian town, but it is also the story of all weekly newspapers. It is the tale of how the *News* influenced public opinion and how it tried to assist its readers as the town grew and prospered. It traces the editors of the weekly over twenty-five years with a view to identifying their backgrounds, editorial opinions and business priorities. *Printer's Devils* is a history of a dying institution in Canadian society as portrayed in one western industrial town. It is also an opportunity to vicariously visit the history of a Canadian town in transition.

It was fun to make that journey. I hope it will also be fun, informative, engaging and occasionally insightful for you as well.

Ron Verzuh
Labour Day 2022

INTRODUCTION

WELCOME TO TRAIL CREEK, CIRCA 1895

Once there was a boom town on the banks of the Columbia River in south-central British Columbia, and it was "filled with rough-and-tumble folks from all over the place." What one thing would such a pioneer town need "as badly as a saloon and a general store?" The answer: "It needs an official soapbox.... It needed a newspaper."[1] And that is what Trail Creek Landing (later Trail Creek and still later Trail) got in the fall of 1895, a weekly newspaper called the *Trail Creek News*.

Printer's Devils revisits the history of the pioneer weekly, capturing the personality, energy, civic-mindedness and sometimes civic blindness that came through its pages, guided by the country wisdom that each new editor brought to the smelter city's reading public.

Trail Creek Landing was typical of many immigrant-packed camps around the West Kootenay, a mountainous district a dozen kilometres from the Canada-United States border near Patterson, Washington. And yes, indeed, it needed its "official soapbox." An American newspaperman named William Fentress Thompson saw that need and filled it with the *News*. It would publish under that name until early in the next century, then undergo a name change to the *Trail News*. And if it did not always add a "touch of civilization" or a "sense of erudition," it certainly provided plenty of space for "pontification" in the boom town that had emerged with the building of a giant lead and zinc smelter on the banks of the Columbia River.[2]

When Thompson arrived, the great smelter's stacks loomed above the ramshackle group of makeshift hotels, saloons, general stores and other business ventures that would service the growing smelter workforce, some having migrated north with American smelter founder F. Augustus Heinze, also known as a Montana copper king.[3] Local entrepreneurs hoped their start-up businesses would serve the needs and interests of a growing population of miners and smelter workers from "all over the place," including a growing community of migrants from Italy and other southern European countries. The entrepreneurs, like Thompson, also hoped to make their fortunes, or at least their living, off mining and smelting families.

When Thompson arrived in Trail, he looked out over a ruggedly beautiful landscape marred only by the noisy construction of the smelter that would sustain both his newspaper and the town well into the future. Local historian Elsie G. Turnbull situated the Kootenay region where Thompson had chosen to settle: "With the Selkirk and Purcell Mountains at its center it is a great island of forest, ice and snow, often called 'The Switzerland of North America.'"[4] Elsewhere she cited the more prosaic view that Trail Creek was "a city of shacks on stilts, stuck in a hole in the ground."[5]

In her history of the West Kootenay, historian Mollie E. Cottingham described Trail as "a camp on the flat above the river." A flood in 1894 wiped out much of the camp, but soon it revived "as a stopping place worthy of development."[6] Historian Donald M. Wilson describes Trail House, "a rough two-storey'd cabin," as the cen-

Trail Creek News office with unknown group posing outside, ca. early 1900s.
Courtesy Trail Historical Society

trepiece of the boom town. It was home to Trail founders Eugene Sayers Topping, sometimes known as Colonel Topping, and Frank Hanna, "as well as serving as a church, meeting hall and hotel." Trail House, "Hanna's blacksmith shop and ore storage shed, and a few miserable shacks were all that welcomed travellers."[7]

Thompson, the first of Trail's printer's devils, saw the region in economic terms in the spring of 1896: "Trail possesses ten good hotels, eight saloons, four restaurants, eight general stores, one big hardware store, two meat markets, four barber shops, two news and stationery stands, one bank, one jewelry store, one drugstore, one tailor shop, two sawmills, two blacksmith shops, a big brewery, bottling works, one billiard hall, two real estate offices, two livery stables, several dray lines, churches, schools, post office, telegraph and telephone offices, one depot and a second soon to be constructed, one bakery," and on he went.[8] He was already proud of his new town.

The British Columbia Iron Works and the Mac Machine Works were operating by then. The British Columbia Smelting and Refining Company, the town's biggest employer, would soon install electric lights and a public water system. Heinze, twenty-seven years old, "a young man of vision, unbounded enthusiasm, determination, and resourcefulness," was among Trail's most influential business pioneers.[9] He was attracted to Trail after Colonel Topping, later to be called the Father of Trail, revealed the wealth hidden in the nearby mountain area behind Trail.

Topping's foresight in making an early and modest investment of $12.50 in local mines, particularly the Le Roi in nearby Rossland, drew prospectors to the region, and they would need the services of merchants setting up businesses along the "Bowery" and eventually on Bay Avenue, the "Broadway of Trail."[10]

They might not have seen the need for a local newspaper, but Thompson did. So did Heinze and Topping and his business partner, Frank Hanna.[11] Frank and his spouse, Mary Jane Hanna, owned Trail House, the town's first accommodation. For Thompson, the new town had plenty of financial potential, and with a population of about 1,500, there were plenty of subscribers to sustain a weekly newspaper. Heinze was good for a standing half-page advertisement about his smelter and other merchants followed his lead. They knew that with a lively newspaper to report its progress, the town would flourish. And it did.

Some early merchants were fly-by-night peddlers offering the latest household device or fashionable bonnet. Others sold snake oil and other supposed magic elixirs. Still others sought fortunes in the liquor trade, later battling prohibitionists and church lay people who saw the growing number of local hotel bars as dens of iniquity. Many of the new merchants and their clientele were Americans, like all but one of the *News* editors we are about to meet. First Nations people were thinning as gold hunters, merchants, and smelter workers migrated north to displace them. Immigrants were not plentiful yet, but over the weekly's life they would increase and feel the sting of anti-immigrant views.

The *News* Followed in the Tradition of Earlier BC Newspaper Pioneers

The *News* came about forty-five years after the *Victoria Gazette*, British Columbia's first newspaper, appeared in 1858 as the new British Crown colony was being established. And while Thompson brought some of his own pioneering entrepreneurial spirit to the task, the *Gazette*, publishing twice weekly and later five days a week, was first to present news that revealed "fascinating side-lights on the character of the people and enabling us to appreciate the conditions existing in a new country."[12]

The *Gazette* editor shared some of Thompson's characteristics. His desk, for example, was "a bundle of printing-paper skilfully poised upon a leather trunk, vibrating with each movement of the writer's hand, and compelling him to double up his person in the act of preparing 'copy' in a manner more curious than graceful."[13] Other early editors, men like Amor de Cosmos, who started his *British Colonist* at the end of 1858, would go on to other careers. De Cosmos became the province's second premier in 1872. Whether Thompson knew of it or not, archivist John Forsyth in his review of the pioneer press, mentions "a scurrilous little paper called *The Scorpion*." Published irregularly in New Westminster by "Josiah Slumgullion," it hoped to emulate *London Punch*, "containing political skits."[14] If Thompson needed models, perhaps this was among them, for the *News* would contain plenty of wit and sometimes downright silliness.

These scurrilous news sheets were members of BC's "once raucous and undisciplined newspapers, willing to tilt at any establishment windmill," as journalist William Rayner put it.[15] Here readers found "tomorrow's history text. Incisive and

— TRAIL. B.C in 1900 —

Early Trail with *News* sign. Courtesy Trail Historical Society

immediate (and sometimes wrong)." Here, too, they would see their memories preserved. "True, the news is raw, often incomplete or confusing, occasionally written in haste and usually blunt in its presentation." Nevertheless, here was "sometimes barely digestible and sometimes merely frivolous" news that "becomes the building block of history."

Rayner referenced the daily press as the "chronicler of history," but in Trail that purpose would be served for thirty years by the weekly *News*. Thompson and the pioneering newspapermen that followed him, printer's devils all, shaped the history of the province and, in this instance, a small corner of Canada that figured in the social and economic development of North America.

In the early years, it was not easy to get to the backwater mining camp of Trail Creek. But by the time Thompson and William K. Esling, who soon joined the staff as news editor, made the trek from Washington State to Trail, there was an ever-evolving transportation network that included railways, sternwheelers and wagon trains. "The movement of Rossland ores necessitated a rudimentary transportation infrastructure," historian Jeremy Mouat explained: "In 1892, the Washington [mining and railway] developer [Daniel C.] Corbin extended his Spokane railway [the Spokane Falls & Northern Railway] to Northport (Washington) and in the same year a wagon road was built to link Rossland to this line. A second wagon train was completed in 1893, connecting Rossland with Trail."[16]

Also integral to the nascent transportation network was the growing fleet of sternwheelers like the SS *Lytton*, the SS *Trail* and the SS *Columbia* that chugged along the broad, swift-flowing Columbia and adjoining Arrow and Kootenay Lakes. These river workhorses supplied goods to the mining and smelter camps of the region and shipped ore to smelters and metal markets.[17] The steamers would offer another source of news and advertising for Thompson and Esling as they played an increasingly important role in the building of the new town.[18] As the network matured, the *News* supplied readers with wagon, train and ferry schedules. Road and river accidents were a source of news as were city council debates on how to prevent drownings, collisions and other mishaps. Thompson and Esling anxiously followed the many railway projects underway throughout the ore-rich Kootenay district.

A decade before they arrived on the scene, the two major transcontinental railways had been completed. "The immediate result," historian Ronald H. Meyer wrote, "was a greatly increased accessibility to the Kootenays."[19] The Northern Pacific Railway line and the Canadian Pacific Railway (CPR) lines would provide reams of news copy for the weekly *News* bringing a flood of new customers and service providers. Also newsworthy was the constant battle to carry Rossland's raw ore to refineries. The Northern Pacific was poised to take it to southern smelters, the CPR wanting to transport locally smelted product to eastern Canadian markets. The rivalry would often play out on the pages of the *News* and other local newspapers. With the coming of the railways came public demand for a better communications system as well.[20]

By the early 1900s, Trail saw a limited increase in the number of telephones being used. Access to telegraphic services was also limited or expensive, preventing the *News* from advancing to the news-gathering capacity that was required for a daily. People living in the upstart smelter city had to rely on news exchanges for information on financial transactions tied to the town's main industry. The exchanges provided news about war, including the Boer War and the "Great War," and the ever-festering labour conflicts that were common to all mining communities in the northwest.

Readers of the *News* could agree or disagree with the editor's pointed political opinions on the editorial page, and they could always count on those opinions, often coming as boldly boxed items on the front page. The trend-conscious reader followed the latest social, fashion, and entertainment trends brought to Trail in the pages of the *News*. And always they could turn to their local weekly to boost their spirits about the future of a town built on hope and the ups and downs of the metal markets.

The *News* was overflowing with bombast, exaggeration, and "pontification," for sure, but it did generate a certain community spirit. As we will see, Thompson left town in 1898, but he left behind his printing equipment and enough of that spirit to sustain the rag-tag collection of residents and instill in them the belief that a future was to be had in Trail Creek.

The *News* Jumped into a Cauldron of Competing Newspapers

Thompson was not the first of the pioneer editors to ship an old Washington hand press to the Kootenays in hopes of making a living with it.[21] In fact, anywhere there was gold, silver, copper and other lesser metals, and people to extract it from the ground, there were newspaper publishers. The US provided several examples. "No citizen was more important to the mining camp than the newspaper editor," noted historian W. Turrentine Jackson in describing mining camps in Nevada. "The paper he published became the eyes and ears of the community recording daily events for posterity. His files became the primary source of information on the social scene, on economic conditions and political activity," wrote Turrentine. "His publication also established contact with the outside world advertising the glories of the isolated camp in metropolitan journals and, in return, learned of national and international events of interest to the hard-working miner."

It might be too much to claim for Thompson's News, but "some editors had the rare gift of making their newspapers the center of intellectual comment or the repository of local literary effort." Where Thompson and those that followed him fit the image best was that "more often than not the newspaper editor supported his community to a far greater extent than the local populace underwrote his enterprise."[22]

The Kootenay district saw its first newspaper six months before the Trail Creek News arrived when Eber C. Smith started publishing the Rossland Weekly Record on February 28, 1895. When it finally got on its feet, the local historian of the day, Harold Kingsmill, said it was "a very credible production, and spoke volumes for the stability and energy of the new town."[23] On March 2, 1895, the Rossland Miner appeared under the ownership of John Houston and C.V. Dake. David B. Bogle was the editor.

Houston, along with Charles Ink and Gesner Allen, started the Nelson Miner, arguably the district's first newspaper, on June 21, 1890, and Houston soon earned a reputation as one of the more combative newspaper editors in the Kootenays.[24] Perhaps most notable was the colourful report of a kerfuffle that pitted Houston against a CPR superintendent named R. Marpole. The CPR man called Houston, whose nickname was "Truth," a liar.[25] A melee took place that stands as one of the great spats in Kootenay journalistic history.

As Thompson reported the incident, Houston told Marpole to leave his office. Marpole refused to go, and called Houston a liar for the third time—and Houston hit Marpole over the head with a ruler, cutting a gash in Marpole's scalp. Marpole threw a dictionary at Houston, and then they closed with each other. Marpole possessed himself of the scissors, and tried to stab Houston, but the others present took the scissors away from him. In the melee Houston was 'biffed' in the eye and Marpole had the end of his finger bitten nearly off. Marpole had Houston arrested, and the editor paid a fine of $10."[26]

The feisty Houston betrayed the Nelson Miner in 1892 when he started the rival Nelson Tribune with C.V. Dake and W.J. MacKay. Houston was destined to become Nelson's first mayor.[27] Bogle, the "virile editor," as Kingsmill put it, started the Mining Review in September 1896 with A.R. Macdonald, but it lasted less than a year.[28] Eventually Bogle moved to a big city daily on the coast.

The *Rossland Miner* was initially devoted to mining news, the quantity of which allowed it to compete with Smith's *Rossland Evening Record*. In July 1895, W.A. Pratt launched *The Rosslander* as the third newspaper in Rossland, which at the time was a much larger and more developed city than Trail. It too was short-lived, lasting only six months. The local miners' union would also join the battle for readers and advertisers in 1901 with the *Rossland Evening World*, a "workingman's journal, framed particularly to protect and advance his interests," but also intended to deliver the news to a "city of busy workers."[29]

The men and women—and yes, there were some women—who launched the Kootenay pioneer press were cut from similar cloth to those who were more established members of the eastern Canadian press of the day. Men like Joseph Howe and William Lyon Mackenzie were the stuff of school history books, while the western tramp printers and frontier journalists of the Kootenays were often on the rough edges of that history. And yet, if those eastern "editors vied with politicians in vehemence of tone and wealth of expletive," the Trail pioneers quickly showed that they were made of the same stern stuff.[30] Perhaps they got their courage and spunk from "Colonel" Robert Thornton Lowery, the "newspaper editor, publisher, financier and tramp printer" who brought one of the first two printing presses to the Kootenay district.

When Lowery arrived in the Kootenays, he was possibly the first printer's devil to penetrate the mountainous region of BC's southeastern interior. His press was one of the "old American army models sent over the mountains by mule," local historian John Adcock explains.[31] The other belonged to Houston, who "used a rowboat to float an army press from Bonner's Ferry, Idaho, to Nelson, BC." Lowery started his first newspaper, called the *Petrolia Topic*, in his home province of Ontario, but sold it and struck out for the Kootenay silver district in 1893. "Buying a *Washington* press and metal type fonts he began his boomtown newspaper career at Kaslo," on the west shore of Kootenay Lake, Adcock writes. His first Kootenay newspaper was the weekly *Lowery's Claim*, but a fall in silver prices put an early end to it.

Meanwhile, more pioneer newspapers were about to be born in the Trail-Rossland mining district. They were part of the opening up of the mining West just as much as were the fur traders, prospectors, homesteaders, homemakers, Asian and European immigrants, and others. "Like the prospector, he was seeking paydirt," wrote local historian Turnbull. "In his case, however, this paydirt involved starting a periodical to extol the new town or mining camp and boost its prospects for success."[32] With that, Turnbull aptly described the pioneer editors of the *News*. Each editor brought his own blend of experience, motivation, political views, and civic duty to the newspaper. Each influenced readership perceptions of the local, national and international scene. And each took care not to alienate their most important clientele, the Trail business community.

Friendly and Not So Friendly Rivalry Existed among Kootenay Editors

Putting out a newspaper, even a weekly, was a demanding task for all Kootenay pioneer editors. True, they did not endure the weekly grind alone. Founding editor

Thompson once published a list of fourteen staff members, excessive perhaps, but every weekly required at least a typesetter, printer, and printer's devil (in this case a printer's helper). Despite having such help on the technical side, editing a country weekly could be unnerving. Often editors shared their particular frustration with readers, and often it had to do with unpaid bills.

Editors often railed against errant subscribers and, as an added cudgel, quoted others on the importance of the local small-town newspaper, partly as a generator of local pride, but more significantly as a nudge to advertisers, subscribers and news sources. "An editor should not be expected to know the names and residences of all your uncles, aunts and cousins, even if he should see them get off or on the train," cried one editor. "Tell us about it. It's news that makes the newspaper and every man, woman and child can be associate editor if they only will."[33] Another example from the *News*: "The local newspaper of the community is the economic physician to the community. It is the progenitor of prosperity and development's most ardent and forceful advocate." A town like Trail, or any other, could hardly be "considered to be on the map at all until it has its local newspaper."[34]

The *Penticton Herald* had this to say about the content of the local paper: "In the old time, John Smith was sure to have a letter to the editor on current topics every once in a while. Mrs. John Smith never forgot to have the visit of a friend from another community duly chronicled." Let's not forget Bill Jones, who "was

Moyie Leader office, ca. 1900, was one of the many weeklies publishing at the time. The *News* reported on their progress in the world of pioneer newspapering. Courtesy Moyie High School Museum

proud to have mention made of the repainting of his big red barn. Then there was that old crack about Ira Brown buying a buggy and the usual addition of 'Watch out girls,' or 'Ira must mean business....'"[35]

Colonel Lowery was perhaps the most acerbic of critics, but he defended his fellow editors. When the *Rossland Miner* changed to daily publication, Lowery praised the editor with one hand and insulted his readership with the other: "We admire an editor of brains and nerve, especially when he lives and moves amongst a community, largely composed of mud-brained people who cannot distinguish between a diamond and a hunk of country rock."[36] Apparently, the "mud-brained" included those who "strike for higher wages or shorter hours," Lowery continued. "While the war profiteers and the wage grabbers are plotting how to squeeze more money out of the meek general public, they just eat their mush and free publicity dope in silence, put another patch on their pants and keep on shoving the pen for the benefit of the hog-like world."[37]

News editor Walter B. Willcox, who bought the *News* from Esling, was only bested by Lowery in lecturing readers on how to submit news. "It is true that the average individual does not appreciate what is news and in consequence is unable to give any news to a newspaper and therefore keeps his lips sealed when asked if he knows any news," he instructed. "That is the case in Trail just the same as in… every other portion of the civilized world." Willcox then offers a list of thirty-three newsworthy events, among them, "Eloped," "Absconded," "Embezzled," "Cracked a safe," "Been arrested," "Robbed a house," and "Stolen a dog or a friend's wife."[38] Much earlier, he opined, "Some individuals seem to have an idea that the chief function of newspapers is to throw either brickbats or bouquets. And it is just that kind that would make the biggest sort of a fizzle of it if they were put in charge of the pen pushing end of almost any kind of publication."[39]

The editors were often easy on themselves and hard on others. When the *BC Federationist* appeared in Trail, the *News* censored it, calling the union paper a "radical socialist weekly… which promulgates doctrines tending to give comfort to the enemy."[40] The *Fernie Ledger* also took a battering. "A rumor is afloat in the Crow [Crow's Nest Pass] that the miners in that section will resurrect the *Fernie Ledger*—that weekly that had a fine plant and plenty of capital a few years ago but no brains."[41] When the miners made good on their promise, the *News* editor mused that "it remains to be seen whether the new-old Fernie publication can accomplish the almost impossible."[42]

Perhaps Willcox was chagrined that the *Ledger* could be revived when so many newspapers had succumbed. An active member of the Canadian Press Association, he attended its 1918 conference in Vancouver where he learned that forty-one BC newspapers had folded since the First World War began. "The average man is apt to think that the publisher of a newspaper has one sublime path of roses; that generally, he has an easy row to hoe and that he is in the habit of making loads of cash at any and all times." Not so, said the editor: "As a matter of fact, exactly the opposite is the case, as those in the business are only too painfully aware. Possibly no calling has been hit harder by the war—and yet there is no real complaint."[43]

The quest to make a living from their enterprise drove the Trail editors, and some succeeded for a time before passing along both the potential and the problems of publishing a small backwoods country newspaper. Many years before the *News* eventually went daily, some editors might have warmed to a series of articles in the *Saturday Evening Post* depicting the role of small-town papers. "Nobody ever heard of an editor having credit. He had to give plenty, though," wrote Frank Parker Stockbridge in recounting his early years as a country newspaper worker. "Subscribers paid up when they like it or not at all. Often as not they would pay in kind—garden truck, cordwood or eggs—and sometimes advertisers did the same."[44]

In recalling his experiences, Stockbridge was telling the *Trail News* editors' familiar story. "Gone are the whisky bottle and the corn-cob pipe," Stockbridge reminisced about the pioneer days of newspapering. Gone is "the ribald jest and the odoriferous spittoon which made the old-time country newspaper shop as picturesque and glamorous."[45]

In describing the profitability of the country newspaper, Stockbridge might have accurately portrayed some of the Trail editors. Certainly, Esling owned many properties as well as the *News* and the daily *Rossland Miner*. He also became a prominent member of the local elite. Thompson apparently earned enough profit to purchase the *Nelson Miner* and considered turning it into a daily. Others struggled to maintain enough revenue to make payroll. Clearly, though, they were not all as prosperous as the editors Stockbridge identified. They could also be seen as beholden to their corporate subscribers.

Thompson felt the wrath of the reading public when it accused him of being too close to smelter-builder Fritz Heinze. "The citizen," he scolded, "who is not of sufficient depth or breadth of mind to acknowledge that a newspaper of the people cannot speak well of an enterprising corporation or of a monied man unless it be subsidized or owned in whole or in part by such 'powers,' has the honest sympathy of the News in said citizens' mental misfortune."[46] Esling, the longest running *News* owner-editor (1898–1915), borrowed this view from an Illinois senator: "The editor in proportion to his means does more for his own town than any other man. He ought to be supported not because you happen to like him or admire his writing, but because a local paper is the best investment a community can make. It may not be crowded with great thought, but financially it is of more benefit than both preacher and teacher. Today editors do more for less pay than any man on earth."[47]

Arthur R. Babington, who edited the paper from 1907 to 1914 while Esling still owned it, regularly published views extolling the virtues of the weekly country newspaper. "Many people who have access to all the dailies, are often heard to speak slightingly of the weekly paper," he noted, but "they forget that the great daily cares nothing for the corner of the world in which you live and that it's the little home weekly that prints all your little doings just like you were 'somebody' and loves and boosts your corner of the world as nothing else does." The weekly, he concluded, is "a faithful friend."[48]

"Bab" also attacked those who thought they knew his job. "Bringing out a newspaper is an easy task," he wrote sarcastically. "An actor who never earned any other plaudit than a soft tomato or an over-ripe egg will give instructions in handling news." Mrs. Babington may not have appreciated him saying that "Any old lady with just sufficient knowledge to get on a street car backwards, had positive opinions on the way a newspaper should be conducted."[49]

James J. Clarke, replacing Babington as Esling's editor, joined the chorus of complaints against local businesses that did not advertise frequently enough. "Poor old Clulow, the shoemaker, used to complain that this paper was 'too small to wrap anything in,'" Clarke wrote. "He was right, but even so, it was larger than the businessmen of Trail wanted."[50] Willcox, as we've seen, often penned the most blistering complaints about advertisers' and subscribers' failure to pay: "An editor states that he works 365½ days per year to get out his paper—that's labor. Once in a while somebody pays a year's subscription—that's capital. And once in a while some dead-beat takes the paper for a year or two and vanishes without paying for it—that's anarchy. But later on justice will overtake the last named creature, for there is a place where he will get his deserts—that's hell."[51]

Elmer D. Hall did not immediately complain about the readers, subscribers and advertisers, but he soon warmed to the task. "If you ever feel like kicking because the paper costs four cents, just remember, please, how many folks and how much time it takes to prepare four cents worth of news, just for you to read," he exclaimed. "It takes a lot of knowledge about mystic things like slugs and human nature, to be a make-up man."[52] He also used poetry as his battering ram against disrespectful readers. Here's a disgruntled father:

He says there ain't a single thing in it worth while to read,
And that it doesn't print the kind of stuff the people need.
He tosses it aside and says it's strictly on the bum—
But you ought to hear him holler when the paper doesn't come.[53]

Gallows humour was also used: "An editor was murdered in Arkansas the other day and the murderer was sentenced to 99 years in prison, while a fellow that killed a lawyer got off with seven years. Prospective murderers take notice."[54]

Shining through all the carping and whining was a dedication to delivering the local news. The editor shoulders the "greatest responsibility" at a country newspaper, according to a pamphlet designed to improve local newspapers. "One of the qualities necessary to make a good newspaper is news," it counselled, "plenty of real, honest country news that interests everyone—church news, school news, sporting news, town news, social news, and every other kind of local news."[55] Trail's editors mostly followed this rule.

Founding editor Thompson and those that followed him were part of a fraternity of "large personalities, unafraid to strongly voice unpopular opinions."[56] Thompson was also unique in that his spouse, Martha, a capable newswoman and compositor, joined him, along with an adopted son who knew his way around a printing press at an early age, a true printer's devil. Neither left nor right politically,

Thompson viewed the job mainly as a booster for a town dependent on what miners could extract from the surrounding mountains.

Esling was also a booster, but he took a serious interest in local real estate. Another Washington State "hustler," as Thompson called him, he would fit the mould of "independent printers" who would feed "a growing market for political debate."[57] Unlike his former boss, he remained a bachelor throughout his life. Like Thompson, though, he lacked compassion for the Asian immigrant community in Trail and was adamant that members of the Doukhobor sect from Russia should leave town. After fifteen years at the helm of the *News*, he embraced political life, running and winning election after election from 1920 in the provincial legislature to sitting in the federal Parliament from 1925 to 1945. He revealed his political leaning early as a Conservative and never faltered from supporting his party in the *News*.

Babington, the only Canadian-born *News* editor, later revealed that he was a Liberal Party supporter, but with Esling as his boss, there was no sign that his editorial policy shifted from Esling's Conservative preference. In fact, there were few editorials during his editorship to indicate where he stood on any political issue, and the paper suffered for it through its blandness and lack of personality. Like Esling, he was an active Freemason. Unlike Esling, he was married and eventually sired several children. He also chaired the school board and participated in some local sports. Clarke also joined the staff under Esling and followed his dictates regarding political allegiance.

Willcox bought the paper in 1915 and turned the lacklustre weekly into a sprightly news machine with a busy editorial page that did not shy from criticizing city council. He also increased the number of pages—it had lingered at four for years—and he improved the design. According to Willcox, he also increased his readership by 20 per cent. What also increased was the quantity of paid advertising, and Willcox, like no previous editor, put extra effort into chastising local businesses that failed to advertise in his paper.

The last of the *News* editors, Elmer D. Hall cut his editor's teeth on several Kootenay newspapers before buying the Trail paper from Willcox in 1919. More than any of his predecessors, he saw himself as the moral compass of the community. Young girls were advised to stay at home and become mothers and homemakers. Young men were told to get a job and hold it. Trade unions were chastened for threatening to strike or for joining the One Big Union (OBU) or the Industrial Workers of the World (IWW). Socialists, Communists and anarchists should be deported. The smelter owner was seldom criticized.

Style, Consistency and Reliability Were Not Always Hallmarks of the *News*

Not all of the *News* editors brought style, flair and imagination to their writing and editing. Thompson displayed some of those qualities, but others, like Esling, used the paper as a political propaganda tool or business promotional sheet. Still others, like Willcox and Hall, brought a raconteur's style to their newspapers. Perhaps they had learned at the hearth of flamboyant men like Lowery and Houston or pioneer Nelson editor David Mark Carley of the *Nelson Economist*, published from 1899 to 1906. "These writers included visceral, poignant or funny details not typically covered in a news report," writes Sean Arthur Joyce. Lowery, for example, with his "acerbic sense of humour, draws us to him, his impatience to get on, his cursing at the mud, his eagerness to collapse for the night in grateful exhaustion in a rough-sawn hotel."[58]

Lowery and Houston "understood the vital role of journalism in holding politicians and corporations to account," writes Joyce. But not all Kootenay newspaper proprietors shared this view, least of all those that ran the *Trail Creek News* and *Trail News*. They were business boosters and their constant boosterism was not purely altruistic; they needed the town to survive so that their newspaper could continue earning them a basic living. Many did not succeed. The *News* was an exception. Perhaps this was due mostly to editors like Willcox who spent much space coaxing, guilting, and cajoling business owners to support his enterprise with ads.

Most of the Trail editors saw their job as supplying their business audience of prospectors, mine owners, smelter managers and backcountry hotel-keepers with the latest comings and goings, including the latest rumour about a gold strike or a sound investment opportunity. They were often in constant debt and forced to work year-round to keep their publications afloat. They knew that their bread and butter depended on how well they covered mining, smelting, transportation and communications developments. The Kootenay papers provided links to the outside world and announced technical innovations of benefit to mines and their owners. Occasionally, the miners and muckers (shovellers) who pried ore from the mountains were briefly mentioned, but usually it occurred when one was injured in a workplace accident or threatened to strike.

"Beyond mining, there [was] a sprawling array of information about shop and hotelkeepers, churches, social events, principal entertainments, and local politics," the late BC geographer Cole Harris explained, but getting outside information in a remote area like the Kootenay district wasn't easy. "The telegraph, which arrived in the summer of 1893, was expensive and unreliable," wrote Harris. "Postal deliveries, initially by pack train, opened the door to personal correspondence as well as to commercial and political news, but most people… had nothing to do with the telegraph and little more with the mail," continued Harris. "Their connections were largely oral," leaving an "ample place for newspapers."[59]

Some of the *News* editors took their civic duty more seriously than others, joining local service clubs, offering editorial advice and engaging in local sports events and clubs. But the *News* was first and foremost a business and its owners were in business to make money. Judging from the real estate holdings of some of them, the paper was highly successful.

What to Expect From *Printer's Devils*

Printer's Devils offers a perspective on what the *News* covered and how it covered it. Differences in how each editor used his news judgment and the application of the general editorial policy reveal consistencies, inconsistencies, and more importantly, the evolution of editorial policy over time. The book provides a glimpse of a wide-ranging selection of articles that testify to the scope and breadth of the coverage area. The reader interested in small-town history, particularly single-industry towns, and the mining and smelting industry in western North America will find the plethora of items cited here stimulating and hopefully useful. For the general reader, less interested in tracking such a huge variety of items, several overarching themes emerge.

Despite playing such a notable role in taming BC's version of the Wild West, Kootenay press pioneers have received little recognition outside Canadian printing and publishing circles. These printer's devils and tramp printers have been relegated to the periphery and receive only brief mentions, if any at all, and yet they struggled to earn their place in the history of Canadian journalism.[60] *Printer's Devils* hopefully serves as one corrective.

This is a book about Trail's pioneer days as seen through the news and editorial columns of the *Trail News*. Through its pages, we meet the men and women who embraced the pioneering spirit of the mining West. We read about their driving ambitions, courage, civic duty, and sometimes, their sheer greed. We witness the town's setbacks and its successes, watch events unfold as the rugged mining camp slides from boom town to the "Metallurgical Mecca of Canada," and finally becomes a First World War producer of war essentials like lead and zinc.[61] We vicariously mourn the tragedy of family members killed at work or at war or yet another child drowned in the Columbia River. We even witness the odd murder. The *News* was there to cover it all.

Printer's Devils plays a double role, first as a social history and second as a history of country journalism as practised at the *Trail Creek News* and *Trail News*. Eventually the paper would become the present-day *Trail Daily Times*, where this story will end. How it got there is a tale of intrigue, with a rough-hewn cast of characters, and an astonishing level of optimism. It is an account of Trail's political development, its citizens' voyage from conservatism to social democracy, and its slow evolution from nativism to tolerance.

Along the way, we see the story of pioneer capitalist entrepreneurs, the migration of thousands of workers, and the resulting class struggle that started with the building of the smelter in 1895 and that still informs the Kootenay region today. This is a story of one small country weekly's attempt to record the first draft of Trail's history with all its mistakes, biases, prejudices, and idiosyncrasies. It is a Canadian story that celebrates a special corner of the past as the country moved step by step into the twentieth century.

1–TRAIL CREEK NEWS (1895–1898)

"WRONG FONT" THOMPSON MEETS THE MONTANA COPPER KING[62]

A Down-On-His-Luck American Launches a Canadian Boom Town's First Newspaper

In the fall of 1895, Trail Creek Landing was teeming with prospectors and ragged-trousered industrial workers who had rushed to the British Columbia mining boom camp in hopes of either striking it rich in the ore-laden hills of the West Kootenay district or finding a job at the new smelter due to open the following year. Eventually joining them would be fortune-seekers of another kind, including bakers, brewers, launderers, hoteliers, restaurateurs and, of course, several practitioners of the world's oldest profession. Among the flood of newcomers was a thirty-year-old pioneering newspaperman named William Fentress Thompson—Trail Creek's first printer's devil. Thompson would seek his riches not in the local mines but by starting "the only home-print newspaper in the Kootenay country!"[63]

Thompson hailed from a breed of mostly men sometimes called "tramp" printers or publishers who swept across the Canada-US border in the late 1880s and 1890s in search of boom towns where they could set up shop. They represented the independent entrepreneurial energy that arrived in many West Kootenay district settlements as the new camps struggled to survive. Thompson was among the pioneering spirits that played a special role in opening up the mining West. Whatever his reasons, Thompson embraced the challenge, as did those that followed him as Trail's pioneer newspaper editors. This is the story of Thompson of the *Trail Creek News*.

Like those who came to the region before him, Thompson spied a journalistic business opportunity and set about founding a four-page weekly newspaper to "be published in the interests of the Trail Creek mining region." He added that it would also be "for the financial advancement of its proprietor."[64] This was perhaps the greater motivator, for a few months before plunging into his new enterprise, Thompson had suffered a substantial financial loss. He was then the editor of the daily *Independent* in Sprague, Washington. On August 3, 1895, fire destroyed the town, including the *Independent* building. Thompson salvaged a printing press and two cases of type and somehow managed to publish a final edition. But he was not insured and lost $2,000 to the fire. It's not clear why he chose to steer north into Canada after disaster struck. Perhaps it was the steady news of gold, silver and copper strikes in the West Kootenay district near the Washington border with BC. He would need to raise enough money to finance the trip, and he would need cash to start up a new paper.

Trail Creek founder Colonel Eugene Sayers Topping, another American, must have greeted Thompson with open arms. Topping, a frontiersman, mining investor and eventually Trail's first mayor, had struck it rich early in the decade, turning a paltry investment of $12.50 in the Le Roi Mine at nearby Rossland into a small fortune overnight. By a lucky break, he acquired what would become one of the most valuable mining assets in the district and beyond.[65] Topping had used his new wealth to purchase land at Trail Creek, and he and business partner Frank Hanna welcomed the prospect of a newspaper. Topping and Thompson also shared a literary bent, Topping having published a history of Yellowstone country in Montana in 1888.[66] Both men knew that a newspaper could help promote the start-up of needed new businesses and bring new investors.

Another welcoming individual at Trail Creek was Butte, Montana, copper king Frederick "Fritz" Augustus Heinze. Thompson would have read the telegraphic service news stories about the precocious million-

Smelter founder F. Augustus Heinze. Courtesy Trail Historical Society

aire before he arrived earlier the same year. Soon Thompson was reporting on the twenty-six-year-old mining *wunderkind* and his building of "a noble structure that is rising foot by foot on the brow of the hill overhanging the beautiful town of Trail."[67] The structure was hardly noble but the metal processing smelter would soon dominate the new town physically and economically. Thompson, four years his senior, would become "a great supporter of Heinze."[68]

Soon the new smelter would be refining ore on the shores of the Columbia River, and Thompson envisaged that the resulting crop of local businesses would need a place to advertise. Heinze was among those with the deepest pockets. His own experience had taught him that a newspaper could be of value in promoting business for his British Columbia Mining and Smelting Company. Young Heinze would prove adept at buying newspapers to promote his business interests, and he would soon invest in several newspapers to fend off his business enemies.

Given his substantial loss in the Sprague fire, it was unclear how Thompson would finance his new venture. He might have borrowed the money, but he had little collateral. He also could have secured advertising contracts to use in negotiating a bank loan, although he had limited time between arriving in town and issuing his first edition. Could he have won it in a poker game? He liked playing, but was it realistic to expect his winnings could finance such an enterprise?

Somehow he overcame the financial obstacles. Years later, his plant foreman, Loss Bernard, shared some insights into Thompson's views on money.[69] "He didn't have the faintest idea of what a dollar was worth," he told Thompson biographer Paul Solka Jr. "No accounting system meant anything to him. He was a marvellously effective promoter and fund raiser, but not a good businessman." Loss, whom the Thompson family had informally adopted in Sprague, added, "To him a business was just as much a gamble as a card game, and it never bothered him to lose at either."[70]

Fortunately, Thompson was also "a born promoter and a mighty fine solicitor for himself as well as any cause he espoused," Bernard added.[71] Furthermore, he enjoyed a major business asset in the form of his marriage to Martha Lavinia Caton, the first of his three spouses. She was the daughter of Judge Nathan T. Caton, a respected member of the Washington State legislature, a relationship that might have placed Thompson in a more respectable light with regard to advertisers. As Trail Creek's first newspaper editor, he could also count on Martha to provide her skills as a compositor (typesetter), presumably for free. One press report called her "an equally able 'newspaper man'."[72] As Thompson noted in his first edition, "Mrs. Thompson is thoroughly conversant with everything connected with a printing office and will assist her husband in getting out the *News* in the future."[73]

Long before meeting Thompson and making the difficult voyage to the Kootenays, Martha had been married twice, first to Robert E. Leete in 1877. Leete died, and in 1884, she married Frank M. Gray, the owner of the *Davenport Times*, where Thompson worked for a time. As Mrs. Lavinia Gray, she had played an active political role, running for election as Lincoln County assessor and superintendent of schools. In 1889, she sued for divorce on grounds of cruelty and adultery and resumed using her maiden name. About 1892, she married Thompson while he was starting the *Westport World*.[74] Born in 1857, she was Thompson's senior by six years.

In early fall 1895, the Thompsons set out from Sprague, about two hundred kilometres southwest of Trail Creek, following in the footsteps of earlier tramp publishers. Thompson had no doubt read news reports of fellow Americans trekking through the Selkirk and Purcell mountain ranges that stretch north of the international boundary not far from the gold, silver and copper El Dorado of Rossland. But a game leg from an injury during a baseball game would prevent Thompson from doing any tramping. He would use a cane for the rest of his life.[75] Still, he and Martha must have been excited about their prospects, unknown though they were at this point. They were probably also flat broke.

The nascent network of railways was the couple's likely transport to the Kootenay district. Although rail passenger service was still limited in the region's borderlands, the Thompsons could have taken Canadian-born James Jerome Hill's Great Northern Railway to Spokane from the temporary station at Sprague (fire had destroyed it, too), then connected with Daniel C. Corbin's Spokane Falls & Northern Railway to Northport, a future smelter town itself. From Northport, the Thompsons could go the rest of the way "by riverboat" on the sternwheeler SS *Lytton*, which had started plying the Columbia River by the summer of 1890.[76] The couple's lives were about to take a new turn. Whether for better or worse they did not know.

Thompson came to Trail Creek with no shortage of skills as a writer and printer. Born at Reed City, Michigan, in 1863, he was soon exploring his prospects in the newspapering world. His father worked in the lumber industry and "attained

"Wrong Font" Thompson as a young man on arrival at Trail in 1895. Courtesy Trail Historical Society

a healthy financial standing in the community," but young William showed no interest in following in his father's footsteps. He attended school in Michigan, but "it is unlikely that he was exposed to the rigors of secondary schooling," notes Solka.[77] While still in his teens, he meandered to the Deep South from Michigan, then west via Arizona, where he picked up his basic writing and printing skills. He worked in San Francisco, then moved to Utah, where he became a newspaper publisher for a short time. After Utah, he landed in Sprague.

Before migrating to Trail Creek, Thompson, possibly sporting a bushy black beard that later became a goatee, had already had a lengthy journalistic career. He was a "jaunty man," wrote Trail historian Elsie G. Turnbull, and he "proved full of energy." His first domestic use of that energy was to use "a shovel, an axe and a hatchet" to construct a "shack, primitive but adequate" on Spokane Street to house his newspaper and double as a matrimonial home for him and Martha.[78] It was a "house of poles, built in the middle of a very stumpy street, with no windows or doors," Thompson later wrote.[79] In true pioneer style, "A latch string secured the door." To open a window, "a board was removed from the side wall" and "to replenish the stove Thompson reached out and tore down a small sapling."[80] Then he turned his energies to producing the first edition of his new paper.

News Is Born, Editor Is Sober, A Chorus of Praise, "Balm to the Nostrils" in 1895

Like many pioneer printers, Thompson used a Washington hand press, possibly one he had salvaged from the Sprague fire, to accomplish the task, and on October 19, 1895, using borrowed wrapping paper from a grocery store, the first edition appeared.[81] He apologized for the inconvenience, saying the *News* "did not expect to greet you in its initial number with clothes on that would look better encircling a yard of calico."[82] The *Victoria Daily Colonist* reported that he blamed "the paper house at Spokane, which, while claiming to sell the majority of the paper in the Kootenay district, yet knows not enough to send a certified invoice with the package, that it may be gotten through customs office at Trail."[83]

Thompson began his journalistic career in 1879 at the Howard City *Snorter*, his Michigan high school newspaper, when he was fourteen years old. He went on to be "editor, manager, and pressman" at the *Lincoln County Times* in 1888, coming from the *Spokane Review* to Davenport. Earlier, he had published "a sporting, society, and dramatic weekly of his own in Tacoma." He also started a daily at Westport-on-the-Sea, where he claimed to have organized the first county press association in Washington State.[84] At Sprague, he not only ran the *Independent*, but also the *Lincoln County Farmer* and the *Lincoln County Democrat*.

He had suffered from alcoholism during those years, but claimed to have gone sober after taking the Keeley Cure before arriving in Trail Creek.[85] Whether he had beaten the affliction or not, his trained eye for the news and his often-florid language made him a suitable candidate to start Trail Creek's "home-print newspaper." Under his watch, the *News* promised to be a serious business and not a home for political zealots or gossip-mongers. He also set an early tone as a booster for his new town, writing admiringly about Trail Creek's prospects, "situated as it is on the banks of the noblest of rivers, whose waters never freeze and where navigation never ceases, centrally located among the fabulously rich ore belts of the new world."[86]

Many early Trail residents shared Thompson's belief in the town's future, "but none declare it so eloquently as the newspaper editor. The first smelter smoke, he said, 'will come… as balm to the nostrils of the progressive North American'."[87] It was not a description that thousands of smelter workers whose arrival he predicted would come to appreciate. Nor was the landscape around Trail something everyone would describe in glowing terms. In fact, it would soon be rendered a moonscape by smelter smoke and river effluents.

Ably assisted by Ralph White as "Mining Editor," W.E. Blackmer as "Travelling Corresp'd't," and eventually William K. Esling as city editor, the *News* editor would provide the boom town with its very own weekly chronicle of the individuals, social events, mining developments, and various skirmishes that marked life among the scattering of buildings on the Columbia River.[88] It was the beginning of a new century and the embryonic days of what would eventually become a daily newspaper for the smelter city.

Editor Shows Pluck, Mine and Rail Rivalry, Editorial Rancour in 1896

Judging from his February 1896 number, Thompson appeared to be flourishing in his new pioneer environment. His confidence must have increased after the *News* was showered with mostly positive comments from other editors around the Pacific Northwest. He had bragged for weeks about his coming "Holiday Number,"[89] a special edition that arrived after the holiday season. It was "a source of monetary loss to us," but its style and content, sporting several illustrations, garnered much positive comment. Ever the booster, a proud Thompson published more than a few of these laudatory comments. John Thomas Wilkinson, also known as "Wings" (so nicknamed for his frequent travels), asked if the *Vancouver Daily World* could use "about $75 worth of cuts" (illustrations) that had appeared in the lauded issue. In exchange he would "write up Trail." The deal resulted in a two-page article on "Trail Creek and Slocan Counties," including an illustration of "Mrs. Hanna's cottage."[90]

Wings had visited the previous November and was ecstatic about the town. "I could scarcely believe it was the same place.... Its growth has been marvellous. A year ago it had only a few inhabitants—I should judge not more than 40. Now its population and that of the vicinity has passed the 1,000 mark, and will soon reach the teens." He thanked both Thompson and Blackmer in his article, saying that the *News* was "thoroughly up to date," before providing a detailed description of Heinze's smelter and his proposed Columbia and Western Railway.[91] Thompson basked in the momentary glory, but the *World* was soon among his favourite press enemies.

Others joined the chorus of praise. The *Sprague Herald*, the surviving newspaper from his old stomping grounds, called it a "very handsome edition [that] abounds with wholesome advice." The *Rossland Prospector* declared that "this specimen of art now before us speaks highly for the enterprise and pluck exhibited by the publishers." The *Davenport Times* said it was a "very descriptive number... that would be a credit to any establishment."[92] The *Spokane Review* called the sixteen-page, magazine-style number "a very creditable production." Even the *Rossland Miner*, another of Thompson's future rivals, called it "the handsomest and best publication which West Kootenay has produced to date." Always a self-promoter, Thompson sang the edition's praises and concluded "the amount of good done for a town by its local paper cannot be over-estimated."[93]

The journalistic pat on the back must have fortified Thompson, for he was soon sparring with other Kootenay rivals over various issues. Criticism from the *Rossland Miner* about a proposed relocation of the customs office from Rossland to Trail brought out Thompson's razor-sharp pen. He called the Rossland paper's support for Heinze's mining and railway-building competitor Daniel C. Corbin "blind egotism," arguing that it had "blundered grossly" in attacking the government for a delay in getting replacement machinery to the War Eagle mine.[94]

When the *Nelson Tribune* called Thompson and his paper "Johnnie come latelies," Thompson shot back "'Tis true we came to British Columbia later than the dyspeptic old wind-bag who inflates the Tribune; but, unlike him, we have not outworn our welcome, and we are apt to stay in this country after he is gone and forgotten." He then called editor John Houston's paper "Grandma Tribune" and the "self-constituted press-censor of West Kootenay."[95] When the *Rossland Miner* questioned Thompson's "intelligence" and claimed him incapable of publishing even a "primer," he spared no venom in counterattacking. "If the distinguished journalist who imagines he is filling a 'long-felt want' in Rossland would come from off his rhetorical stilts, from which he is engaged in talking over the heads of the select few who comprise the subscription list of the Rossland Miner," he wrote, "the Miner would enjoy a better standing in the limited area in which it circulates." For good measure, he added "the Miner could not publish a primer that any school book house in the world would accept."[96]

By the end of February 1896, Thompson shared with readers his plans to "build a two-and-a-half-story cottage" near a fresh water stream: "The building will be only 13 X 24, and there will be but two people in it." Perhaps as a gesture to Martha, he added that he would make it "the prettiest one in Trail."[97] Soon to be more comfortably housed, the Thompsons were well primed to deliver all the news that he saw fit to print, including rumours of a gold strike in Washington, a prospector's suicide, a report on the firemen's masquerade ball and a half-page advertisement from Heinze's British Columbia Mining and Smelting Company offering to buy gold, silver and copper. The Heinze ad, consistently the largest to appear regularly, was perhaps part of the reason why Thompson announced that the *News* would have a massive new printing press in operation by April. Meantime, there were also some minor setbacks. "The editor of the News is hostile, and is looking for two timber thieves," Thompson railed, and he promised a "life-subscription" reward to anyone who could identify the thieves.[98] It was the sort of personal comment that readers would get used to over the next three years along with accounts of journalistic encounters with angry readers.

Thompson, for example, commented on an altercation involving a fisticuffs brawl between *Nelson Tribune* editor John Houston and a Canadian Pacific Railway director (see Introduction).[99] With his index fingers no doubt speeding across the keys, Thompson wrote disparagingly of the now-classic country newspaper incident. "It seems strange that the editor of an able newspaper and the superintendent of a great system of Transcontinental railways are not possessed of sufficient sense to settle their differences without blows and curses, with police-court accompanyment [sic]," he asserted. "Brute instinct seems to be king over intellect."[100] Perhaps the *News* editor had forgotten his own past skirmishes as a Washington State newspaperman.

In 1888, for example, he, his future father-in-law, Judge Caton, and another man were charged with assaulting Davenport newspaper editor Frank Knight who apparently published "a rumor… to the effect that owing to the relations existing between Thompson and the wife of his employer [that is, Martha] the latter had fled the country."[101] Editor Knight claimed that Thompson and his fellow assailants had attacked him and that Thompson had pistol-whipped him. Thompson claimed he had no pistol. "It was a red hot fight for a time," the *Spokane Falls Review* reported, "and the air was blue with sulphuric sentiments, loosened whiskers and country exchanges."[102] Nevertheless, the local sheriff jailed all three and they were fined five dollars.

It would not be the last time Thompson ran afoul of the law, but for the moment, he would produce a weekly newspaper for the town "where smelters grow." According to the other slogan on the front banner, it was also a "good town to tie fast to!" How long he would tie fast to Trail Creek was as yet unknown. There was also the question of who or what the *News* would tie fast to. In the early editions of 1896, possible answers began to surface.

In March 1896, the *News* published a complaint about a proposed 2 per cent provincial tax on mining, calling it "oppressive." Both Topping as a mine owner and Heinze as a railway and smelter owner stood to lose if the tax was imposed. The *News* argued that it should not. The *Spokane Review* article suggested Heinze was being "accused of doing something," but the newspaper provided no proof.[103] Thompson gave it sarcastic coverage in another of many instances where the editor stepped in to support Heinze on his front page.

The local press was another favourite editorial topic. Thompson reported that Eber C. Smith of the Springdale, Washington, *Statesman*, had bought the *Rossland Evening Record*.[104] Smith's paper shared similar goals to Thompson's *News* in that it "thrived on controversy, with an idiosyncratic style that regularly featured personalized attacks on institutions and individuals, including editors of other papers."[105] It was a combative style that Thompson quickly adopted, including regular ambushes of the Rossland press.

Perhaps Thompson had Smith in mind when he commented on the journalism wars that were raging around the West Kootenay, fueling discontent with the *Nelson Tribune*'s Houston by describing his paper as "at war with all mankind."[106] Still recalling the glory of the Holiday Number, the *News* began reprinting articles from it. Also appearing regularly was news about the new Trail Board of Trade. Thompson supported the board and welcomed the printing and advertising revenue. And the *News* regularly announced the appearance of a nw brewery, bakeries, a bottling works, and several hotels. Trail Creek was booming, and Thompson was telling the reading public about it. He was also beginning to realize his initial hope of "financial advancement."

By May, the Thompson family had moved to the new cottage. It wasn't yet finished, but "it will be more desirable as a residence than their old quarters in the *News* office."[107] The move did not seem to slow the publication of mining news, which increased in regularity, as did the items praising Trail as the new mining and smelting mecca. With the promise of Heinze's railway to Rossland and beyond,

Thompson ran a rare poem commemorating the stagecoach that had been used to carry passengers and freight to Rossland from Trail Creek Landing. "Goodbye, old stage, your days are o'er," wrote a local poetaster. "We've adopted new, more modern ways;/We need your creaking frame no more,/We've done with all your jolts and sways." The poem finishes with a salute to Heinze's coming Columbia and Western Railway: "We are trav'ling now with hissing roar/ To Rossland's golden, snowy crest."[108] The only thing that might have sullied the poet's vision was Heinze's failure to reach an agreement with the provincial government on the required railway land grant. By the end of May, however, Thompson was optimistic that the *News* would be "turning out the stationery for the new road."[109]

Thompson filled his June 1896 numbers with mining and smelting news from around the world and plenty of civic boosterism. But the editor occasionally reined in his enthusiasm, warning workers not to believe the tall tales published in the "sensational" daily press. Despite his boasts of great opportunities, Thompson worried that hopeful newcomers would be disappointed if they came to Trail Creek in search of their fortunes. "There are enough working men here to fill any demand that might arise this year," he wrote.[110]

The Fourth of July was celebrated in the *News* pages, but Thompson sheepishly announced that it was merely a delayed celebration of Dominion Day. In fact, there were as many Americans in town as any other nationality, probably more. In Rossland, however, editor Smith proposed that the city celebrate July 4 for that very reason: "Because other nearby places were having formal celebrations on the Queen's Birthday (May 24) and Dominion Day (July 1), Rossland should do something different."[111] The *Nelson Economist* was not amused, calling the proposal "exasperating impertinence" and "blatant hostility to Canada."[112]

The Western Federation of Miners (WFM), an American trade union, also received coverage, but mostly to announce the winners of an election or to highlight the annual picnic organized by Rossland's WFM Local 38, among the first mining unions in the district. Seldom, if ever, did the pro-business editor publish articles favouring unions. Curiously, the International Typographical Union (ITU) would organize Local 335 in Rossland near the end of 1896 with eighteen members.[113] Yet Thompson gave readers little hope of the *News* becoming a union shop under ITU organizer George H. Howell.

The 1896 US presidential election race also found a home on the *News* front page, with Thompson giving Democratic candidate William Jennings Bryan plenty of space. It may have reflected a liberal tendency in Thompson, but more likely he knew a newsworthy diatribe when he heard one. Republican William McKinley, who more than likely garnered Thompson's support, won the presidency. In September, Thompson joined various white institutions and some legislators in the call for "total exclusion" of Chinese people. He also found himself on the defensive when he blamed a Captain Gore of the steamboat *Nakusp* for failing to help a drowning man. The death was met with public protests and blistering local newspaper editorials. His old nemesis, the *Nelson Miner*, claimed the *News* had "directly implicated the Captain of the *Nakusp* in an abominable deed."

Thompson denied the charges, saying "The Miner (abominably) lies."[114] The *Nakusp* and the *Trail* would soon join the *Lytton*, plying the Columbia River and the Arrow Lakes, carrying freight, passengers (although sometimes uncomfortably), and the coal so important to fueling the smelter.[115]

While Heinze continued to press the provincial government for rights-of-way for his expanded rail plans, Thompson announced that Major W.E. Blackmer, Thompson's business partner, had resigned, and Ralph White, "the well-known mining man," would continue as the *News*'s mining editor.[116] The editor also joined the heated debate over the gold versus silver standard, arguing for a bimetallist solution that allowed both metals to be used as legal tender. As he did with so many new businesses, Thompson hailed the opening of the Arlington Hotel as "the best furnished" in the BC Interior.[117] It was one of at least eight serving the travelling public.

In October, Frank Hanna, one of the mining camp's founders, made the front page with news that he now owned the Frank Hanna Liquor Company. A reprint from the *BC Mining Record* supplied a short biography of the Illinois-born Hanna, who, with Colonel Topping, had erected the first building and first hotel in Trail Creek five years before Thompson arrived.[118] The month marked the end of the first full year of publication, with Thompson boasting "the News has done its duty by the town of Trail."[119]

Autumn numbers saw profiles of other prominent citizens, including Ross Thompson, no relation, "the Father of Rossland," regular news reports about Heinze's attempts to secure loans from London financiers to further invest in Trail Creek, and where to buy everything from chewing tobacco and liquor to lingerie. Trail, it was announced, had formed a whist club, a new hospital was under construction, and two drugstores were open for business. A "lady" barber was rumoured to be moving to town. And the California Restaurant seemed to have an unlimited supply of fresh Baltimore oysters. Electricity was on its way, thanks to the smelter, and new telephone lines were promised.

In anticipation of future advertising, Thompson increased the paper's size to eight pages. His defence of Heinze also intensified. "When the Rossland papers run short of sensations they print a lot of rot about Trail's smelter," he wrote, "and not once in a coon's age do they hit it right."[120] Clearly there was no détente established between Thompson and Eber C. Smith.

In September, the *Rossland Miner* was sold to a group that Spokane mining and rail magnate Daniel C. Corbin was allegedly supporting financially. Corbin's Columbia and Red Mountain Railway opened in December 1896, connecting Rossland to the proposed Northport smelter and carrying ore, freight and passengers to Spokane and elsewhere. Corbin used the *Miner* to promote his railway and to support his claim to ownership of land outside the original townsite of Rossland where many mining families had settled. Thompson's allegiance to Heinze compelled him to editorialize in the Butte industrialist's favour, and he did not hesitate to defend him against the *Miner*.

As 1896 wound to a close, mining editor Ralph White proved his worth, filling the *News* with announcements of mining discoveries, financial ventures and technical advancements. Meanwhile, Thompson ensured that the public was aware of a new Baptist church, new fraternal societies such as the Knights of the Maccabees and the Freemasons, and the need for a proper sewage system. He also devoted many column inches to talk of several new rail lines coming from all directions. One of those directions was the Heinze proposal; the other was Corbin's. Thompson would eventually find himself in the middle in more ways than one.

In November, uncharacteristically, he published a short front-page item on the deadly Leadville strike in Colorado in which he seemed to argue against employers' efforts to "break up the Miners' union."[121] Such seeming support for the unionized miner was not soon repeated. Political news was also gaining prominence in the *News*, with full coverage of politicians' visits to Trail from Victoria and Ottawa. In another departure from his editorial policy, Thompson ran a story on the Armenian Massacre that called on citizens to donate to the Armenian Relief Committee.[122]

Thompson's *News* had indeed pleased local merchants. "Not one of them has ever taken his advertisement out of the *News* for a single issue," the editor gushed. He told them there was no need to ship printing work to Spokane when he had a "handsome power press... numbering machines, power staplers, pasting machines, bronzing machines, [and] perforating machines."[123]

A New City Editor, *Miner* Inconveniences and a Heinze Collaboration in 1897

As he and Martha settled into their new home—"built of logs" with "a cupola on the roof surrounded by a verandah"—they had much to look forward to in 1897.[124] Thompson hailed the newly hired William K. Esling as his city editor, declaring him a "hustler."[125] In addition to Blackmer, himself, White, and Esling, the *News* could boast a large staff, including reporter Charles Martin and press room foreman Loss Bernard, the fifteen-year-old who had come to Trail with the Thompsons. Martha and two other women worked as compositors along with a female stenographer and bookkeeper.

"The News at all times supports fourteen persons, including the wives and families of employes," Thompson boasted.[126] He was gaining momentum as a promoter that businesses could count on, and with competent new blood on the editorial staff, a reliable advertising clientele, an increase to six or eight pages, and a full array of new job printing equipment, it seemed Thompson was in charge of an unstoppable success.

By New Year's 1897, Ralph White had disappeared from the masthead. Major Blackmer was still listed as a travelling correspondent and, if his beat included writing about proposed new railways in the district, he must have been busy. Thompson used his first editorial to wax optimistic: "Today the smelter has grown until the furnaces are in sight that will treat 600 tons of ore per day; the railroad is completed to Rossland and one twice as long is in course of construction to connect Trail with the CPR at Robson.... Trail has a machine shop and foundry, a 50-barrel brewery, two sawmills, and many other industries."[127] Business was becoming so prosperous in the smelter city, Thompson opined, that "Trail needs a chartered bank."[128]

The *News* editor, who had spent most of December on a buying spree in the East, reported that he was "the happiest man in Canada" now that a powerful new press and much additional equipment was on its way by CPR rail and by the steamer SS *Trail*. So large was the "complete new outfit of everything needed for the newspaper and job office" that the freight charges alone "will make a $1,000 bill look mighty sick."[129] Where he got the money to invest in such an expensive "outfit," he did not say. Perhaps the CPR was lending a helping hand? Then there was always Heinze, "the youngest and most enterprising businessman in Canada."[130] Could he be showing his appreciation for Thompson's sycophantic defence of the mining and rail millionaire?

By mid-February, Thompson sat alone in the masthead identified as publisher. Esling remained unidentified, but a blurb revealed him preparing to launch a real estate business.[131] Editorials continued boasting about the *News*'s new printing equipment and Thompson was touting his latest special number, "The Commercial History of Trail."[132] He seemed unthreatened by the appearance of a second weekly, the *Trail Creek Miner*, which was "issued under difficulties yet reflects credit upon the publisher," Conner Malott.[133] The threat, if it ever was one, soon disappeared after R.D. Anderson took over the *Miner* using equipment he bought from Thompson. Malott soon joined Esling on the city desk at the *News*.[134]

A dispute over who controls Trail's water supply occupied Thompson in March when his old colleague Major Blackmer got up a petition against Heinze's plan to establish a second firm in competition with R.T. Daniel's Trail Water Supply Company. Seventy-eight local businessmen signed the petition, including Thompson. However, he struck back at the petitioners once he realized he was in opposition to Heinze. The petition, he wrote, "is simply a covert declaration that F. Aug. Heinze desires to supply Trail with water, and it declares that every business man in the town that Mr. Heinze has made by the investment of his means, is arrayed against him and on the side of R.T. Daniel." They were supporting a man "whose Trail holdings, as compared to those of Mr. Heinze, and whose power to control, for weal or woe, the future of the town of Trail, also in comparison with that power possessed by Mr. Heinze is in about the ratio of 1 to 1,000,000."[135]

In mid-March, Thompson weighed in on the issue of Sunday closing. A local clergyman had urged businesses to observe the Sabbath so store workers could have the day off. Thompson, after much consideration, especially from "a religious standpoint," took the view that "each one must regulate his own business to suit himself, but the clerk or employe should have his day of rest, and the employer will lose nothing by allowing him it."[136] With that, the publisher declared that *News* employees would continue to have Sundays off.

Heinze's business partner Carlos Warfield made the *News* in April in a front-page reprint from the *Toronto Globe* in which the Butte, Montana, mining mogul spoke of the untold riches yet to be tapped in the Kootenay district. The smelter now had electricity and was "brightly lighted," and Thompson used the welcome change to boost Heinze and his enterprise as another example of how he benefited Trail Creek. Colonel Topping spearheaded the founding of a brass band for the city. The Knights of Pythias joined the growing group of service clubs. The Methodist Church was now part of the array of religious denominations. Trail's baseball team was bidding to join the Washington and Kootenay Baseball Association. And Frank Hanna let the contracts to build the Trail Opera House. The smelter city was coming of age in myriad ways—all duly reported in the civic-minded *News*.

Once again, the editor blasted the *Rossland Miner* for failing to support Heinze and for favouring plans for a Northport smelter that would compete with Trail's smelter. "Up to the present time the papers of the Kootenay, and those of Rossland especially," he argued, "have shown more favor to the idea of a smelter at Northport than they have to the actual and active smelter at Trail."[137] Once again, Thompson stood fast in his support of Heinze, and he went a step further, advocating "Canadian ores for Canadian smelters."

By mid-April, the editor complained that "for the past three months the News has been run at a financial loss." To resolve the problem, he announced that advertising rates would increase 50 per cent. If Heinze and other advertisers rejected the rate jump, "we will be compelled to cut the paper down to a smaller size."[138] Then he addressed the rumours that he was in Heinze's pocket.

"Owing to the publicity given to the private affairs of the publisher of the News by some of our esteemed contemporaries," he railed, "and to the speculation that such publicity has created as to said publisher's connection with deep-laid schemes of national importance, the writer finds it advisable to state the following startling truths." In response, he stated categorically that "neither Mr. Heinze nor any man who ever saw Mr. Heinze, save the publisher of the News, has a mortgage on the News, or any interest in the paper, or any control over it in any way."[139]

Thompson then announced that he had "purchased an interest in the Nelson Miner, the oldest newspaper in West Kootenay."[140] To finance the purchase and to pay off his debts, he explained that he had sold his real estate interests in Trail. Then in June, Thompson got more bad news when his dream of an evening daily faltered in light of the CPR telegraph company's refusal to run a telegraphic service to the smelter city that would have provided the necessary national news service. "That means that Trail cannot have a daily paper until the second line is strung between Revelstoke and Trail," he explained in an editorial dripping with "disappointment."[141]

By mid-1897, Esling still was not listed in the masthead. However, in addition to his real estate interests, he was now a resident agent of the CPR's accident insurance company.[142] It also appears that he had assumed a role in communicating the city's resolutions regarding Heinze's proposed railway linking Robson with Penticton. Thompson, always favouring Heinze, criticized the BC and federal governments for not providing the industrialist with a grant to proceed with construction. Acting as the copper king's chief defender in the Kootenays, the editor found another Heinze ally in the *Kaslo Kootenaian*. He quoted the paper asking if all the criticism of Heinze was "getting just a little bit sickening?"[143]

Although union activity was evident in the Kootenays, the weekly seldom reported any news about union organizing attempts. And yet by the time Heinze's smelter was being built, Western Federation of Miners (WFM) organizers no doubt had an eye on the six hundred or more workers "up the Hill." The radical union had earned a reputation as a tough negotiator that did not back away from a fight. News of violent union wars in the mining camps of Idaho, Montana and Colorado came north in letters, newspapers, and by word of mouth.

Whether or not the WFM followed Heinze to Trail Creek, his smelter was already exhibiting a clear need for such worker representation, especially regarding workplace health and safety. As the smelter was "blown in" (started up) for the first time, for example, the *News* reported "the Butte boys at the smelter are not having the best of luck." The brief item described how "Harry Fay had the ends of his two fingers on his left hand cut off while examining the blower too close." George Quyle "tore a great hole in the fleshly part of his thigh while being lowered for an elevation."[144]

If Thompson considered working people at all, it was to promote employer benevolence toward them rather than encourage unionization or health and safety legislation. "The voluntary increases of wages have continued," he noted that summer, "and the number of unemployed workmen has been visibly decreased."[145] The idea that a unionized workforce should have something to say about their workplace and its wages and working conditions never occurred to him. Nor did their views on the development of Trail Creek.

Any suggestion that socialism could provide an answer to unemployment or any other social problem was *verboten* to Thompson. These were the concerns of the employer and of free enterprise capitalism. "Eugene V. Debbs [*sic*] has abandoned his scheme of locating his camp of hobos and Coxeyites in the state of Washington," he crowed in one edition.[146] "No system of socialism has ever proved a success, and history repeats itself. There is no royal road to fortune, and [until] Debs' following realizes the fact that hard work, and that alone, is the foundation of success in life[,] it will be chasing a hopelessly distant chimera."[147] It was an attitude that would prevail throughout the life of the paper.

When a Northport smelter was approved and would process ore from Corbin's and other Rossland mines, shipped there on Corbin's railway, the *News* criticized the CPR "for permitting American roads to capture business that should remain on this side." In the same edition, it also criticized the *Rossland Miner* for failing to support rail projects that would keep Canadian ore in Canadian smelters: "The *Rossland Miner*, ever ready to strike a blow at Canadian institutions outside of Rossland, and anti-Canadian and anti-British in all its sympathies, is endeavoring to gracefully back down to the desires of the alien share holders of the Le Roi Company, which means smelting Kootenay ores in the United States."[148]

Klondike fever struck the front page of the *News* at the end of July. "Billions in gold await those who care to undertake the perilous trip," ran a front-page headline.[149] So enthusiastic was the *News* that it seemed the editor was also contemplating the possibility of getting rich in the Yukon. He said as much in his editorial: "If any of the readers of the News know of any man, woman or child that will trade a ticket to the Klondyke and a year's outfit of grub and clothing for a newspaper claim, they will be doing us a kindness by telegraphing the News at our expense."[150]

Yukon gold rush news continued to dominate the front page in August, as did support for Heinze's concerns on the editorial page. Thompson penned two long editorials lambasting governments, the province's newspapers, and the "loud-mouthed opposition" to Heinze. Let them "show their enterprise before they attempt to belittle the efforts of a man whose achievements are a matter of public record and of the greatest importance to British Columbia."[151] As for the newspapers, "for some time past they have taken occasion to belittle Mr. Heinze's progressiveness, and to insinuate that our enterprising townsman is farming the Provincial and Federal governments, rather than seeking to advance his interests along commonly recognized business lines." Thompson then demanded a "fair and honorable discussion of the subject."[152]

A short item in one of that month's editions noted that Esling was the *Rossland Miner*'s new Trail correspondent. Given the constant bickering between the *News* and the *Miner*, the new appointment of the *News* city editor might have signalled the possibility that changes were afoot. Indeed they were. In mid-1897, Corbin lost interest in the *Rossland Miner* and Heinze took ownership as a silent investor. As historian Shearer has noted, "in August, 1897, it was announced that 'editorial and business management' of the paper had been purchased by Fred Moffatt, a Toronto lawyer who had come to Rossland as correspondent for the *Toronto Globe*. Not announced was that the deal probably had the financial backing of Corbin's rival, Augustus Heinze." At that point, the editorial policy changed radically, with Heinze using the *Miner* to promote his business interests.[153]

Whether or not Thompson knew of Heinze's secret ownership of the *Rossland Miner*, he took regular pokes at the paper. In September, for example, he noted that the Rossland paper "had changed hands several times in the past two years," and he roiled at the rival paper's suggestion that the *News* was for sale: "From Rossland the story was wired to the Yankee papers—in short, the publicity given to the fairy tale is all the fault of our esteemed Rossland contemporary."[154] Did Heinze instruct *Miner* editor Moffat to prod Thompson into selling? Could the copper king, a vigorously acquisitive capitalist, have intended to monopolize the local press?

The *Kaslo Kootenaian* attempted to sort out the situation when it "announced upon good authority, that C. [Charles] E. Race, editor of the Nelson Miner, had been offered and will accept the editorship and management of the Rossland Miner, the leading newspaper in the Heinze, Thompson, Jowett, Mowfatt [sic] syndicate."[155] Thompson treated the claim with sarcastic disdain, rejecting the notion that he was part of any syndicate: "If you were not such a 'josher,' Dave [the *Kootenanian* editor], Thompson would feel highly complimented by your connecting his name with 'the big 'un'."[156] Still, given Thompson's almost weekly efforts to praise Heinze, perhaps some observers had good reason to believe there was a strong connection between the two men.

At the same time, hostilities between Local 335 of the Rossland ITU and *Rossland Evening Record* owner Eber C. Smith were boiling over, with Smith insisting that his unionized workers stay only in his boarding house. In the resulting imbroglio, Smith taunted the union in his editorials, and the union responded by declaring the *Record* a non-union shop. In a union town like Rossland, losing that status meant the loss of advertising revenue, and that could be deadly.

As the labour trouble escalated, the ITU local produced the *Evening Union* to discredit Smith and build community support. Not to be outdone, Smith formed his own union, but it failed to resolve his labour problems. Soon WFM Local 38 withdrew its patronage from Smith's paper and pledged to support the ITU.[157] Typical of Thompson, who generally avoided labour issues, the whole affair was left untouched in the *News*. Perhaps he did not want to draw the ITU's attention to his paper? Perhaps he was biding his time in hopes of getting some of the advertising revenue that was being denied Smith's paper?

Financial Woes, Pressure from Heinze, Smelter for Sale, Gold Rush Fever in 1898

"As the town cannot support the News of today, the only thing remaining for its publisher to do is to discharge all his help, cut the paper down to the commercial size of the town and do the best he can do under the circumstances," he wrote.[158] Did this mean Esling would no longer work for the *News*? Would Thompson run the technical and editorial side of the operation? Would Martha be enlisted to run the presses? It seemed unlikely, but the publisher was out of ideas for how to sustain the *News*. "There is no other newspaper in Trail, or we would be willing to quit," he lamented, citing the poor outlook of the city's economy.[159] The situation was grave.

Financial woes, however, did not stifle his jabs at the *Miner*, especially on the issue of railways. He criticized the paper for "its tirade of abuse" against the CPR for, among other things, not building a line to Rossland fast enough. The other things amounted to the rail company's refusal "to make a reasonable traffic arrangement with the Columbia and Western system."[160] Therein lay the main concern: the C&W was Heinze's railway. As a *Miner* owner, the copper king appeared to be influencing the editor to support him on three contentious issues. First, he wanted the *Miner* to back his bid to have a significant tax imposed on exports of raw copper and gold ore that would discourage exports and thus promote local smelting. Second, Heinze wanted editorial support for a government subsidy to build his proposed railway from Robson to Penticton. Finally, he wanted the *Miner* to pressure the CPR to speed up the extension of its lines into the Trail area. This, he knew, was vital to reducing the cost of coal and coke from the Crow's Nest Pass to feed his smelter.

Given his predisposition regarding the press as a personal vehicle to support his business ventures, Heinze may have quietly invested in the *News* and the *Nelson Miner* before the *Rossland Miner* became available. As historian Shearer has suggested, Heinze may have seen that "control of the two papers would have facilitated the spread of his message to a wide audience across the region."[161] Thompson always denied being an insider when it came to Heinze's many ventures, but the

Rossland press battles of 1897 surely must have shaken his confidence and given him pause with regard to his future as the *News* owner. Either he was lying about his financial relationship with Heinze or he was naive in rejecting allegations about Heinze's possible plan to buy the *News*.

As more articles about the Klondike filled the pages of the autumn editions, did the *News* editor perhaps spy an escape route from his predicament at the money-losing weekly? Rumours were spreading that Heinze and Carlos Warfield were negotiating the sale of their Trail and Rossland properties as well as the Heinze railway from Rossland to Robson. They were negotiating with none other than the CPR, "the big railway monarch."[162] In a long editorial in mid-December, Thompson rejected those rumours. He admitted that he had no inside knowledge, but insisted that Heinze's smelter was "not about to be sold." In fact, he offered the uplifting view that he was satisfied that it would be business as usual in the smelter city, and that he "expects to spend the remainder of his life in Trail."[163] Meanwhile, the Klondike beckoned.

Enticed by tales of untold riches, the editor had taken steps to invest in a "proposed Klondike enterprise" with the intention of moving to Alaska. However, he soon abandoned his plans: "Mr. Thompson gave away all his Klondike maps and papers and has already made great progress in the effort to forget that there is any such country as the Klondike."[164] Thompson had heard so many get-rich dreams from fellow travellers that he set aside his own dreams: "He will from this time be found hard at work in his office at Trail, and the man that mentions 'Klondike' to him will be unmercifully snubbed."[165]

Apologizing for the Christmas number being less "pretentious" than in previous years, the *News* editor wished Trail a Merry Christmas. He lamented not being able to celebrate previous Yuletides because he worked in the "poorest-paying business on earth" and had to work those holidays.[166] With that, he announced that this year would be different. The *News* would close for the holidays and the staff would have the week off.

Less than a week into 1898, Thompson was back at his usual denial of any attempt by Heinze to sell the Trail smelter and his constant promotion of the copper king as the city's saviour. He also continued his attack on other newspapers. This time it was the *Toronto Globe* that incurred his wrath for portraying Heinze as a "grasping, grinding monopolist" who was attempting to "squeeze the life out of a poor little struggling competitor like the CPR."[167] Although he steadily claimed not to have any direct pipeline to the smelter owner, he was quick to defend him in spite of rumours that Heinze was considering the sale of his Trail smelter to the CPR. Then, at the end of January, after months of denying any knowledge of a smelter sale, Thompson finally admitted that the sale was on and that the CPR had bid about $800,000 to purchase it. Heinze's Columbia and Western narrow-gauge line running from Trail to Rossland and his standard-gauge rail line from Robson to Rossland were to be part of the deal.

In a supplement, the *News* announced "the Trail Smelter has been sold for good this time, and the CPR gets it." Thompson was ecstatic: "No better news could come to Trail," for it is "now a CPR town" and the CPR will bring "power for the good of the community." Thompson predicted that "Trail will be the CPR City of the Kootenay—We're On the Up-grade Once More, and Nothing Can Stop Us, Now."[168] The comment seemed as much directed at his own future as that of the town. Whether or not he saw the sale assisting his ailing newspaper, he did not say. In a final editorial salute to Heinze, Thompson was effusive. "Mr. Heinze is due all praise and all respect," he wrote. "Mr. Heinze built the smelter at Trail, and the smelter built the town." In a typical Thompsonian tribute, he concluded: "He is of the stamp of Western hustlers that never quit until they have won, and to whom nothing seems impossible. To him Trail owes all."[169]

With Heinze out of the picture, Thompson returned to Corbin with Canadian nationalist fervour. Corbin had continued to seek government support for his Kettle Valley Railway, and Thompson continued to lecture the *Rossland Miner* on its failure to see that such a railway would have no benefit to the Golden City—as Rossland was known. The *News* had long harangued the Trail Creek neighbour about sending Canadian ore to the American town of Northport for smelting. "We defy anyone to point a way in which the granting of a charter to Corbin for a road into the Boundary Creek country can help Rossland," he chided. "Not a dollar's worth of the Kettle River Valley business will ever go to Rossland." He then lamented that "Trail could have benefitted from a Canadian railway into that section, but now there is no hope for us in that direction. Another blow at Canadian smelters has been struck, and Rossland has done all it could against us."[170]

It was probably Thompson's last kick at Rossland and the *Miner*, for the man historian Turnbull glowingly described as the "irrepressible, flowery-penned newsman, the rustler, eighteen carats fine" would soon disappear from the *News* masthead.[171] On April 16, 1898, he announced that he was leaving the paper in the hands of William de V. leMaistre, a local barrister and solicitor.[172] On May 6, Thompson's hustling city editor Esling joined forces with his travelling correspondent Major W.E. Blackmer to become the new publishers.

For all his pledges never to leave Trail, Thompson seemed ready to depart his adopted city, but to where exactly? The previous April he had been in Nelson, leading to speculation that he "has become financially interested in the Miner Printing and Publishing Company."[173] However, if he had invested in the Nelson paper, it was short-lived, for the *Miner* reported in April 1898, only a few weeks before Thompson sold the *News*, that he had "disposed of his interest in The Miner to W.A. Jowett."[174] Jowett, a real estate and mining broker had been at the paper since at least the fall of 1896.[175] In late August 1897, the *Vancouver Daily World* confirmed the *News* sale and indicated that Thompson would "confine his attention to his Nelson property."[176] He and Martha moved to Nelson's Phair (later Strathcona) Hotel.

It appears that Thompson was involved with the Nelson weekly for six months or so, but his role there remains unclear. That spring or summer, perhaps recalling the launch of the *Rossland Daily Miner* in late December 1896, Thompson supposedly set his sights on converting the *Nelson Miner* to an "afternoon daily."[177]

The *Victoria Daily Times* interpreted the move as showing "his confidence in the future of the Kootenay country."[178] When the Nelson paper first went daily on May 10, 1898, it was unclear whether Thompson was still an active participant.[179]

Details of the *Miner's* complicated ownership history as reported in the *Nelson Tribune* reveal that Jowett, imagining "he was a born newspaper man[,]... gained control of the Miner company by trading [Clive] Phillips-Wolley real estate at Trail for his shares."[180] He ran the paper alone before selling a controlling interest to Thompson, who supposed that he would be allowed to control it as business manager. The *Tribune* mentioned that "Disagreements followed," but did not elaborate.

"In the fall of 1898," the *Nelson Tribune* reported, "Jowett became financially embarrassed and a deal was arranged by which the late D.J. Beaton assumed control as editor and manager."[181] Beaton announced in his December 1, 1898, edition that "the Miner passes to the control of a new management."[182] Thompson was not listed as a shareholder nor identified in any other capacity.[183] Nor was Heinze.

During the ownership squabble, Thompson, perhaps recalling the many glowing articles he had published about the goldfields, decided to move to the Klondike where he "established the first paper... at Glenora, on the Stikine Trail."[184] Clearly, Thompson, Martha, and Loss Bernard left Nelson quickly, for they would launch the first edition of the *Glenora News* on June 3, 1898. Thompson's biographer, Solka, suggests that his parents supplied some of the funding for the venture, and others in the Michigan lumber trade also invested.[185] It was the beginning of another storied phase in the life of W.F. Thompson.

His three years in Trail Creek go almost unmentioned in obituaries, but perhaps those years best epitomize the active editorial mind and business ambitions of a BC newspaper pioneer. Meanwhile, back in Trail, the new publishers of the *News* pledged to "be untiring in their efforts to promote public interests and will endeavour to give the people of Trail a newspaper, creditable to the chief smelting point in Canada, and one to merit generous patronage and approval."[186] It was a pledge that Thompson would have seconded wholeheartedly for he was ever the smelter city's biggest booster.

The Tacoma "Hustler" Makes His Mark in Kootenay Newspapering

"Wrong Font" Thompson was the first journalist to chronicle the south-central British Columbia mining and smelting community of Trail Creek, recording its rapid transformation from grubby boom town to the thriving industrial centre of Trail. Within about three years, however, the founding editor of the *Trail Creek News*, the new town's first newspaper, was struggling to keep his business alive. Although he had often pledged never to leave the smelter city, Thompson was restless. In the spring of 1898, he and his spouse, Martha, both proven newspaper people, moved to Nelson, leaving the paper in the hands of the city editor, William Kemble Esling. Thompson

had earlier hailed Esling as a "hustler" and "one of the best known newspaper men in Washington."[187] Now, members of Trail Creek's newspaper reading public would get a chance to judge for themselves.

Esling's father, Lemuel Theodore Esling, died less than two months after his son was born in Philadelphia on February 19, 1868, but his mother, British-born Jane Catherine Esling, survived to old age.[188] Perhaps due to her spouse's early death, she enrolled Billy at the City of Brotherly Love's historic Girard College, a preparatory school where he studied for seven years from 1876 to 1883. The school opened in 1848 after a long construction period. Its benefactor, shipping and banking magnate Stephen Girard, one of the richest men in the US at the time, intended it as a

Trail Creek News owner William K. Esling as Kootenay member of Parliament. Courtesy Trail Archives

school for "poor, male, white, orphans."[189] At an early age, Billy grew accustomed to a segregated environment devoid of females, African Americans, or other people of colour. We do not know how he fared at Girard, but as its founder wished, Esling was schooled in "the purest principles of morality."[190]

Esling left the college at fifteen in 1883, moulded into a life-long conservative. He then served a three-year apprenticeship with the Philadelphia book printer Jas. Grant. "His were long hours, hard work and small pay," an Esling obituary commented. "His 'master' saw that he not only did the work of the proverbial 'printer's devil', but that he was able to stand up at the case and stick type."[191] Following that, he worked at the *Philadelphia Record* until the fall of 1889, when he moved to Washington State. The *Olympia Tribune* funded the trip, having hired Esling to succeed a Major Barton as city editor of the *Morning Olympian*, the soon-to-be state capital's first evening daily.[192] He remained in that position for four years.

While in Olympia, he was an active Freemason and secretary of the Olympia Board of Trade. On December 11, 1891, he was listed on the National Guard Enlistment Register as a twenty-four-year-old "reporter," living in Thurston County, Washington. He was five feet, three inches tall and had a "dark" complexion. He was discharged on May 11, 1893.[193] Three years later, in 1896, after stints as a reporter at the *Tacoma Ledger* and the *Seattle Post Intelligencer*, he migrated to Trail Creek. He was twenty-eight years old when Thompson appointed him news editor.

Three more years passed, then Esling rather suddenly bought the *News* in the spring of 1898 in partnership with Major W.E. Blackmer, who hailed from the *Ritzville Times* in Washington State. Blackmer had been with the *News* since 1896. The sale was completed on April 16, 1898, but Thompson's name continued to appear in the masthead throughout April. On May 6, 1898, the masthead named "Blackmer & Esling, Publishers."

The new proprietors made a similar editorial promise to the one penned by their previous employer. They would be "untiring in their efforts to promote public interests and will endeavor to give the people of Trail a newspaper, creditable to the chief smelting point in Canada." Also like Thompson, they made it clear that the *News* would "merit generous patronage and approval." Interestingly, the owners added, "The paper will speak for itself."

With Thompson's departure, Esling and Blackmer initiated editorial and style changes at the *News*. Larger, more artistic headlines identified sections such as "The Local Mines" and "Trail News Notes." Illustrations began to embellish articles more regularly. A large quantity of US news continued to cater to the substantial American population in the district. The more frequent appearance of poetry might have suggested a change was afoot, as did the occasional illustrated short story. However, these were almost always reprints from other publications. With the new ownership came a "Woman's Realm" column adorned with woodcuts, offering advice to the homemaker. It was a short-lived innovation, but it indicated a possible shift in policy to include more news about women. The paper sometimes featured children's essay contests, a local touch tucked into the abundance of American-based articles. At first, Esling seemed less combative when referring to other Kootenay newspapers, preferring to quote them on newsworthy events. What did not change noticeably was the paper's undying support of the local business community, especially the CPR and its smelter.

Esling did not appear in the masthead of the first post-Thompson editions, perhaps relying on Blackmer to edit the paper. The new ownership arrangement was further thrown into question when an April 16, 1898, front-page blurb reported Esling leaving "this evening for the coast where he will probably remain." The item added "He stopped in Trail yesterday and today, in order to issue The News this week, and only regrets that it is not possible to again become a permanent resident of Trail."[194] Presumably, he still resided at least some of the time in Tacoma with his mother, but there was no indication that his older sister, Mary, or his older brother, Lemuel Jr., lived there with them.[195] Could it be that Esling travelled to the coast, perhaps Vancouver or Victoria, to apply for Canadian citizenship, a goal he eventually achieved?

War With Spain, Prohibition, Fractious Politics and Chinese "Highbinders" in 1898

Editions in early 1898 showed little change in editorial policy regarding trade unions. Like his predecessor, Esling consistently sided with employers over employees. In mid-April, he cited a "pleasing incident" where a pastor in New Bedford, Massachusetts, furnished "idle hours" recreation to striking cotton mill workers: "All were welcome who would refrain from discussing the strike or other labor matters."[196] Fritz Heinze, once Trail's chief employer, was still newsworthy. As he receded from the industrial scene, however, Walter Hull Aldridge gained prominence as the CPR-owned smelter's general manager. He went on record promising $100,000 in improvements to the company's Trail properties. Town founder Colonel Eugene Sayers Topping also maintained a steady presence in Esling's *News*.

On April 30, 1898, the *News* announced that W.F. Thompson, "a wide awake enterprising newspaper man and good editorial writer," had "severed his interests"

First smelter general manager Walter H. Aldridge.
Courtesy Rossland Museum & Discovery Centre

in the paper. He was "a man of strong convictions, fearless and determined," Esling further noted, and both he and Mrs. Thompson, "one of the best literary women of the age and capable of editing two newspapers herself," would be "missed in the social circles of Trail."[197] Esling praised the founding editor for "putting in one of the most complete job printing and bookbinding plants in both the Kootenays."[198] The front-page announcement wished the couple well in their new home at Glenora in northern BC.

Telegraphed news reports of war dominated the editorial page in late April as US President William McKinley asked Congress to declare war against Spain. Future president Theodore Roosevelt's Rough Riders went unmentioned, but would soon be featured across North American front pages. In May, the *News* ran reports on railway construction; two lead stacks for the smelter; new steamboats; the Northport, Washington, fire; a liquor sale at the Trail brewery; another essay writing contest; and another suicide by drowning. The Trail Dramatic Company was set to present a new play at the Hanna Opera House, and a new Kootenay history book fondly remembered "Father Pat," the district's first clergyman.[199] Whether Blackmer or Esling were writing the editorials, they were redolent of Thompson's bold Trail boosterism style.

In June, the new town of Brooklyn on the Lower Arrow Lakes got front-page treatment with the prediction that "it will be a bustling little city."[200] "Last week it was a forest, today it's a small city," said a follow-up item lauding the new townsite.[201] Five days after the town was born, the two *Trail Creek News* entrepreneurs published the first edition of the *Brooklyn News*. Blackmer was in charge of the new operation, while Esling stayed in Trail. Brooklyn served as the construction headquarters of the Columbia and Western Railway while a new line was built to Midway in the Boundary Country.

Life in the pop-up town, endowed with a hospital and a jail, was "hectic," wrote local historian Elsie G. Turnbull. "Games of blackjack and poker were in session every night and bars were always crowded." She added that "on Sundays the steam launch Oriole ran excursions up the lake while Presbyterian missionary John Munroe held a service in what the newspapers called the 'Brooklyn Tabernacle'."[202] The *News* owners "considered Brooklyn would be a likely and a lively little town," pulsating with newsworthy events and much advertising revenue.[203]

In August 1898, Esling and Blackmer sold the paper to W.B. Willcox, another American, and a man named O'Reilly. By mid-November, rumours were flying that the railway's head office was leaving town. The last edition of the *Brooklyn News* appeared on November 2. By September 1899, the camp that at first consisted of "but one cabin, an unfinished hotel and a dozen tents" was all but dead.[204] Willcox would reappear much later in the unfolding history of the *Trail News*.

Back in Trail Creek, Heinze again appeared on the editorial page. While he had "ceased active operations in this immediate vicinity," an editorial noted, "he is not, by any means, done with British Columbia."[205] Under Esling, the *News* would continue to be a big copper king supporter. A short item on the same page apparently shed some light on Esling's own political views. "Trail seems

Interior of the first electrolytic lead refinery in Trail ca. 1902. Courtesy Rossland Museum & Discovery Centre

to be pursuing a wise course in not rushing pell mell into politics," he wrote. "Its conservative political action is evidently bearing fruit."[206] It would be many years before the *News* editor was elected to the provincial legislature and then the Canadian Parliament as a Conservative, but already there were hints in that direction. More clarity came with Esling's editorial endorsement of independent Government candidate John McKane. With the provincial election scheduled for July 9, the *News* advised voters to cast their ballots "for a man who will support the general progressive policy of the Turner government, but who, so far as questions particularly affecting Kootenay are concerned, will be free to act, independent and irrespective of party."[207]

Political parties did not identify themselves as Conservative or Liberal at this time. But voters knew a vote for the party of Victoria businessman John H. Turner was a vote for continued conservative government. Until 1903, BC had no political parties and elected candidates were free to cross the floor. Conservative candidates were known as "Government" candidates and Liberals as "Oppositionists." As the election neared, Esling's editorial rhetoric intensified.

Stumping hard for the "Government" candidates, Esling wrote that any other outcome would be "disastrous to the best interests of Kootenay."[208] He criticized the "Rossland rowdies" who had "obstructed, interrupted, and insulted" Premier Turner on the campaign trail. He then called Turner's government "the working-man's friend," when in fact it had obviously been a party favouring big business and special interests such as railways and mines.[209] In a final judgment, Esling called the Opposition's criticisms "simply a desire to bark," concluding "there is no issue upon which the government should be overturned. Not a single one, and not a single principle."[210] It did not fly with the West Kootenay electorate.

One day before the election, the *News* ran a two-page supplement called "The Premier's Manifesto." Inside, Esling interspersed coverage of Dominion Day celebrations with snippets promoting his candidate and listing the Turner government's accomplishments. "If you want progress and prosperity... vote for John McKane," stated one. "If you are indifferent, then don't vote at all."[211] The clamour continued on the editorial page with even greater force, with Esling culling supportive statements from other Kootenay newspapers.

To Esling's chagrin, Turner was defeated in the 1898 election, bringing to an end "a dynasty that had assumed power in 1883."[212] But Turner remained premier until Charles A. Semlin assumed that role. James Martin, the Opposition candidate for the riding of West Kootenay-Rossland defeated Esling's candidate, marking a rise in the political importance of elections for the region. Somewhat graceful in defeat, Esling expressed surprise that the smelter city had voted for the Opposition, but conceded that it now is "time to forget political differences and settle down to business for the upbuilding and advancement of a busy and prosperous Trail."[213]

A week after the election, the *News* reported the visit of Governor General Lord Aberdeen and Lady Aberdeen, the founder of the Victorian Order of Nurses. Trailites greeted the couple with "loyalty and love," although Rossland may have celebrated with slightly more pomp and circumstance.[214] Street improvements were underway, the Columbia River took another life, new prospecting discoveries were rumoured, a new road was being blasted out of the rocky Kootenay terrain, and the Reverend Glassford reported that the Presbyterian Church had a "most prosperous" year.[215]

Then it was back to politics with a front-page letter signed with the initial "E" that held out hope of a change of results. On the editorial page, Esling suggested Turner might hang on a while longer as premier. Perhaps Semlin would consider forming a coalition government, he speculated. But Trail readers' attention was soon shifting to the new Yuengling Brewery, copper mining developments in Brooklyn that Major Blackmer was reporting, and the increased demand for laborers to work as railway navvies.

The August heat might have prompted Trail's hotel owners to want to raise the price of beer to 12½ cents from 5, but the decision to do so was postponed, no doubt to hear the reaction of the city's thirsty smelter workers. Another missive from the mysterious "E" advocated a coalition government. John McLin reported sighting W.F. Thompson in Glenora with news that he was heading still farther north. By mid-August, local news was supplanted by international news on the front page. One such item told of the wounding of Colonel Theodore Roosevelt during the attack on San Juan Hill.

The Canadian Smelting Works, the new name for the CPR-owned smelter,

2-TRAIL CREEK NEWS/TRAIL NEWS (1898–1907)

was "blowing in" the improved operation. Esling ecstatically greeted the development: "The people of Trail… had the pleasure of seeing smoke from the furnaces at the smelter."[216] It was less loquacious, but sounded like Thompson's earlier line about the putrid fumes being "balm to the nostrils."[217] Meantime, another victim succumbed to the Columbia's powerful undercurrents, and a dog poisoner invoked the wrath of a "dog fancier." The dog's owner wanted the "contemptible cur" and "base vermin" to "come forth."[218]

In September, another visitor returned from the Klondike reporting a sighting of W.F. Thompson on his way to Dawson City, Yukon. In mid-September, Trail welcomed the Honorable Mrs. E.K. La Barthe. A member of the Utah legislature, she had "the distinction of being the first woman who ever introduced a bill in a legislative assembly, it being the Anti-High Hat bill now a state law in Utah." In an unusual show of interest in women's affairs, Esling quoted La Barthe liberally. "Experience has shown that women, by the exercise of the franchise, lose none of their lady-like qualities," she told the *News*, "and in holding office, they in no sense deteriorate from the high standard of good mothers and house wives."[219] As we will see, a later *News* editor would disagree.

The September 23 edition noted that Esling's title had changed to "manager" and the masthead named "Esling & Worth, Proprietors." An editorial explained that Major Blackmer "has withdrawn from the Trail Creek News… his interest having been purchased by James M. Worth, the real estate and insurance broker." Esling continued with "the business management and general direction of the paper." Worth retired from the *News* in April 1899 to devote himself full-time to the real estate business in Trail, leaving Esling the sole proprietor.[220] In an attempt to boost circulation, Esling announced that his subscribers would also receive the *Toronto Weekly Globe*.

Trail participated in a federal plebiscite on the prohibition of alcohol in late September with thirty-eight citizens voting for prohibition and twenty-six against, with two spoiled ballots. The plebiscite passed with a majority of 40,000 votes, but the item did not say what might happen as a result.[221] Esling and other Kootenay editors would later oppose legislated prohibition.

Trail celebrated Labour Day late, with Rossland hosting the annual sports competition, which included a drilling contest, tug of war, a "wet test" of how well the firemen handled their hoses, and a "hub and hub race." The Columbia consumed yet another drowning victim in October, a "Young Men's Club" opened, the dramatic club was rehearsing a new comedy, an "immense consignment of fine cigars" was on sale at Charlie Bates's store, the *Rossland Miner* was publishing seven days a week, and "Charlie, the Chinese laundryman" had flown the coop with "the wife of a brother celestial."[222]

The Trail "hive" of the Ladies of the Maccabees saluted their departing Lady Commander and the Trail Court of Foresters heard from their past Chief Ranger.[223] The Salvation Army opened its new barracks on the Bowery. Nick Burley, "the pug who met Coolgardie Smith in a ten-round contest at the International [Rossland's main entertainment hall] last Monday, crept quietly out of town yesterday morning."[224] A.L. Poudrier, who had enticed many to seek their fortunes in the Klondike with his front-page articles in the *News*, committed suicide. And the CPR launched its newest steamer the SS *Moyie*.

November's editions offered the usual mining and railway construction news mixed with reports on the Knights of Pythias Lodge's masked ball and a report on the visit to the Trail lodge from the Grand Master of the Ancient Order of United Workmen (AOUW).[225] Yet another newspaper, the *Kootenay Mining Standard*, had started up, vandalism had occurred at the Methodist and Baptist churches, a young railway labourer had hanged himself by his suspenders, and a talk on nuts was given to Mrs. Wilkes's kindergarten class.

Tragedy struck the West Kootenay district in early December when the flat-bottomed steamer SS *Ainsworth* sank in Kootenay Lake. Nine people died, including two unnamed Italian labourers. Esling did not offer an editorial on the incident, preferring to dwell on the amount of taxes the region contributed to government coffers. "As a result of [the] anti-Chinese agitation [by white miners] in the Slocan," noted a short item, "the Sandon miners are considering the formation of a union."[226] In another story involving the Chinese community, E. (Elijah) J. Choo was reported fleeing for his life after the Chee Kung Tong, a Chinese freemason-style secret society, called him a "highbinder."[227] The story was apocryphal, according to the reprinted *Montreal Star* item. The *News* added that it was Choo who lent Charlie the money to leave town.

At year's end, Esling called 1898 a year of "shadows and sunshine, and although there may have been at times, many discouragements, the businessmen of Trail have much to be thankful for."[228] He also foreshadowed the marriage of the most prominent of those businessmen, smelter general manager Walter H. Aldridge, early in the New Year.

Cityhood Coming, Masonic Lodge, *Miner* Jousting, and Buying the *Record* in 1899

As 1899 began, Esling seemed in a foul mood. At the end of January, he published a front-page editorial chastising local businessmen for failing to attend a mass meeting. "It is simply disgraceful," he wrote in a sharper tone than the often sycophantic Thompson had ever used.[229] Elsewhere he pressed the issue of Trail's incorporation as a city, the value of the two-cent stamp and freezing water pipes at the *News* office. Inspired by an old-timer's letter in support of his earlier tirade, Esling berated citizens for not backing the politician who strives to achieve more. He then urged more public clamour about the need for public services, none greater than an improved postal system. Late in the month, a second mass meeting was better attended, allowing a further opportunity for Esling to press home the importance of Trail officially becoming a city.

The editor was in a better mood in March, perhaps because he was helping establish a Masonic lodge. Frank Hanna had promised new shows and new space at the opera house and the Twentieth Century Club was scheduling regular lectures on various scientific and medical theories of the day. However, the editor was irate

Trail Creek News office, ca. 1896. Courtesy Trail Historical Society

at the government for not providing a nighttime police officer. Poetry continued to appear. One from a local woman had a temperance message: "The man who takes the red, red, wine, shall never glue his lips to mine. The man who chews the navy plug, will in this parlor get no hug."[230]

Once again echoing Thompson, Esling took up the cause of Canadian nationalism in April, blasting the *Rossland Miner* for supporting the business interests of Spokane mine and rail magnate Daniel Corbin, adversary of favourite *News* patron F.A. Heinze: "It seems a little odd that such a journal should so far forget its interests in a district which gives it such a generous patronage, for in advocating the granting of the Corbin charter [for a railway from the Kootenay-Boundary district into the US]… it advocates a measure which will aid in building up interests across the line and ruining the business of men who have planted their money, time and energy in Rossland."[231]

The railmen's rivalry tracked back to at least 1893, when the two titans of train transportation vied for exclusivity over shipping ore to markets. "Heinze had completed his narrow gauge line from Rossland to Trail in the face of opposition from Corbin," historian Millie E. Cottingham explained. "He [Corbin] had acquired massive land grants from the BC government covering the Rossland area and he wanted Heinze to pay $5,000 for access…. Corbin, at this juncture made a masterly stroke to put Heinze on the defensive," Cottingham continued. "He obtained a writ from the supreme court of the province, overruling Heinze's injunction and enjoining his Trail Tramway Company from trespassing on Corbin's land."[232]

When Corbin's Red Mountain line was completed, it cleared the path for Rossland ore to be shipped to Northport. Meanwhile, Heinze was preparing to extend his tramway to the ore-rich Boundary Country under his Columbia and Western Railway company.

In another editorial reminiscent of the Thompson era, Esling chided the *Miner* for supporting individuals who act "for personal reasons and not for the public good." Esling pointed out that the Trail smelter was only processing half the ore from the Rossland mines, the rest going south. He wrote that "Northport is growing at the expense of Rossland and Trail, because the high treatment charges, maintained by Mr. Heinze, who owns the *Rossland Miner*, made it necessary for the Le Roi company to build a smelter of its own, and Mr. Corbin, who was so largely interested at Northport, used his influence and his railroad to place it there."[233]

Esling had clearly taken up the Trail booster's banner abandoned by his departing predecessor. In mid-April, he produced a front-page editorial replete with a complex sketch to illustrate Corbin's unfair rail advantages in carrying ore out of the Kootenay district. The editor also took the *Miner* to task for lamenting the CPR's high shipping rates. After comparing rates when Heinze owned the smelter and the railway line to Rossland, Esling found the *Miner*'s lament "laughable," reiterating "Mr. Heinze owns the *Rossland Miner*, and that paper has a mission in its crusade against the CPR."[234]

Later in the month, Esling escalated his editorial jousting with the *Miner*, repeating that Heinze was using it for his own gain. How the *News* had changed in its editorial stance from its early days when Heinze was portrayed as a man who could do no wrong. Now, under Esling's masthead, he could do only harm to the smelter city, while his newspaper, "Rossland's leading daily very discreetly steers clear of the facts."[235]

Esling also announced the dissolution of his partnership with J.M. Worth and posted an advertisement for "a complete newspaper outfit."[236] Thompson's old Washington hand press was among the items for sale. Incorporation was again front-page news, with Esling supporting the required petition. An optometrist now served the city. And "Harry Ross, the Chinaman arrested for posting obscene literature," had hired a lawyer.[237] He would eventually be acquitted. By April's end, an increasingly civic-minded Esling had joined the group planning to form a lodge of the Independent Order of Odd Fellows. D. Jelly addressed the Twentieth Century Club, after which a lively debate ensued regarding the "cause of and cure for the ills of the working man."[238]

Throughout May, the editor's pen was hard at work analyzing the lead market and mining industry, the editorial bread and butter of Kootenay newspapers. Meanwhile, the weekly's front page was peppered with notices of workplace fatalities at the smelter, in local mines and on the railways. Esling appended a note to his editorial on BC's eight-hour law adopted on February 27, 1899, as an amendment to the Inspection of Metalliferous Mines Act. As might be expected, he supported the employers who complained that the law spelled profit losses. He "regretted that the legislature has seen fit to disturb the existing harmony, to interfere with the growing prosperity of the mining districts, to reduce the wage-earning power of the men employed, and to interfere with the free right of contract hitherto enjoyed."[239]

The front page of the *News*, always a grab bag of advertising promotions, gossip, rumours, investment speculation and obituaries, noted in late May that four murders were being tried in Nelson. Heinze, "the hustling young capitalist," might be looking for a new smelter location. An Indigenous person, "much the worse for liquor," had been "badly kicked in the face" by a horse. And Trail's football (soccer) team beat Nelson and tied Kaslo in games played over the Queen's Birthday holiday.[240] Esling opted to use his editorial page for the edification of Trail's literature lovers with a lengthy reprinted short story called "The Abbe's Cloak."

Police court, church, political and social news dominated the June editions, and unlike earlier years, Fourth of July celebrations were notably absent from the *News* pages. Instead, Esling provided a brief history of Dominion Day. At the end of the month, the editor blasted Attorney General Joseph "Fighting Joe" Martin during a disagreement over Martin's controversial eight-hour day and alien exclusion laws. Apparently, the honourable gentleman had slandered a gathering of leading citizens at a banquet, including Trail's "father," Colonel E.S. Topping.

Martin's eight-hour-day legislation took effect on June 12, but the mine owners ignored it. This led to a Western Federation of Miners (WFM) strike in the Slocan Valley mines that quickly grew into a full-scale regional labour war. An ancillary result was the rapid increase of WFM locals in the district to thirteen, with a membership of 3,000, many of the members refugees from the violence-prone strike in Coeur d'Alene, Idaho. The employers' defiance strengthened the union, leading to the formation of WFM District 6. The Slocan strikers stayed out for nine months. Meantime, strike talk in Rossland would boil over in mid-1901.[241]

Political fallout from the Martin fiasco and general squabbling within the government persisted throughout July, culminating in Martin's resignation at the end of the month. In early August, readers learned that "the greatest social event in the history of Trail" was to be a ball that the "union miners of Trail" were to organize. All proceeds were to go to the Coeur d'Alene Miners Union.[242]

In spite of Joseph Martin's unpopularity in Victoria, the lieutenant-governor would soon name him premier. He lost the election a few months later, pleasing Esling, who called Premier Charles Semlin's short-lived government a "political side-show," and a "circus." Although he would one day immerse himself in the same political scene, the *News* editor now opined that "the government seems to have placed itself in such ill-repute with its obnoxious tactics, that men with any respect or interest for their political welfare, fight shy of the alluring bait of office."[243] And in the lost-but-not-forgotten department, the "Personals" column noted, "Mrs. W.F. Thompson is in town [as] a guest at the Spokane" hotel.[244]

Late in August, Esling purchased the *Rossland Evening Record* from the iconoclastic Eber C. Smith, flipping from Smith's populist style to an editorial policy that would become "ultra-conservative" as opposed to Smith's "virulently anti-conservative" posture.[245] The *Nelson Daily Miner* wished Esling would produce "a very bright and prosperous paper." The item included a note from Smith, calling Esling "a newspaper man of wide experience" who "will no doubt improve the Record."[246] The *New Denver Ledge* hailed Esling, saying "It is about time someone took hold of the sheet. For months it has looked more like the tattered remnants of an advertising fake than an evening paper."[247]

On September 1, 1899, Esling published his first *Evening Record*. His opening editorial stated "the Record will be a clean paper, free and devoid of sensationalism." Under Esling, the daily would "do all in its power to increase the prosperity of the community by presenting its resources in the [best] possible light."[248] The pledge may have been sincere, for a month later he posted a message to the Rossland Trades and Labour Council on his front page. In it, he stated that his paper is not "hostile to organized labor." Esling then declared that the *Evening Record* was "thoroughly a union paper, conducted on union principles, and that the new management is in most hearty accord with every movement having for its object the maintenance of a wage scale which fully remunerates a man for his labor." He then boasted that "for the past eighteen months, this same management has conducted his other newspaper on a union scale, in a town where no unions existed or exist, and where there was and is no obligation to do so, beyond the conviction that the laborer is worthy of his hire."[249] The other paper was, of course, the *Trail News*.

Esling pressed the point further: "It was entirely voluntary, and there was nobody to interfere. Had he chosen to run it on a non-union basis, he could have done so at a much lower wage scale, and consequently with better financial results to himself." The argument did not hold up. The dispute continued for another year, but ultimately the print and typographical unions, as well as the council, declared a boycott that forced the *Record* out of business in December 1900.

Back in Trail, the *News* seemed to experience a crisis of identity. With its first September edition, the masthead read *The Trail News*, with no explanation for the name change. Then the paper announced that J.C. Rathbun of the *Seattle Times* "takes the management of the Trail Creek News." Had Esling hired a bill collector? Included was a pledge to give readers "a good local paper," but Esling added a warning to those "who are willing to profit by the energies of their neighbours."[250] It brought back memories of Thompson's pleas for support to keep the *News* alive.

The October 14 edition marked volume 6 of the *News*, and front-page commentaries were designed to bring Trail out of a slump as the Kootenay winter started to blow in. Rathbun was gone from the masthead, perhaps suggesting that the doldrums had set in at the *News*, too. Was Esling devoting the lion's share of his time to the daily *Record*? It seemed possible, since the *News* was clearly adrift editorially. He was having difficulty managing two newspapers, and it showed in the *News*.

An early December comment might have seemed like déjà vu, with Esling slamming the *Rossland Miner* for again advocating that East Kootenay ores be smelted at a new smelter in Moyie, BC, rather than in Trail. A few days before Christmas, the front page focused on news of Britain's bloody Boer War. There were no Christmas greetings. Even the final edition of the year had a ragtag feel to it. Yet another booster comment hoped that "Trail is again beginning to travel towards prosperity and good times."[251] The smelter city was at the gates of a new century, but was its weekly newspaper up to the task of guiding it through them?

Late 1900 saw the end for the Esling daily. The suspension of "the Oldest Daily in the Interior" was "due to the stand the paper took during the labor troubles of last spring," the *Nelson Tribune* reported. The union town implemented a boycott "from which the Record never recovered." It had, as the *Tribune* editor noted, "Gone to the Boneyard."[252] However, Esling would not follow it. In 1905, he was back in the daily newspaper business as the owner of his old nemesis, the *Rossland Miner*. Seemingly having learned a lesson from his earlier encounter with the labour council, the paper took a "more conciliatory tone."

A City Is Born, Party Politics, and the *News* Swerves Right in the New Century

Missing volumes of the *News* mean we can only guess that Esling continued to use both his Rossland daily and his weekly to do battle with the *Miner*. We can also assume that he continued his unswerving support for Conservative candidates and devoted much space to criticizing Joe Martin during his short period as Liberal-Conservative BC premier. Liberal Prime Minister Sir Wilfrid Laurier also felt the sting of Esling's editorial whip. "It is with a feeling of shame that one speaks of the gross and scandalous corruption of the Grit Party," Esling wrote as the country was about to go to the polls in November 1900. He hoped voters "will pronounce an emphatic verdict of 'guilty' on this gang of pirates."[253]

His support extended to Colonel Topping's bid to incorporate Trail as a city, with Esling claiming "the sooner we break loose from this cheese-paring, thin-skinned government, and run our own municipal affairs, the better for us." He called for more public spirit from local businesses, earlier calling them "idle and irascible." In late December 1900, a mass meeting discussed incorporation and some citizens expressed concern about increased taxes. These were dismissed when it was shown the new city would benefit by increased revenues for local improvements.[254]

Despite his carping about the lack of public spirit, another safe assumption is that Esling's papers would remain in strong support of business over labour. His *Evening Record* did sport a typographical union label in its masthead, but there was little else to suggest sympathy with the local working class amidst stories about workplace fatalities, suicides, murder trials, hockey, cricket and tennis tournaments, and ads for "Laxative Bromine Quinine Tablets." The latter was said to cure a cold in one day. The business of mining, smelting, and railway development, not the labour movement, supplied the meat and potatoes of Esling's *Record* and presumably his *News*.

Front-page *Record* coverage of the ongoing Boer War in South Africa, in which some Rosslanders were fighting, would have been reprinted in the *News*. So would the steady flow of anti-Chinese patter. In one instance, the *Record* editor hailed union men "for attacking the Chinaman in his tenderest spot, his pocket—by starting a co-operative laundry."[255]

During the labour dispute over the eight-hour day, Esling's daily consistently took the side of the mine owners, who argued that contract labour should not be undermined by the shorter work hours that the BC legislature had instituted for underground workers. An editorial commenting on the Canadian Mining Institute's objection to the eight-hour law said it "interferes with the freedom of contract by restricting the hours of labor underground which has led to the closing down of many active mines in this Province and has caused a disturbance of the cordial relations which had hitherto existed between capital and labor."[256] During the latter part of 1899 and throughout 1900, Esling persisted in supporting privately contracted labour over the miners' collective bargaining rights.

By early 1900, members of WFM Local 38 in Rossland, already long riled by the *Rossland Miner*'s vicious attacks against unions, had also run out of patience with the *Evening Record*. In 1899, the union bought the weekly *Industrial World,* and on May Day 1900, changed the name to the *Rossland Evening World*. It then began publishing in direct competition with the other local and regional newspapers.[257] By 1901, the *World* was well established as the miners' newspaper and would serve in that role for the next three years. It was the weapon the miners' union needed as strike clouds loomed over the Golden City.

The strike began on July 4, 1900, while a Northport smelter dispute was still simmering. The next day, between 1,200 and 1,400 miners were out on strike, reported the *World*. It also noted that the Rossland News Boys Union refused to deliver the *Miner*, which, along with the Rossland Board of Trade, formed the backbone of opposition to the strike. The newsboys then struck in sympathy with the miners' union.[258] The *World* referred to the *Miner* as the "Morning Whiner" and called it a "warm supporter of the Miners' Union and union principles under its former owner Augustus Heinze." However incongruous that seemed, since Heinze was never a union man, his sale of the paper to the Le Roi Mining Company in June would ensure that the *Miner* "quickly adopted a bitterly anti-union line."[259]

As Trail historian Turnbull notes, Trail was incorporated as a city on Dominion Day (July 1) 1901. Colonel Topping was named the city's first mayor but would remain so for only a year. Starting in July, the new city council, mandated by a seal of incorporation that displayed the motto "Gold Must Be Tried by Fire," passed bylaws governing tradesmen, liquor sales, and dogs.[260] Before incorporation, "vice was tolerated," Turnbull noted. "Horses and cattle thronged the main thoroughfares" and "the town was slovenly, its streets and bridges in disrepair."[261] The *News* had supported incorporation, Esling arguing that "Trail is waking from a long Rip Van Winkle sleep and is getting a move on. She has been known as sleepy hollow long enough."[262] On a sad note, the weekly reported the death of the beloved Father Pat (Henry Irwin) in Montreal. Sometimes called the Cowboy Pastor, he had "conducted the first religious services in Trail."[263]

On February 12, 1901, the *Vancouver Province* reported that E.H. Lewis had acquired a half interest in the *News* and that it "has manifested signs of vigorous growth and a disposition to develop into one of the best weeklies of the upper country." The coast daily added that it "will be wholly a home-printed production."[264] Real estate and financial agent Lewis would supervise business interests, while

C.S. Clarke acted as *News* editor.[265] How long they remained in those positions is unknown. However, on Dominion Day 1901, they had much to report. "Heaven favoured the town on that day," wrote Turnbull. "Everywhere gleamed the gold and black of the city's colours."[266] The sun shone brightly as the Trail baseball team defeated Rossland. Children enjoyed numerous races in the streets. Hundreds of Rosslanders came on the morning train. Lacrosse teams fought it out. And everyone enjoyed the great Calithumpian Parade.[267]

What the *News* was like in 1902 is beyond retrieval apart from the snippets of news that appeared in a weekly column called "Trail 20 Years Ago." Even then, the selected items were often of a social nature. We

Eugene Topping, the father of Trail. Courtesy Trail Historical Society

may, however, assume the *News* covered the Rossland miners' strike that ended in January 1902, with the union all but decimated. If the *Record* is any indication of how the *News* might have covered labour activities, it seems doubtful that Esling's pro-business editorial posture in the *Record* would have differed greatly from that shown in his Trail weekly. Meantime, although extant editions of Esling's *News* did not appear again until January 23, 1904, the intervening years were significant ones.

We know that Noble Binns, a local businessman, replaced Topping as mayor in early 1902, but he resigned within a year to become a police magistrate. His replacement was James Hargrave Schofield, another businessman, who stayed as mayor until 1907 when he was elected to the provincial legislature. City council focused on an agitation in the Gulch where many smelter workers, including several immigrant families, were essentially squatting. Council reached agreement with the CPR, which owned the land as part of its railway land grant, and the squatting workers were able to purchase land to build their homes. Council also reactivated the ferry service that had once carried passengers across the Columbia when Heinze owned the smelter. Apparently, it was no luxury voyage, with passengers complaining that it ran infrequently.

Though councillors were keen to make improvements, there were still "wooden sidewalks and dusty thoroughfares" in the smelter city, as historian Turnbull described it. "Small frame houses clung precariously to the lower slope of Lookout Mountain, while on a bench above the town stood a neat white schoolhouse. Spires of a few churches mingled with the big barnlike halls and, down at the river's edge, a grandstand and ballfield were used for sports in summer and a rink in winter. Only the occasional sternwheeler now called at the boat landing," she continued. "Over all hovered thick yellow smoke from the smelter, its acrid fumes scorching trees and flowers."[268]

The 1903 volume was also lost, but some local news coverage could be found in the coast papers. On February 2, 1903, for example, the *Vancouver Daily World* reported that Esling "has left Trail to assume an important position in Tacoma, where his family resides. The city will miss a bright, cheerful and energetic businessman." He was presented with a "handsome purse of gold."[269] Whatever Esling's intentions, he was not gone long, and the *News* apparently continued to appear. We can be certain that the weekly and its Conservative owner hailed the election victory of Richard McBride and his Conservatives on October 8, 1903.

Esling's Return, Chinese Bashing, WFM Local 105, and a New Name in 1904

In January 1904, Esling was back in the *News* masthead. Still Trail's biggest booster, the hustler from Olympia strived to attract new residents to its "population of 2000 at least," enjoying "a pay roll of $75,000 a month." Esling now listed James D. Anderson as his co-publisher. The two businessmen also co-owned a local real estate firm. As an inducement to migrate to the Kootenay district, they shared the following assessment of the smelter city:

> What other city in the world has no poverty, no liability to famines, pestilences, floods, blizzards, cyclones, earthquakes, or rainy seasons, no Sunday laws, debts, boodlers [corrupt politicians], advertising doctors, Dowieites, or other brands of religious cranks, mediums, faith cureists, spiritualists, business men doing business in their wife's name in order to defraud creditors, food faddists, anarchists, christian scientists, or patent medicine men.[270]

Esling's editorial did not mention trade unionists, even though many Trail residents would become members of the smelter's Western Federation of Miners (WFM) Local 105 as soon as it formed.

Several balls and an ice carnival marked the leap year in February. Hockey had joined football and baseball as significant pastimes in the city, a skating rink having been opened sometime between 1900 and 1904. A new telephone exchange had also opened and users were issued with numbers rather than having to use their names. "Not a single Chinaman has been reported as having paid the $500 poll tax for entry into Canada," the *News* commented about the Chinese head tax adopted in the legislature early in the year.[271]

March brought another smelter fatality and a worker's left arm was severed, harbingers of what was to come if workplace safety hazards went unchecked. An editorial claimed Trail's opera house was "the most dangerous in Canada and perhaps the world" because of inadequate fire escapes.[272] Summer editions focused on school honour rolls, church and social club events, and what would become customary negative coverage of the Doukhobors, the Russian religious sect that would move to BC from Saskatchewan in 1908. An item about the new rifle club may have missed the notice of some readers. It recorded the score of a newcomer named Selwyn Gwillym Blaylock.[273] He had arrived in Trail in 1899 at twenty years of age, fresh from his graduation at McGill University in Montreal. He would stay for the next forty-six years, rising meteorically in the smelter hierarchy, and would have a massive influence on the smelter city.

In early October, Trail's baseball team was declared "Undisputed Champions of the Kootenays" after defeating Fernie.[274] Coverage of the Russo-Japanese war appeared sporadically. From its earliest days, the *News* sometimes gleefully reported the problems of other Kootenay newspapers. In one example, John Houston, editor of the *Nelson Tribune*, was sued for libel and the raucous trial was covered in the *News*. Poetry continued to surface with verses scolding Russia for attacking Japan and Sir Wilfrid Laurier for being a Liberal.

On November 19, 1904, the weekly became the *Trail News*, although the masthead still showed the *Trail Creek News* being "published Saturdays by [W.K.] Esling & James D. Anderson." The publishing year ended December 24, and the lack of editorial comment throughout the year may have made readers wonder if anyone had been at the switch. With the paper's name change to match the shortened name of the city, the readership might have expected improvements in the *News*. Alas, there were only minor adjustments, mostly to accommodate increased advertising.

Sharp Shooter Blaylock, Labour Disputes, Murder and Cricket in 1905

Finally, on January 7, 1905, the *Trail Creek News* banner disappeared for the last time, thus further erasing the legacy of W.F. Thompson. Like a ship without a captain, the weekly continued into the New Year with heavy emphasis on hockey and mining but not much else. The front page of the *News* was increasingly filled with display advertising, leaving even less room for news. The editorial page mostly avoided comment on local issues. One spring edition reported "the shingle mill at Salmo has discharged all whitemen and introduced thirty Japanese instead." The news item noted that police had escorted the Japanese workers to the mill, but that despite the anger among the displaced mill workers, "no disorder occurred though one C.M. O'Brien 'Socialist Organizer,' counselled resistance to the police whom he called the servants of capital and the real enemy of the working men."[275]

One name kept reappearing amidst the proliferation of ads for supposed medical cure-alls, real estate deals, and legal notices. It was S.G. Blaylock. His star was rapidly rising as a defenceman in the hockey arena when in January he scored the first goal for the home team against Rossland in "a spirited tussle with the puck."[276] Blaylock would become a lifelong supporter of Kootenay hockey and the Trail Smoke Eaters, the smelter city's future world champion amateur team.

In May, Esling and Anderson provided a glimpse of pioneer Trail Creek with a reprint from the *News* of ten years earlier that revived memories of founder W.F.

Smelter president S.G. Blaylock. Courtesy Trail Historical Society

Thompson's first impressions. The article gave due credit to city founder Colonel Topping and his business partner Frank Hanna for their role in the "much talked of town."[277] The flood of 1894 was remembered as it had wiped out much of Topping and Hanna's buildings. Heinze, a lesser-known Trail figure than he had been in Thompson's day, was recalled as the smelter's builder. In sports news, Blaylock continued to improve his rifle range shooting scores.

A murder in early June on Red Mountain near Rossland received the *News*'s full attention, replete with graphic details of the deadly wounds inflicted "with a pick handle covered in blood."[278] It was the first big news story to appear in the weekly in months. Blaylock made the sporting news again with his performance in a tennis tournament with Rossland. The news hole continued to shrink with many items cribbed from the *Rossland Miner*, which Esling bought in 1905.

Heinze proved he could still command a front-page spot in mid-July when it was rumoured that his Butte, Montana, copper company was about to be absorbed after a long and bitter fight that involved "the loss of many lives."[279] Drownings, fires, workplace fatalities and suicides stayed on the front page, along with the usual array of titillations. For example, a butcher in Belleville, Ontario, "in a fit of coughing threw up a lizard five inches long."[280] A borrowed item from the *Nelson Tribune* scolded the Crow's Nest Pass Coal Company, saying it exhibited "a combined heartlessness and trickiness which it would be hard to match in the annals of the industrial world."[281] Such tough pro-worker stances were usually non-existent in the Trail paper.

Cricket joined other sports on the front page in the fall. More than 207,000 Russians and more than 155,000 thousand Japanese had been killed during the sixteen-month-old Russo-Japanese war, the *News* noted in "Facts and Figures."[282] Once again, readers learned of a labour dispute, this time in Nanaimo where miners had agreed to a two-year settlement so that the city "will be free from the evil results of the strife between capital and labor."[283] In late October, Granby smelter workers met with the employer to discuss an eight-hour day. The smelter at Grand Forks, BC, founded in 1899, was processing ore from nearby Phoenix.[284]

The masthead was missing from editions late in the year, but Esling and

Anderson kept advertising sales active. A self-serving article quoted an Illinois senator: "a local paper is the best investment a community can make. It may not be crowded with great thought, but financially it is of more benefit than both preacher and teacher. Today editors do more for less pay than any man on earth."[285] In mid-December, the *News* noted that there were eleven licensed hotels in the smelter city. At year's end, the masthead had still not returned and again the usual seasonal greeting to readers and an annual news roundup were noticeably absent.

The Value of Lead, An Earthquake, Heinze's Return, Fruit Lands Boom in 1906

The *News* began 1906 with an expansive article on the Trail smelter's "output for the year."[286] The value of its production of gold, silver, copper and lead topped more than $7,000,000. The new Huntington-Heberlain process of lead smelting was touted as part of yet higher profits. Perhaps the smelter's financial success was the most fitting way to welcome the New Year. As the smelter business went, so went the new city of Trail. That had been the credo of the weekly since it began in 1895, and Esling and Anderson were determined to hold to it.

Earlier in the week, an earthquake had rocked the smelter city, setting "the glasses and crockeryware to tinkling," but no great damage was done. For several editions, Esling and Anderson had been broadcasting the presence of fruit land

Rossland Miners' Union Hall, built in 1898, served as the meeting place for union conventions. Courtesy Rossland Museum and Discovery Centre

buyers from Manitoba and Alberta. A New Year's item suggested they look for the land in the Trail area rather than Nelson. It was less a news item and more a covert advertisement for land sellers. Hockey dominated the front page, with S.G. Blaylock providing "an almost impregnable defence" for the Trail smelter team.[287]

In late January, the *News* announced the merger of several industrial interests to form Canadian Consolidated Mines, Limited. The deal would merge the smelter and Rossland's power company with several mines. It was the first concrete hint of what would become the Consolidated Mining and Smelting Company of Canada (later Cominco).

As one of the mildest winters in memory subsided, F.A. Heinze again adorned the *News* front page in March. Perhaps it was no surprise for readers to learn that the copper king had invested in the Bulkley Valley in northern BC, where Colonel Topping had been exploring mining possibilities for months. Once again, the *News* offered its negative opinion on trade unions when it reported the arrests of WFM leaders for the murder of Idaho's governor, Frank Steunenberg, "because he enforced the law at the time of the famous Coeur d'Alene outrage" by the WFM.[288]

The Trail Mill and Smelter Union WFM Local 105 now represented about 1,000 smelter workers in the smelter city. Rossland's WFM Local 38 had existed since 1895 and was the most active miners' union in the Kootenay district. The local was possibly the first Canadian union to join the radical Industrial Workers of the World (the Wobblies). Civic-minded and politically aware, the local had built the Rossland Miners' Union Hall, which opened in 1898. In mid-March, the *News* noted "that blatant anarchist E.V. Debs, in a long shriek to his 'comrades' in the 'Appeal to Reason' says that Governor Steunenberg got only his due and if the leading officials of the Western Federation of Miners—who are accused of assasinating [*sic*] and are now under arrest—are convicted, that there will be an armed revolution in the United States, and that he will bring it about."[289]

The *News* also took oblique shots at the Opposition party. For example, the paper noted in late March that "Mrs. Jimmie Anderson, another celebrity that Trail has produced, is threatening to horsewhip Mr. J.A. McDonald, the leader of the opposition in Victoria, and each and every newspaper man in the province who has called her 'a female adventurer' because she engineered the Kaien Island deal. She states she is a lady."[290] A scandal emerged after McDonald's Liberals were accused of collaborating with the Grand Trunk Railway to gain them an advantage in purchasing Kaien Island.[291] On the same page, the weekly reprinted a *New York Times* poem about F.A. Heinze: "Everybody works but Heinze./He sits around all day,/Figuring up his profits/To while the time away/."[292] Ten years after his arrival in the Kootenay district, the copper king was still showing up in the *Trail News*.[293]

Judging from the number of front-page articles in April and May on fruit lands for sale in the district, Esling and Anderson must have been enjoying the resulting real estate boom. The weekly also regularly tracked views on new federal legislation such as the "Lord's Day Observance Bill," which the paper did not support because "it will be illegal to shoot at anything on Sunday, play baseball, publish a Sunday paper, run Sunday trains, etc." It slammed "the sanctimonious, clerical sneaks who are thrusting this tyrannical law down the throats of the indifferent majority and the progressive minority differ very little from the clerics who burned and imprisoned those who differed with them in religion."[294]

However, Esling and Anderson did support "the bill to protect the poor and ignorant from the fraud practiced on them by the patent medicine companies." In a moment of civic-mindedness, the publishers lauded the bill, saying "all decent magazines and many newspapers are refusing to [any] longer be a party to the defrauding of the unfortunate by carrying the ads of these concerns." It was not clear if the *News* would carry the ads, but "the yellower and rottener the paper is the greater the number of these fraud ads you will see in it."[295]

In June, Upton Sinclair's *The Jungle*, an exposé of the meat slaughtering industry in Chicago, was highlighted and despite the book being "a socialistic one," it was reviewed favourably.[296] Women's suffrage, usually dismissed in the *News*, was attacked head on in a piece that accused British suffragettes of "hysteria."[297] Late in June, the weekly announced that 1,400 men were employed in Rossland and Trail. The paper also noted that Mrs. J.C. Esling was visiting her son.

In September, nuptials were celebrated when Colonel Topping married his former business partner's wife, Mary Jane Hanna.[298] The couple was to live in Victoria, ending their long association with Trail. In another blast from the past, the *News* welcomed the arrival of the *Tanana Daily Miner* in Fairbanks, Alaska. The editor? None other than *News* founder W.F. Thompson.[299]

By mid-November, the United Mine Workers of America's two-month-old coal strike in Fernie was over. Buried on the back page was news that "mechanics on the hill have been granted a nine-hour-day with no reduction in wages." The *News* credited the company for acting "in a spirit of fairness" and the union for "the reasonableness of the request."[300] After months of absence and with no explanation, Esling had returned to the masthead.

Tory McBride Wins, Esling Bows Out, Bab Babington Comes Aboard in 1907

The front page of the first edition of 1907 was packed with wire service copy in a column called "Right Off the Wire." Ads were more plentiful than ever. Then, in late January, Esling penned his first editorial in over a year in support of former Trail mayor James H. Schofield, a Conservative candidate in the provincial election. He also noted the promotion of S.G. Blaylock to manager of Nelson's Hall Mines smelter, reporting that he would leave his job as assay office chief on his way up the corporate ladder.

The following week, Schofield was victorious, as was the Conservative party of Premier Richard McBride. Esling was elated, writing that "cheer after cheer rent the air."[301] Esling's dislike of Doukhobors resurfaced in the *News* in March with a report on a dispute over taxes in Yorkton, Saskatchewan.[302] Heinze, too, was facing a lawsuit brought by Sir Thomas Shaughnessy regarding Columbia and Western Railway land. Another rail luminary, James Jerome Hill of the Great Northern Railway, born a Canadian, was the subject of an editorial when he claimed prosperity was ending. Esling differed and suggested that perhaps the rail magnate was using the prophecy of doom to stave off wage demands. It was to be his last editorial, for on March 9, 1907, Esling disappeared from the paper's masthead altogether.

Esling would carry on as owner of the paper until 1915 when failing eyesight forced him to give up his newspaper career, but the little hustler from Tacoma had definitely demonstrated that he had staying power as the second of the early printer's devils to come to Trail. He had marked out a permanent patch in Kootenay newspapering. Now he would concentrate on publishing the daily *Rossland Miner*, making his mark in local real estate and business enterprises in Rossland and Trail, and eventually in politics.

3–TRAIL NEWS (1907–1914)

A CANADIAN STEERS THE NEWS AS THE GREAT WAR BEGINS

Trail's Only Newspaper Struggles to Please Workplace, Household and Business

W.K. "Billy" Esling had catapulted himself into daily publishing with the *Rossland Miner*, relegating Trail residents to second-class reader status. With Esling focused on the larger Rossland readership and advertising clientele, he needed to find someone to handle his *Trail News* operation. Early in 1907, he found such a man. Without fanfare on March 16, 1907, Arthur Richard Babington bumped Esling from the masthead to become "Manager" of the twelve-year-old weekly, the first Canadian-born editor to do so.

Much had happened in Esling's world since Thompson had hired him in 1896 as city editor. He had cultivated a strong presence in one of the two local Freemason's lodges, he attended various Board of Trade banquets, and like his predecessor, he was an unstoppable city booster, urging people to move to Trail and partake of the blossoming economic miracle. He was building a real estate and newspaper empire that required his full attention. He needed a manager who would do the hard work of producing the Trail weekly, while also bolstering the Conservative party provincially and federally.

In 1907, Babington was twenty-nine years old, ten years younger than Esling. He arrived in Trail in 1904, a stranger to the city, an outsider.[303] It is possible that he found a job with the *Rossland Miner* when Esling bought the daily the following year. So Esling may have been familiar with his skills. Babington's string of previous jobs at various Ontario newspapers also gave him an understanding of a small city's collective mindset, idiosyncrasies and prejudices. However, he lacked knowledge of life in mining camps and boom towns. What he also lacked was a sense of Trail's evolving place in the country. His new post would test his ability to adapt.

Babington was born in the small town of Tara in Bruce County, Ontario, on August 21, 1878, the youngest son of

Trail News editor A.R. Babington as mayor of Melfort, SK. Courtesy Melfort City Hall

Irish immigrants.[304] He went to school in nearby Invermay,[305] later learning the printing trade at the *Hepworth Journal,* a weekly in the small village of Hepworth, near Wiarton, the main town on the South Bruce Peninsula. By the time he arrived in Trail, Babington had worked on at least four other newspapers: the *Ingersoll Sun,* the *Lindsay Watchman-Warden,* the *Huntsville Forester,* and the *Port Arthur Chronicle.* Apparently, he proved his worth for at least one employer.

In June 1902, C.F. Campbell, publisher of the *Wiarton Canadian,* and presumably also the publisher of the Hepworth paper, attested to Babington's printer's devil skills, noting that he was "a very tasty job printer with modern ideas and a fast man on the [type] case." Campbell added, "I have used him on local reporting and have found that for a young man he was fully up to the requirements." Campbell paid Babington $9 a week and "consider that I had him cheap." A further inducement to hire the young man: "He is one of those kind of men who do not think of time."[306] The Campbell letter, sent to T.A. Bellamy, publisher of the Ingersoll paper, would have impressed Esling, for he needed a workhorse to hold down both the printing operation in Trail and to cover any significant news events. What Campbell failed to add was that Babington could not type. He used what he jokingly called the "hunt and hope like Hell" method that was not uncommon among pioneer editors, who were more adept at setting lead type than operating a typewriter keyboard.[307]

Eighteen months after he became the *News* manager, Babington married British-born Mary Freeman in Nelson on November 30, 1908.[308] The couple would

Kee Chinese Store in Rossland, BC, ca. 1898. Courtesy Rossland Museum and Discovery Centre

have five children, as well as a stillborn daughter in 1911.[309] Unlike Esling, a life-long bachelor, Babington was a family man with family interests. He soon became Trail's school board chair, a position he held throughout his time at the paper. Board activities were regularly reported, often on the front page of the paper, and children's activities at school and in church were well covered. Boy Scout and later Girl Guide events also received ample space. Perhaps sponsored by Esling, Babington also joined the Fidelity Lodge of the local Freemasons and was installed in several executive positions. Both men were community-spirited and both seemed to share a conservative political outlook, although Babington joined the Liberal Party after leaving Trail.

By 1907, whether he was ready or not, Esling handed him the reins. But no one could call it a great start. There were few editorial innovations and fewer design improvements. It almost seemed that Esling was holding the puppet strings, quietly dictating policy. Of course, he had a right to guard his major business asset and to monitor and approve any changes that Babington might contemplate. They seemed to agree that heavier coverage of trade unions was a sound business decision in a town full of unionized readers. It wouldn't match the massive imprint of the mining and smelting coverage, but occasionally labour stories appeared side by side with business ones. There was also the mutual concern with promoting a head tax on Chinese workers and favouring the restriction of immigration to Canada. The issue would explode in September with the anti-Asian riots in Vancouver.[310]

As he began his new job, readers might have wondered what to expect of the new manager. Would he climb out from under Esling's thumb and turn an increasingly dull four-page newspaper into one that Trail readers would find useful, entertaining and informative? For the next seven years, readers would watch and wait for signs that their local newspaper was transforming into more than Esling's weekly dose of often one-sided material plucked from other newspapers and telegraphic news services.

No Dowieites, Chinese Immigration, Heinze Downfall, and a Smelterman's Ode

In his first edition, Babington included old age pensions on the front page. An editorial noted the passing of John Alexander Dowie, "a self-styled modern Elijah," who led a religious cult.[311] Esling had promised potential new residents that, among many undesirables, they would find no Dowieites in Trail, and Babington would oblige by avoiding any positive comment and by publishing news about his own St. Andrew's Anglican Church and the four other mainstream Trail churches.

Business continued to take up space on all four pages, as it had under Esling. Now, however, the editorial page allowed for some political commentary. Babington even took a mild nationalist approach, arguing that Canada need not "look for favors from the capital of the American nation."[312] He also obliged his boss by borrowing from Esling's *Rossland Miner* to promote land purchases in the district.

When labour-friendly member of the provincial parliament Parker Williams, first elected as a socialist in 1903 in the Vancouver Island riding of Newcastle, introduced a bill in the legislature calling for pay days every two weeks instead of monthly, the *News* manager argued that "such a law... would only hamper the mining, smelting and lumbering industries."[313] In May, the *News* told workers not to be concerned about new technology in the mines, for it would be to their advantage. "It is not enough that a man should master a single machine and confine himself to its use," the article said.[314]

The Chinese immigration question continued to interest Babington. "Mongolian farm laborers are asking and receiving as high as $50 a month and board," he noted in one article.[315] Clearly, Babington had no disagreement with Esling regarding the Chinese, but labour might have been a different matter. That summer he devoted space to WFM Local 105's smoker, calling it "a grand success and one continuous round of pleasure from start to finish."[316] The "splendid musical program" included a poem called "Ode to the Union Smeltermen" sung to the tune of "Auld Lang Syne." The *News* said it "brought down the house." One stanza stood out, with its cheer to the WFM:

> With unity and stable minds, the workman should progress.
> And arbitrate all grievances, which leads to sure success. Be loyal to your order, to each brother lend a hand. Like true men strive to aid, cement the federation band.[317]

While union smokers were men-only social events that focused on musical programs and other forms of entertainment at an affordable fifty cents, they could occasionally stress the larger social goals of trade unionism. The poem was one example.

The Rossland miners' strike of 1901 had left lingering bad feelings about employers and the apparent weakness of unionism in the wake of powerful government agents. But it also created strong memories of how the workers "should progress" and it would become clearer as the years passed that a smelter union like Local 105 would need to build on the resulting solidarity. In August, labour issues stayed in the *News*, with a "Labor Circles" column offering mostly US items, but one item reminded readers that the national Trades and Labour Congress would hold its twenty-third annual convention at Winnipeg. The main issue would be immigration, "one of the most difficult problems confronting organized labor, affecting as it does wages, hours of labor, in fact every condition that surrounds workers in the sale of their labor."[318]

Showing some initiative, Babington also introduced a "fashion letter" as a regular feature, contributed by "a Lady writer."[319] A reprint from a New York journalist was reminiscent of earlier boasts from Esling and Thompson. "The only real and truly independent press is to be found in country towns or small cities," wrote John Swinton.[320] The press got further attention: "the man in public life and the man who writes in the public press shall, both of them, if they are really good servants of the people, be prompt to assail wrongdoing and wickedness."[321]

In midsummer, labour hit the front page with a resolution from Local 105 calling for a stop to the export of local coal so that the Crow's Nest Pass Coal

Company could continue to supply the necessary fuel to the smelters and mines in the Kootenays. Babington also repeated the call for everyone to attend the Labour Day celebrations and gave the day good coverage, calling it "a pronounced success."[322] Rivalry between Trail and Rossland burst onto the front page when Trail won the baseball tournament and Rossland won the football competition.

In November, the *News* joined the world's press in covering the fallout from the Heinze Brothers-induced Wall Street Panic of 1907.[323] "Heinze's Downfall" reported "the crash of the Heinze interests, which led to the recent financial upheaval."[324] Another Local 105 smoker took place and "a splendid program was rendered by local talent, including several Irish jigs."[325] Local 105 formed the Trail Rochdale Co-operative Association and Richard Parmater "Parm" Pettipiece of the typographical union assumed his position as western organizer of the Vancouver Trades and Labour Council. Pettipiece helped found the Socialist Party of Canada and was editor of several publications, making him a printer's devil of a different kind.[326]

Never short of diversions, the *News* noted that "Mr. Cranbourne-Pugh, Palmist, is desirous of thanking all those ladies and gentlemen who have so kindly recommended him." Sibbald the Jeweler advised readers "to get one of those elegant gold and silver headed Umbrellas."[327] And Pauline Johnson, "the famous Indian entertainer," would perform at the Trail Opera House. A "desperado" wanted for murder was killed near Kamloops. A John Ruskin anti-war poem appeared on the editorial page, but if you discounted the pacifist Doukhobors, which the *News* often did, conscientious objection to war was largely absent from the weekly.[328]

In late November, Babington returned to the more serious subject of a Rossland miners' vote to accept lower wages due to sagging metal profits. Since July 1906, wages had "been $4 a day for machine men and $3.25 a day for shovelers."[329] The miners would not have appreciated an article in the same edition in which future Prime Minister William Lyon Mackenzie King espoused conciliation boards as a way to settle workplace disputes. "In strikes affecting the public welfare the government has the right to interfere," King declared.[330] Miners recalled his disastrous role during the 1901 strike when he turned on the strikers and refused to recommend compliance with the Alien Labour Act prohibiting foreign workers from undermining the strike.

In December, Babington reported the Vancouver Trades and Labour Council's demand for the dismissal of Lieutenant Governor James Dunsmuir. The reason: as president of the Wellington Colliery company, he had hired 500 Japanese labourers. As the year ended, the addition of so much labour coverage marked a clear departure from what readers had come to expect from Esling. But was Babington's *News* any more sympathetic to the union cause in a town brimful of unionists? As his years as manager wore on, the answer to that question would become increasingly clear.

Sam Gompers, Big Bill Haywood, Doukhobors, and a New Mayor in 1908

Babington's second year saw the usual plodding efforts to report mining and smelting news, much of it cribbed from other sources, most of it addressed to corporate interests. The "Local Notes" column gladdened those who appeared in short items on marriages, funerals, promotions, movements in and out of town and other social news. City council meetings got their own weekly column, with newly elected Mayor Fred G. Morin holding court as council considered agenda items to do with water, sewage, police, and fire. The latter was of great interest to the *News* editor, and he challenged council to fix the problem of weak hose pressure that had led to failures to save several buildings. Even historic Trail House, the first hotel in the smelter city, went up in flames.

One noticeable change was the lack of sassy comments about other Kootenay newspapers and their editors. From Thompson on, the *News* had used this jocular sense of humour in describing some of its competitors. One reason for the change was probably Esling's ownership of the *Rossland Miner*. The paper had long been a target of competing editors, especially when the Le Roi mining company owned it. When F.A. Heinze assumed ownership, it also took some harsh criticism. Now, however, Babington did not dare comment negatively on the daily. Its owner, after all, was his boss.

Babington had learned quickly that Trail was a sport-mad town, and he generated much-craved articles on hockey, curling, boxing, baseball and lacrosse. Reports regularly appeared on the local cricket and rifle clubs. City council passed an early closing bylaw, but councillors rejected a motion to remove bawdy houses from the Bowery. WFM women's auxiliary No. 2 thanked supporters for helping with its first dance, held at the Swartz dancing pavilion, and the weekly announced that the US labour movement would soon have a national newspaper syndicate.

Supplementing its labour coverage were reports on immigrant activities. In one item, it might have appeared that Babington took a sympathetic view when the *News* reported that 50,000 Italian workers in the clothing trades were prevented from acting as strikebreakers against the United Hebrew Trades.[331] Elsewhere, however, an editorial explained "How the Hindoos Are to Be Kept Out of British Columbia."[332] Hindu immigrants were treated as unwanted and undeserving. Readers could also depend on reports on Chinese men arrested for gambling or involvement in the Black Hand.[333] BC Indigenous leaders' attempts to engage in the decision-making process regarding white settler encroachment on their ancestral lands were always viewed as insignificant curiosities.

Babington generally but not always adopted Esling's negative position on Doukhobors, considering it his civic duty to report on their activities. To that end, he noted that sect leader Peter "Lordly" Verigin was searching for property where his followers could settle. The *News* advised that "they are communists as regards property, and are all vegetarians, as their religion forbids them to kill any living thing."[334] By July, the sect's presence in the district impressed Babington, for he noted their "wonderful results" in agriculture. He added, "returns from their produce are not just individual gain. It all goes to a common fund, and all share in its benefits."[335] Was the *News* softening its views on socialism?

Near the end of July, the weekly included an item about a scientist who had developed a way to salvage profits from smelter fumes, arguing "it will mean practically all these values will be added to the profits."[336] It was an early sign of what would happen decades later when company president S.G. Blaylock salvaged smelter waste to produce Elephant Brand fertilizer.

Always conscious of the need to cater to smelter workers' spouses, Babington reported an "insidious menace to feminine morals which lurks in silk petticoats."[337] Also for the women of the house, Mademoiselle Leone, the celebrated palmist and astrologist, was in Trail to display "her clairvoyant gifts."[338] An editorial describing Trail, and particularly the Gulch, as "the dirtiest and most unsanitary place in Canada" might have shocked residents used to hearing nothing but praise for the smelter city. "Festering, germ polluted piles of rubbish and filth have been allowed to accumulate in various quarters and exhale their nauseating effluvium," the article added.[339]

Though it showed civic concern, it was contrary to the booster message readers had come to expect under Thompson and Esling. The issue linked with a nativist prejudice among the majority Anglophone and American population against Italians and other southern European immigrants. Many of them lived in the Gulch and had long complained about the contentious practice of Rossland dumping raw sewage into Trail Creek, which flowed straight through the community.

Esling and other local Conservatives got bad news with the election of Sir Wilfrid Laurier's Liberals on October 26. "Vote for Better Terms and a White British Columbia" was one campaign slogan in the *News*.[340] Clearly, the national electorate disregarded it. The *News* rounded off the year with a puzzlingly positive editorial, arguing that the Chinese are "strangely reasonable" and abhor militarism.[341] With hockey season about to commence, Babington noted that a BC Hockey League had formed in Nelson. And in the spirit of Christmas, a column advised readers "How to Get Rich."

Neither Babington nor Esling appeared in the masthead through much of 1909, rendering the *News* a kind of rudderless ghost ship. There were few editorials and much of the news copy was increasingly about Rossland rather than Trail. Trail readers could still count on seeing city council decisions, Board of Trade discussions, and school board reports. But they could also count on news pages filled with plenty of sales pitches intended to entice readers to buy local products, land and services. There was nothing wrong with advertising. That's how newspapers survive. It was the seamless blending of news with ads that was questionable.

The November provincial election returned a solid slate of Conservatives. James H. Schofield again won his seat in Ymir and continued as the region's political voice in Victoria. For years to come, he would serve in that capacity and grow influential in various other local positions. Conservative Arthur S. Goodeve, a pharmacist, remained the region's Member of Parliament. Federally, the Liberal Laurier government was still fair game for the *News*. Babington continued as treasurer of the Masons' Fidelity Lodge. But his political views seldom appeared in the paper.

The Outlaw Bill Miner, Socialism, Smelter Fumes, and Heinze's Indictment in 1909

Under Babington, the *Trail News* was a long way from matching the quality of Thompson's *Trail Creek News* as 1909 began. Yes, he also focused on aggrandizing business interests and he was also intent on bolstering the public image of the town. Now though, with loyalties divided between the larger mining city of Rossland and the smelter city, readers were served a messy mixture of items mostly from the US with occasional peeks at British and European developments. It had gone from being a paper that was distinctly for Trail readers to one catering more to Rossland's interests. Apparently, the *Trail News* had become a dumping ground for whatever Esling's daily *Rossland Miner* wanted to hand down at the end of the week. Perhaps the main similarity was the weekly's inability to say no to F.A. Heinze. Even when he and his brother crashed the New York stock market in the Wall Street Panic of 1907, the weekly was prepared to forgive him and cheered when his various indictments failed to lead to convictions.

In January, the "Labor World Notes" column featured the American Federation of Labour president, Sam Gompers. Next to stock market news, the usual mining report, and Chamber of Commerce battles against tariffs, BC teachers got some possible good news when a pension scheme was announced. An editorial hailed the migration of BC Hindus to Louisiana and encouraged a similar departure to California for local Doukhobors. Despite noting that they "have proven themselves to be a thrifty and industrious people," they were still pariahs.[342] The long-promised "Fashion Letter" finally appeared. The new curling rink, another Babington interest, and the Italian community's new fund for survivors of the earthquake in Italy were both newsworthy.

In February, the *News* published articles on Canadian caviar, a whale's capture, the Diamond D Ranch in the Bulkley Valley, the regular "Wit and Wisdom" column, and "the vagaries" of getting too fat. One editorial took issue with a *Toronto Globe* journalist's "unmerited reflections on a British Columbia mining camp."[343] Under "Civic Topics," a judge had thrown out the entire city council "owing to the conduct of the returning officer."[344] Late in the month, an editorial outlined BC socialist James H. Hawthornthwaite's Women's Franchise Act in the legislature.

The outlaw Bill Miner, reputedly Canada's first train robber, was covered next to an item about Christian Scientists, faith healers, and others who practise medicine without a licence. "Woman and the Home" was on the editorial page in March, offering home remedies for many concerns. Mayor George F. Weir and his council were re-elected in a repeat election. The *News* regretted one incident where an overly enthusiastic Weir supporter burned one of the opposition candidates in effigy. And Heinze appeared again, as he faced charges of misappropriation of funds: "It is evident that those who are fighting the ex-copper king, not satisfied with getting his money, are anxious to send him to the penitentiary," the *News* declared.[345]

Prime Minister Sir Wilfrid Laurier introduced a department of labour in May with future prime minister William Lyon Mackenzie King as minister. An evangelistic campaign had arrived in Trail, but as Babington noted, "the average citizen takes his religion pretty much the same as he does everything else—with indifference."[346] A Supreme Court hearing in Rossland in June dismissed a suit against the CM&S "to recover damages for alleged loss sustained by the plaintiff [E.C. Smith] through having fruit and other crops destroyed by smelter smoke."[347] The court would reserve judgment in the case.

In other news, the paper relayed rumours that John Houston, once the Nelson mayor, might run for the legislature. The local constable had arrested ten Chinese men "on a charge of gambling and frequenting a gambling house."[348] In an uncharacteristic move, the News ran a positive feature about the Doukhobors: "At Brilliant, formerly Waterloo, they have laid the foundation of a thrifty colony by clearing and planting 350 acres—intend to keep working till they have cleared 4,700 acres—2,700 acres to be devoted to orchards—they are vegetarians, teetotalers, and are opposed to war and violence of all kinds—religion and other particulars of interest—are from the cradle of the Aryan race." Pinched from the Rossland Miner, the article did not reflect Esling's later views when the article added that "those who are interested in humanity and how man is working his way to a higher destiny, can find food for reflection in this simple, plain and god-fearing community."[349]

Summer delivered new charges against Heinze for conspiracy "to obstruct the administration of justice."[350] Once the hero of the smelter city, the former copper king was losing his shine. A miners' strike at Greenwood won union recognition, an anti-discrimination clause and a new wage scale. Indigenous people at Hazelton rebuffed white settlers homesteading on Crown land next to their ancestral land. An editorial backed the use of convict labour to build BC roads. A twenty-three-year-old Italian smelter worker died in a vat of sulphuric acid. And Babington published a warning that young white girls who tutor Chinese men in Victoria need protecting. It was a practice forbidden by law. An article warned of a world-wide increase in divorces, but BC was relatively safe "because of the generally high moral condition of a majority of the residents, and because there is no conjestion [sic] of population, which nearly always brings with it a train of evils."[351]

The WFM's Big Bill Haywood was in Trail near the end of August to speak about the WFM before "a small audience." He was "loudly applauded when he stepped forward to speak and he began his oration by a strong appeal in favor of Socialism."[352] The Trail Rochdale Co-operative Association was declared a success. A Labour Day message called for "a spirit of brotherhood and humanity."[353] The Union Moving Picture Company offered its first weekly performance of movies and vaudeville before a large audience in the Trail Opera House. And after weeks of debate, city council passed a bylaw allowing the city to develop its own public water system.

Indictments against Heinze were dismissed in October. "Mr. Heinze's lesson has been well deserved and his punishment severe enough," the WFM journal Mining World commented.[354] The Grand Trunk Pacific railway wanted to use Asian labour to build its lines into BC. Indigenous leaders were "on the legal warpath… to enforce the proposal that they are entitled to an interest in all the lands of the province under the terms of Confederation."[355] And another BC election was scheduled for November 25.

By mid-November, the *Miner's* anti-prohibition campaign had spilled over to the *News*. An editorial stated that the Richard McBride government was for "preserving this province as a white man's country and preventing the employment of Asiatic labor on large public works."[356] McBride was again elected as BC's Conservative premier. MLA Schofield held his seat with help from the *News*. More Doukhobors would be coming, the *News* informed its readers in December. Again, the paper praised the sect's industriousness. Halley's Comet would be visible during the month.

Blaylock Returns, Eight Hours, Father Pat, and "Any Old Lady" in 1910

In early 1910, the *News* manager was an office-holder not only in the local Freemasons but also in the Loyal Orange Lodge. He entered his second year as school board chair and was listed as a member of Rink No. 8 of the Trail Curling Association. The weekly, meanwhile, continued to suffer from lack of attention. The news pages still promoted local mining, smelting, and fruit growing. Indigenous Peoples, Chinese and Italians often appeared in local courtrooms. Hotel saloons were the scene of drunken brawls, sometimes resulting in charges against the proprietor.

Walter H. Aldridge, the CM&S's first general manager, moved on, and R.H. Stewart took his place. S.G. Blaylock would return from his mission at the company's St. Eugene and Sullivan Mines to serve as assistant managing director. He was in his early thirties. Heinze beat his various indictments for bad business behaviour. The mayor and council congratulated themselves on securing government approval and funding for a new bridge. And the first Trail Boy Scout company was formed, with the *News* publishing a speech by Scout founder Lord Baden-Powell. The WFM District Association No. 6 held its twelfth annual convention in Trail, chaired by Local 105 President John A. McKinnon.

There was no doubt that Esling was influencing news selection without being named in the masthead, and clearly his interests in real estate were ever more present in the *News*. His Conservative politics also ruled the editorial page, with strong anti-Laurier articles federally and pro-McBride ones provincially. Conservative MLA Schofield and MP Goodeve both benefitted from Esling's support in the *News*. Interestingly, Goodeve spoke in favour of the eight-hour day in the House of Commons.

A freight elevator crushed a smelter worker in March and iconoclastic pioneer editor and politician John Houston died at Quesnel. The *News*, previously so admiring of the Doukhobors, turned on them for not becoming British citizens. A front-page report on the sect later described it and its communal lifestyle in detail. The death of King Edward VII in May got the full treatment. "General Jottings" had appeared as a grab bag of news tidbits, such as a Mount Etna eruption and an earthquake in Costa Rica. Greenwood miners were again on strike, this time to protest the employer's failure to fire non-union workers. And elsewhere cannibals killed and ate a Presbyterian minister. Babington (or was it Esling?) was frustrated in June and expressed it through three items on the importance of newspaper advertising and paying the proprietor.

An article appeared in Italian, a rarity, accompanied by a brief note explaining that it referred to a christening in Rossland. Perhaps it showed that Babington recognized he was failing to cater to the large population of Italian mine and smelter workers and their families. Dominion Day was "quietly observed in Trail."[357] The "Fashion Letter" moved to page 1. "Fads and Fashions" appeared on page 3. "The Best Way" returned readers to the old days of boosterism, counselling residents to brag about their city. In mid-July, smelter superintendent Jules Labarthe announced that he was leaving town. Esling was one of two "eloquent champions" thanking Labarthe. "Babbington" [sic] spoke for the press.[358] He was also named secretary of the Trail Boy Scouts.

Father Pat, Trail's pioneer clergyman. Courtesy Trail Historical Society

Business was so slack during the summer months that the *News* published an editorial on the matter. "Suppose that the newspapers should, when the summer comes along, adopt the attitude that it was the time in which to slacken off. Suppose that they cut down to the lowest possible limit all their news dispatches and reports and special features. What a shout there would be!"[359] It was another call out to local business to keep buying ad space. "The newspaper is a law for the indolent, a sermon for the thoughtless, a library for the poor and an admonisher for the lawless," the article continued. "It may stimulate the most indifferent, but it cannot be published without cost and sent to subscribers. This is no joke."[360]

Then an unusual item appeared, profiling a new movement in Britain to create "a workingman's international anti-war organization." Behind the formation was a socialist trade unionist named Maurice Hewlett who outlined "the theory that all financial aid to the warring nations will be denied if a world strike of the unions would go into effect upon the declaration of war."[361]

In September, for the first time in three years, Trail celebrated Labour Day with a Local 105 program. Union secretary J.A. MacKinnon spoke, but his remarks were hardly those of a firebrand. "A working man who did not belong to a union was not doing his duty by himself, his family and his fellow working man," he told the crowd. But "they had no need to strike," he said. "The time of strikes had passed."[362]

Perhaps it was a portent of a defanged WFM to come. A front-page comment in mid-September hinted at Babington's rising frustration and feeling of being unappreciated: "Bringing out a newspaper is an easy task. Anybody can do it. An actor who never earned any other plaudit than a soft tomato or an over-ripe egg will give instructions in handling news. Any old lady with just sufficient knowledge to get on a street car backwards, has… opinions on the way a newspaper should be conducted."[363]

In October, CM&S net profits hit $400,000. Father Pat (Reverend Henry Irvin), the pioneer Kootenay clergyman, was memorialized at the consecration of the new St. George's Church.[364] The Church of England priest had "travelled over forest trails and mountain paths to preach the gospel… in railway construction camps and rough mining communities."[365] He had conducted Trail's first religious service in February 1896 and encouraged the building of the city's St. Andrew's Church in 1899. A November editorial warned that "In spite of the heavy poll tax, the wily Chinee has been sneaking into Canada in fair numbers."[366] Credit for keeping Asian labour out belonged to the Conservative McBride government, the *News* opined. Immigrants continued to serve as editorial fodder in December. Babington was re-elected the Freemasons' Fidelity Lodge treasurer.

Doukhobor Rampage, Borden Wins and Women Incite Violence in 1911

Readers were still confused about who was running the *News* as 1911 began. Babington was often absent from the masthead and Esling's hand was clearly evident. An editorial urged investment, for example, but in Rossland, not in Trail. Another revealed Esling's influence in a lengthy editorial that called on local residents to patronize home merchants who were urged to "advertise consistently."[367] City elections were afoot, and Babington again ran successfully for school trustee. Blaylock was back in Trail in January and had already registered for the St. Andrew's Church vestry committee. His father, Thomas Blaylock, was a Church of England (Anglican) minister. Blaylock the younger won praise as a man with "the right stuff" as he assumed his new, elevated role with the CM&S.[368] At the same time, the WFM district convention was held in Nelson, and delegates passed resolutions about the conditions of BC workers. A few years hence, Blaylock and the smelter union would become bitter adversaries.

Whether Esling was playing puppet master or not, it was to both men's advantage to boost the paper's support. To that end, an article advised that "it's the little home weekly that prints all your little dealings just like you were 'somebody' and loves and boosts your corner of the world."[369] In spite of Babington's later affiliation with the Liberal Party, both men did their share of Liberal bashing, particularly regarding the Laurier government. Both men were active in their civic roles. Babington, for example, had just returned from a convention of school trustees where delegates debated the pros and cons of homework. In January, Esling attended the annual banquet in honour of the 150th anniversary of Scottish poet Robbie Burns's death. For years, smelter workers had been so honouring the working-class poet and his revolutionary songs of egalitarianism with Scotch whisky and haggis, the traditional Scottish dish.[370]

Once again, frustration surfaced in the *News* pages when an article encouraged readers to submit news items: "If your wife licks you, come in and let us see your scars and tender sympathy through the paper." The article summed up as follows: "whatever makes you feel proud, sad, lonesome or glad submit it to our twenty-four carat wisdom and see our matted locks part and stand up on end with gratitude, which will pour from every pore like moisture from a dew 'besprinkled earth'."[371] Perhaps it inspired this similar plea from Babington. "Maybe your editor does not belong to your church or lodge or agree with you politically," said the article, "but he is doing a lot more to keep your town on the map." He then urged readers to help him by "telling him the news instead of criticizing him or trying to take business away from him because he does not happen to see things as some of them do."[372]

MP Goodeve denounced trade reciprocity between Canada and the US, stressing the need to stay close to Mother Britain and avoid an American take-over. Reciprocity threatened jobs, Goodeve later argued. A new law would grant municipalities the power to abolish saloons. A letter from the ministry of health noted that 50 per cent of Trail's schoolchildren are not vaccinated against smallpox. Sightings of bears marked a sure sign of spring. A Trail Improvement Association had formed, with Babington representing the Riverside block.

Spring editions revealed that reciprocity had so riled Babington that he issued a call to arms in anticipation of a fall federal election. The call was to oust the Liberals or "submit calmly to the bartering away of their prosperity to the great nation to the south of us."[373] The anti-reciprocity movement regained space in August with the Kootenays hailing MP Goodeve as a champion of that cause. *The Squaw Man* was playing at the Trail Opera House.

Babington must have cringed when the WFM resolved that the Scouts are "a pious fraud" that encourages "a spirit of militarism which tends to incite and foster the willingness to shoot, maim and murder their fellow men at the behest of the master class, under cover of a corrupted and corrupting spirit of so-called patriotism."[374] It made sense to some, but was unlikely to win Kootenay WFM locals many friends.

Robert L. Borden's Conservatives won the federal election on September 21, thrilling the *News,* which would soon gleefully report that defeated Liberal Prime Minister Laurier might retire. Reciprocity was again the subject of the lead editorial. The Liberals supported it, the Conservatives not so much. An item on the British strike of 75,000 dockworkers and teamsters said "women were the chief inciters to violence in the present troubles."[375] A report on the June Canada Census showed that Trail had a population of 1,460. Rossland had 2,830 and Nelson had 4,473. In December, a Doukhobor rampage was reported in Grand Forks. Members of the sect were protesting the government forcing its laws on them.

Another Smelter Death, Socialist in Town, *Titanic* Tragedy, Roosevelt Shot in 1912

Babington continued in the role of Esling's editorial clone in 1912. Increasingly, the paper simply borrowed and republished items that appeared in the daily *Miner.* The odd photograph adorned some editions, particularly of local MLA Schofield. Political coverage continued to slant to the right, often filling the front page with Conservative propaganda. The defeat of the Laurier government was cause for

Empire Day 1914. Courtesy Greg Nesteroff Collection

prolonged cheering, but there was regret that Goodeve had accepted a position on the federal rail commission.

With the frequent absence of Trail news and comment, readers might have wondered if the *News* was Babington's part-time job. Could he be working at Esling's Rossland daily and simply cobbling together *News* editions from scraps on the newsroom floor? And yet there were no letters complaining about the low quality of the weekly. True, Babington never failed to publish city council decisions, and he always reported on Board of Trade activities. He promoted local initiatives like the new bridge and especially the new school. Sports and cultural events all received regular coverage. So did court appearances for liquor licence abuses at local hotels, poultry club contests and developments in the fruit-growing industry.

The *News* returned to its city booster role in January, boasting that the smelter had 600 employees and a payroll of $60,000 a month. One of those employees, another Italian worker, fell into a flue chamber at the smelter and died. The payroll was part of what made the past year the most prosperous in the history of the city.[376] The Federation of Labour called for the eight-hour day and six-day week, separate schools for Asian children, electoral reforms and improvements to the Workmen's Compensation Act. Doukhobors were dubbed squatters because they refused to become naturalized Canadian citizens. And items on preparations for war between Germany and France were starting to appear.

In March, Trail electors heard socialist candidate Parm Pettipiece criticize the McBride government and present "the usual lecture on Socialism."[377] Schofield easily won re-election. A front-page article asked hopefully, "Is Trail About to Become a Metropolis [?]—All Signs Point That Way." A new ice rink was discussed. The new $45,000 school opened on schedule to much applause. S.G. Blaylock was named honorary president of the Trail baseball club. Trail resident William Hesketh sent Babington an account of the SS *Titanic* disaster in May while he was on vacation aboard the SS *Baltic*. Empire Day was celebrated on May 24. Conservative businessman Robert Francis Green was acclaimed in the June 20 by-election as MP for the riding of Kootenay. The miners' annual union picnic program was published, but it was from Rossland's WFM Local 38, not Trail's Local 105.

That summer, W.D. Wilkinson, president of the BC Federation of Labour, visited Trail. Negotiations between Local 105 and the CM&S concluded with labourers getting a raise to $2.75 from $2.50. William Blakemore was investigating complaints about the Doukhobors, who were often savaged for their refusal to obey the Public School Act, register to vote, or abide by land management laws. Local 105 secretary J.A. MacKinnon resigned and gave a "rattling good address on Industrial Unionism" at the union smoker, stressing that the WFM was "one of the most progressive independent organizations on the American continent, and were known as the fighting organization and were continually endeavoring to remedy conditions for the working class."[378]

In October, the CM&S declared a net profit of $310,345 for the year. Teddy Roosevelt was shot in the chest. Blaylock was again elected honorary president of the hockey club. A November editorial discussed Democrat Woodrow Wilson's US presidential election victory and the rise of Teddy Roosevelt and the Progressive Party. The background of the Balkan War was outlined. Heinze was attempting to squeeze out back taxes on his share of the land in the Columbia and Western Railway deal. And a British suffragette organized a Rossland branch of the BC Political Equality League. As the year closed, Babington was again installed as an officer of the Freemasons.

Union Smokers, "Strange Sect," Women's Vote, and Lead Poisoning in 1913

Babington's name reappeared in the masthead for most of 1913, but the editorial content of the *News* had not altered. Significantly, the "Labor World News" column had completely disappeared. Babington still included labour-related articles, but these were either informational (a union election or smoker) or about a violent strike involving mine workers elsewhere. As usual, Doukhobors and Asians were a constant source of negative comment. Women fared little better, often bearing the brunt of male humour. Unsigned editorials and too few bylined columns prevented readers from discerning whose opinions they were reading.

Esling was no doubt happy to have someone at the helm in Trail while he commanded his daily galleon in Rossland. Still, his financial interests in Trail, including two new stores, meant keeping a close watch on municipal affairs. And Babington was raking in ad revenue as never before, so much so that at times there was little room for news.

When William Blakemore's Royal Commission report on the Doukhobors appeared in January, the *News* dubbed them a "strange sect" but chose not to incite further nativist fears.[379] Blakemore called for an end to the sect's military exemption, children's return to public school, appointment of a "permanent Doukhobor Agent," and the sect's strict observance of all legal registrations such as births, deaths, and marriages.[380] But he did not recommend forcing them to abide by the law.

Among the resolutions at the WFM convention in Nelson was a demand for a $3 minimum wage for smelter workers. WFM Local 105 president George Cantell was elected second vice-president. Peter Verigin was turned away at the US border at Marcus, Washington, accused of being an anarchist. A rare letter to the editor urged candidates in the forthcoming local elections to "take a definite and resolute stand against drunkenness and vice."[381] Dr. D.J. Thom was elected mayor. Babington was again acclaimed school board chair.

The sixteenth annual BC Curling Association bonspiel was held in Trail for the first time, and Babington topped his announcement with "A Curling Ditty" in a Scottish brogue. Premier McBride assured the labour federation that he was opposed to Asiatic immigration. Several letters on the sins of the local tavern appeared. WFM Local 105 sponsored a lecture by Lewis LeClair, president of the National Co-operative Sanitary and Label League, on "Child Labor, Prison Labor, and Other Economics of the Day."[382] A concert was organized to help set up a branch of the Label League in Trail. The Rex joined the Star, giving Trail two cinemas. And the BC legislature's last act before ending the session was to defeat the women's suffrage bill twenty-four to nine.

With the Le Roi mine having petered out, the Le Roi 2 had opened and was reporting favourable production levels at Rossland in March. Still, shareholders wanted costs reduced and that usually meant wage cuts. The bars were ordered to close by 11:00 p.m. and the "girls in the Red Light district" were to leave by Saturday night.[383] The West Kootenay Association Football League was organized. The Eagles planned to meet in Trail. The Rod and Gun Club elected MLA Schofield honorary president in April, and the Improvement Association elected Noble Binns

Le Roi Mine, Rossland, BC, ca. 1900. Courtesy Rossland Museum and Discovery Centre

president and ordered seventy-nine chestnut trees. Future Communist Reverend A.E. Smith of Nelson's Methodist Church told the second Label League gathering about social unrest. Mrs. Bernice Golden Heinze, previously an actress, died of nephritis.

A BC government labour commission visited Trail in May and heard WFM Local 105 endorse a call for the extension of the eight-hour day to all men working in mines and smelters. "Questioned by Mr. Blaylock, Mr. Campbell [Frank Campbell of Local 105] stated that men at the refinery were subject to lead poisoning," the report noted.[384] Campbell also stated, "wages had not advanced in the same proportion as the cost of living and a man with a family earning less than $3.00 a day must work 365 days in a year in order to break even." Blaylock testified "he did not know what percentage of men got leaded. The company was doing everything in its power to prevent it." He did not agree "with Mr. Campbell's statement that half of 140 were affected by lead fumes." He also said, "A minimum wage scale of $4.00 per day would be disastrous."[385]

In mid-May, the Star showed Leo Tolstoy's *Resurrection*. The renowned Russian author had pledged that profits from his novel would go to assist the Doukhobors. Theatre manager Hackney had also booked "another great lesson picture show on Wednesday next, *The Wage Earners*, a three-reel picture of Labor vs. Capital." Hackney explained that "this shows the interior of a great steel plant and the strike of 5,000 men." It was a curious offering given the smelter employer's dominance over Trail. Late in the month, the machinists and boilermakers "laid down their tools… and drew their time at the office, on being refused a raise of wages."[386]

Babington's frustration with his job again reached the boiling point that summer. "Most any man can be an editor," began one comment. "All the editor has to do is to sit at a desk six days a week,… and 'edit' such stuff as this: 'Mrs. Jones, of Cactus Creek, let a can-opener slip last week and cut herself in the pantry'."[387] The item listed other mundane incidents, many sounding exactly like what *News* readers had been seeing since the paper began.

Heinze was being sued for $1 million, Doukhobors were criticized for a midnight burial, coal miner riots broke out at Nanaimo on Vancouver Island, and the militia was called out to quell violence associated with what became known as the Great Coal Strike.[388] On Labour Day, Local 105's J.W. Bennet told the gathering, "the old struggle of lord and slave was still in progress, despite the fact that many people resent that they are called slaves."[389]

An editorial called for a federal network of agencies for the unemployed. In refreshing sympathy with jobless people, Babington argued that "it would be hard to overdo the care of men and women out of work. Far too many people… have been robbed by unscrupulous employment agents."[390] Local 105's Frank Campbell wrote a front-page letter to correct an impression that mine workers' wages elsewhere were lower than those in Trail. In November, comments on a government report on Grand Forks Doukhobors were falsely attributed to an official. The *News* reported the falsehoods, but also reported all the false accusations. Babington was again elected to the executive of the Freemasons' Fidelity Lodge. Blaylock was to represent Trail at the Kootenay-Boundary Hockey League meeting in Grand Forks. Trail won the cup at the West Kootenay Divisional Football League championship playoffs.

United Mine Workers of America leaders were indicted in connection with a Colorado coal strike in December. The *News* reported allegations of lawlessness and violence. The occasional philosophical item on journalism or journalists suggested that the editor was less than satisfied with writing about the latest squabble at city hall, a late-night fight at one of the local hotel bars, or a new prospector's mineral strike. Whether Babington knew it or not, this was to be his last full year at the *News*.

Signs of War, McBride Cup, Typhoid, Prizefighters, and Doukhobors in 1914

War drums were already beating in Europe but if the *News* followed its current path, most of the coverage about it would be reprints from the *Rossland Miner* and the *Nelson Daily News*, a daily since 1902. Meanwhile, hockey was on Trail's mind, and the home team had beaten Rossland in the first game of 1914. The CM&S announced another $400,000 in net profits. A notice called on all union men to support Michigan's striking copper miners by buying a ticket to a benefit dance. "Show the enemies of labor that there is some solidarity in the ranks of labor unionists the world over," urged the notice.[391] Former city councillor Frank E. Dockerill was elected mayor.

Hockey again dominated the news in February with Trail on top of the league standings. The team would win the McBride Cup at the Kootenay-Boundary hockey championships. Cartoons appeared in the weekly for the first time. BC's crime rate was on the rise. Doukhobors took more abuse for not becoming "good citizens in the Dominion."[392] The sect fought back, threatening to engage in public nudity if forced to abide by laws that would force them to send their children to school and other practices that violated their beliefs. The fight to force the Doukhobors to comply with the law continued with a new bill supposedly to protect women and children living under communal conditions.

Heinze lost his earlier appeal and had to pay taxes on more than 300,000 acres of land in the Kootenay-Boundary region. Italian prizefighter Charlie Lucca won against Barney Mullen at a fight in Trail. An editorial urged residents to clean up their city and another urged them to eat more fish. Blaylock continued as honorary vice-president of the poultry association. A visiting missionary to Formosa (now known as Taiwan) defended the Chinese to Kootenay audiences in mid-April, saying "they never were known to carry arms, and they were much less inclined to crime and evil than were the English races themselves. For these reasons there was more common sense in the exclusion of English or Scotch, for the Chinese were more law-abiding than they."[393]

Real estate activity was again highlighted in May. Rossland again beat the Trail baseball team. And a local blacksmith blew himself up. Babington, again playing a positive civic role, warned of the spread of typhoid fever and how to avoid it. Trail's population rose to 2,100 with 1,342 citizens of Anglo-Saxon origin, according to the Trail police chief. On the labour front, Babington borrowed an item from the

Toronto Star, quoting millionaire John D. Rockefeller Jr. on the right of employers not to recognize unions. But the story had a strange new twist for the *News*. "Is he, and are those associated with him, concerned for the welfare of workers?" the item asked. "Are they not determined to retain the advantages which they derive from having workers in an unorganized mass to deal with?"[394]

Then on June 27, 1914, Babington disappeared as quietly as he had appeared on the smelter city scene. Perhaps he was motivated by the possibility of owning his own newspaper. Indeed, that was the case. He moved to Melfort, Saskatchewan, where he bought the *Melfort Moon*, a weekly paper not dissimilar to the *News*. Bab Babington was finally his own boss.

Another New Manager, *Komagatu Maru*, Heinze and the Pope Die in 1914

On July 4, 1914, James Joseph Clarke, known as J.J., arrived from Waskada, Manitoba, and before that from the *Enderby Press and Walker's Weekly*, where he had worked as a printer from January to August 1913. No title was given in the masthead, but later in the year, he became "Manager." The *Waskada News* or the nearby *Delormaine Times & Star*, founded in 1887, could have been where he furthered his newspapering credentials. But there is no clear record of his newspaper service in Manitoba.

Clarke was born in Grantham, Lincolnshire, England, on April 3, 1873. He left school at age thirteen to start a printing apprenticeship, worked as a compositor on some large newspapers, and was a staff photographer for a Warwickshire journal. He moved to Canada in 1910 and began work on the *Trail News*, presumably as a compositor. Like many pioneer editors, he learned his journalism on the job. Before arriving in Trail, however, Clarke had earned a reputation in a field other than newspapering. He was Britain's first saxophonist. In the late 1890s, he toured Britain with the then famous Robin Hood Band, wielding what was thought to be the only saxophone in the country at the time, a gift from his brother George. He also played for the Yeomanry Band.[395] His wife, Elizabeth, and a son joined him in Trail.

The musical side of the new *News* manager might have influenced his choice of items with a special interest in events at the Trail Opera House and band concerts. But otherwise, the Clarke paper made few detours from the bland mix of mining news and social notes that readers had grown accustomed to over the past seven years. Shadow editor-in-chief Esling showed no interest in changing his formula, and Clarke did his bidding. With Clarke, the paper reverted to the safety of one-paragraph squibs about the local smelter, union elections, council meetings, and annual picnics. As before, short editorials were often drawn from the *Miner* or big city dailies. In his early editions, he crowded the weekly with sensational local news. A man stabbed his dog to death before committing suicide. An Austrian smelter worker was brutally beaten to death. An eleven-year-old girl drowned. And a horse thief was jailed.

Perennial editorial issues remained in place. For example, Clarke hailed a federal order-in-council prohibiting Chinese immigration and a further decision to bar Sikh immigrants on the *Komagatu Maru* from entering Canada.[396] He also weighed in on the bottled liquor amendment allowing the sale of liquor outside the bar. Taking a prohibition stance, the *News* suggested that "it would seem reasonable that the average man of intelligence could drink enough at the bar to satisfy his inclinations, without packing away a bottle. It's more than likely that the 'workingman's' wife and family would look at it in this light."[397]

Nothing had changed regarding local politics either, with Clarke quick to support Conservative candidates and announce the public roles of local business leaders. CM&S assistant managing director S.G. Blaylock became president of the Kootenay Tennis Association, for example, and would later appear as a vegetable-growing champion at the Fall Fair, among other local competitions. Sports were almost always on the front page. In the summer of 1914, for example, Trail won the West Kootenay Cup in soccer. Court news also was featured. For example, the trial of former smelter worker Joe De Cesare was headlined for murdering Italian grocer Louis Bianchi.

Soon, however, the First World War began to usurp the front page with Clarke announcing that Trail men were enlisting and that the paper had "arranged for a special telegraph service covering the daily happenings of the war."[398] Trail's Italian community held a parade to support the war, and new duties were placed on cigarettes, sugar, coffee, beer and ale.

In September, city council accepted Esling's proposal to lay cement walks in front of three lots on the east side of Bay Avenue. Another editorial praised the CPR and CM&S as responsible for how "much better off we are than thousands of communities of similar size throughout Canada."[399] A local branch of the Canadian Patriotic Fund would assist families suffering war losses. An editorial suggested optimistically that the "War Probably Will Be of Short Duration." A second call to arms was issued, a soldiers' tobacco fund was organized, the local Red Cross found office space, and a second contingent of eight men was bid goodbye. Also highlighted was the death of smelter founder F.A. Heinze.

The CM&S again beat the odds in court when the judge found it not guilty of smoke and fumes pollution. Blaylock told the court the company had made efforts to render the smoke harmless. It wouldn't be until the 1930s that an International Joint Commission would force him to do something about the pollution by imposing fines on the CM&S.

Another New Mayor, *Miner* Sold, Wounded Soldiers, Fire on the Bowery in 1915

Hockey championships, curling bonspiels, union dances, and choral society concerts were regularly covered during Clarke's second year. Another new mayor, Sidney Butler, was elected. "A terrible whisky man," the *News* reported, because he supported the bottled liquor sales amendment. The new Diocese of Kootenay elected a bishop.[400] An editorial cheered the Chinese head tax for curbing immigration, and local non-Doukhobor house builders complained that Doukhobors were undermining their business by outbidding them.

In March, Esling sold the *Rossland Miner* to W.A. Elletson.[401] But the usual *News* fare continued unabated. "Do your wartime duty" items were on the front page, along with war casualty lists. Elsewhere were notices for women's auxiliary fundraisers, Red Cross donations and calls to support the war effort. Mining still took up the lion's share of the news hole. The rifle club sponsored a renewed call for recruits. The Methodist Church congregation heard an address on votes for women.

Despite the strains of war, life went on much as always in the smelter city, and Clarke now settled into the humdrum of covering mundane events. "Mrs. W.J. Palmer, living near Fruitvale, had an exciting adventure one morning last week," a typical item explained. "When she went to feed her ducks there was a large lynx in her duckhouse killing the birds."[402] It might have enlivened his routine somewhat to report on a local debate about abolishing capital punishment and to note that Trail was against it. But his days were probably numbered as manager. At least he could feel some pride when the *News* turned over its subscription list to the Red Cross and the women's auxiliary to raise money for the Patriotic Fund.

As summer wore on, Trail observed the first anniversary of the start of war. The Italian Red Cross continued to raise funds, as did the Rifle Club and the Smelter-men's War Fund. The women's auxiliary supplied soldiers with food baskets, knit-wear and other helpful items. Readers learned about life in the Vernon military training camp. The *Miner* started a fund to buy a machine gun for C Company. The *News* did the same.

A wounded soldier brought the war home to Trail with these words: "I have heard that A. Morgan has died of wounds. I did not think he would live when we got him out of the trenches. I got 3 wounds in left leg, one in right hand, 1 in right arm, and 2 in the chest. All my wounds are nearly well. I may lose my left thumb, it's no use anyhow, and it will be the less to wash. All the boys have shown wonderful metal, and every praise is due to them."[403] A second letter was equally jarring: "To be hit by shrapnel feels like being badly burnt all over. To be 'gassed' is fearful."[404]

On the home front, fire destroyed the Bow Win (Lee's) Laundry on the Bow-ery. A new Catholic Hall opened. The Star Theatre was sold and the new owners promised improvements. Zinc production was to begin at the Trail smelter. "Can-ada will not only make shells for the Allies," read the announcement, "but will also produce and refine[,] for the first time in this country, the zinc and copper required for this ammunition."[405] Attorney General W.J. Bowser planned to introduce a BC workers' compensation act, allowing for a widow's pension, and union locals struck a committee to explore forming a labour council. It came on the heels of a union member's death from strychnine poisoning at his home.

That fall, an editorial discussed the coming plebiscite on prohibition, and the paper's bias was evident. Clarke asked smelter workers to vote with their con-science "as to whether the bar is an actual necessity, whether the money so freely thrown across it could not be devoted to more essential purposes and whether the home would not be brightened, the children better clad and domestic happiness fostered, if the bar is abolished."[406]

In October, Esling made the front page over a dispute about street grading in Trail. He argued against the proposal, and at first it appeared he had lost. "The discussion became rather impulsive and the Mayor put the question," the report explained. When Mr. Esling demanded his say on the matter, the mayor ordered him to "sit down." Unrelenting, Esling said he would not sit down "but will stand here and say what I have to say." The mayor called on the police but no damage was done.[407] Then Esling, soon to be back in the masthead as "Editor and Prop.," got in his licks: "It's amusing to note how freely the city council can incur an expense of four or five thousand dollars when the money does not come out of their own pockets."[408]

Late that fall, a complaint in the paper challenged the local hotel owners' plans to raise rents. Vacancies were so lacking that smelter workers could be seen walking the streets at night. CM&S "management is threatening to take a hand in the hotel business unless the old rates for board are restored."[409] An editorial suggested that this was "pretty good evidence of interest in the welfare of the employees, and ought to have a salutary effect."[410.]

The Trail Choral Society, Patriotic Fund, Poultry Show and Star Theatre were all front-page items in late November. Clarke was still manager. An editorial again urged people to do their patriotic duty. Trail had a new dentist. A large ad offered war loan bonds at 97.5 cents. There was nary a hint that the *News* was about to change hands.

As the *News* began its third decade, Thompson was tramping through Alaska leaving newspapers in his wake. With the sale of both his papers, Esling's journalism days were over. His failing eyesight would not allow him to continue, but he could focus on both his business interests and his eventual entry into political life. Clarke would later resurface as co-owner with Elmer D. Hall of the *Trail News*. For now, however, he would become part of new owner W.B. Willcox's *News* as the smelter city weekly turned a new corner in the midst of an ever-bloodier world war.

4—*Trail News* (1915–1919)

A Spokane Man Migrates to the Smelter City

The New Editor Refreshes a Moribund Weekly with Critical Commentary

From his first edition as the new owner of the *Trail News*, Walter Beach Willcox, a Spokane, Washington, newspaperman, breathed new life into a fading weekly that had been sliding into oblivion. As a business sheet, focused on company booster-ism, it was as good as ever. As the political voice of the Conservative Party, it didn't miss a beat. As a country newspaper, it left much to be desired. Now things would change. William K. Esling had remained at the top of the masthead as "Editor and Proprietor" until December 3, 1915, when he introduced Willcox as a "clean, capable, conscientious and energetic newspaper man."[411] He had known him since at least the *Brooklyn News* days.

Esling, who had been with the *News* almost since its beginnings under found-er W.F. Thompson, was finally passing the torch. In doing so, he reflected on his "twenty years as publisher" and urged the reading public to "recognize that the local newspaper reflects the spirit of the community and [that] a sense of pride and loyalty should prompt co-operation with the ambition and efforts of the new publisher."

Willcox welcomed the challenge "to support every movement that in our judg-ment deserves the same—and we invite the co-operation of residents generally to this end." He added, "We may make mistakes—who does not? But at least we will

Editors W.K. Esling and business partner W.E. Blackmer started the *Brooklyn News* in this short-lived CPR town near Trail. Courtesy Trail Historical Society

have the satisfaction of knowing that, if we did not hitch our wagon to a star, we have done our best."[412] The weekly would appear on Fridays under a new company name, the Trail Printing and Publishing Company, with Willcox as "Manager."[413]

Willcox was born in St. Louis, Missouri, on September 3, 1862, but left River City at a young age with his mother, Sarah Jane Willcox (née Beach).[414] They lived in Stamford, Fairfield, Connecticut, where she had acquired a property in 1868.[415] The 1872 Stamford city directory shows that Walter's father, Wallace C. Willcox, held a mortgage there. Where young Walter went to school is not clear. It might have been at the eight-grade Central School, but it also might have been any of the fourteen schools operating by 1870.[416] Where he acquired his printing skills is also shrouded in mystery. Could his father have been engaged in that trade? By 1889, Walter and his father were in New York City where they eventually boarded a transcontinental train for a cross-country journey to the west coast.

The memory stuck with him and eventually young Willcox migrated to Spokane to become managing editor of the *Spokane Chronicle*. When the paper was destroyed in the great Spokane fire of August 4, 1889, he "wrote the story on a kitchen table and set the story in type saved from the building."[417] Many decades later, Willcox recalled the moment: "Having arrived in Spokane but three weeks previously, straight from New York City, the writer was something of a tenderfoot at the time of the fire."[418] He was proud that his newspaper never missed an edition; even famously setting up a tent office until rebuilding could begin.[419] He would need such perseverance as he pursued his career in the West Kootenay district about two hundred kilometres due north.

In 1897, he had edited the *Slocan City News* in the ore-rich Slocan Valley near Nelson. In 1898, as we've seen, he bought the *Brooklyn News* from Esling and his business partner Major W.E. Blackmer.[420] In his August 6, 1898, editorial, he declared, "the new editor and manager will devote his entire time to the *News*, and will make it as complete as possible in every respect. Particular attention will be given to news and notes of the railway construction."[421] This was a given since the camp had sprung up around the CPR's extension of the Columbia and Western Railway from Robson to the Boundary Country.[422] Brooklyn lasted only as long as it took to complete the line, and in 1899, Willcox moved to Cascade, a CPR boom town near Grand Forks, BC, where he edited the *Cascade City Record*. Willcox soon saw greener pastures in the mining town of Phoenix where he and former *Rossland Evening Record* owner Eber C. Smith started the *Phoenix Pioneer*. At the same time, Smith was publishing the *Gazette*, a new daily in Grand Forks. Smith soon ended his association with the *Phoenix Pioneer*, and by mid-December of 1899, he had sold his share to Willcox.

Willcox's separation from Smith was a blessing, for the latter was soon to face labour problems at the *Gazette* when he failed to pay his employees on payday, asserting that he did not have the money. With no pay forthcoming, the *Gazette* printers formed a union and struck the Smith paper. There were lawsuits for unpaid wages and counter-suits, with Smith arguing that the walkout was illegal. Ultimately, the union declared the *Gazette* "an unfair office."[423] The union statement implicated Willcox's *Pioneer* in the dispute, but he issued a disclaimer and it worked, with Willcox escaping the wrath of the printers' union. Willcox had made the right move, one that may have guided him later when he managed the Trail weekly.

Willcox continued to gather much newspaper experience on the *Pioneer*, including some tough times at the beginning when "the leading voice of Phoenix" was housed in a building "*sans* doors or windows for nearly a week."[424] Along the way, he acquired a spouse, the German-born Elizabeth "Elsie" Crawford, ten years younger. They had married in Grand Forks on October 3, 1900, while he was still editing the *Pioneer*, and they had one daughter, Elizabeth. The Willcoxes stayed in contact with acquaintances in Spokane as they settled into almost a decade in the mining world of the mountainous BC Interior. By 1908, however, they were ready to move on. That fall, Willcox sold his share of the *Pioneer* to his partner Thomas Alfred Love of Winnipeg and struck out for an apple ranch in North Yakima, Washington.[425] By spring 1909, he had returned to Spokane where he was working for the Franklin Press printing office.[426]

At some point he became a member of Spokane Lodge No. 34 of the Free and Accepted Masons, an association that he likely continued at one of the two Masonic lodges in Trail.[427] Joining a lodge was not new to Willcox. As early as 1891, when he was twenty-nine years old, he was elected recording secretary of Washington Camp No. 3 of the Patriotic Order Sons of America.[428] As the name implied, the order was dedicated to patriotism, but its roots extend to the Know Nothings, a far-right nativist political party. Founded in 1847 in Philadelphia, the order welcomed men who supported its anti-immigrant and anti-Catholic views.[429] As a Spokane businessman, Willcox would have been welcomed into the group.

By the time Willcox bought the *Trail News*, then, he was a seasoned pioneer newspaperman, and he was ready to apply his skills and knowledge to the smelter city's only newspaper. Overnight, the *News* was transformed into a new publication with proper headline type, a carefully organized front page, and a clearly identified editorial page. All had long been missing under Esling's largely absentee helmsmanship. A "News and Comment" column also added to the organized look of the paper, now a six-page sheet, soon to be eight, after years of being stalled at four pages.

Esling Bows Out, Blaylock the Hockey Man, and "Our Boys in Khaki" in 1915

The front page of his first edition on December 3, 1915, still focused on local sports with an encouraging item on the Trail hockey team's prospects for 1916. A soldier named Charles McInnis, formerly of Trail, described life in the trenches. Brewmeister August Mueller died. Like his predecessors, Willcox believed that Trail was "entering on a new era of prosperity," that "its future as a substantial, progressive community is assured," and that "being located in what is now literally the melting pot of Western Canada, we also are confident that good will come of it."

Esling made a rare appearance on the editorial page to welcome the new publisher: "The writer has always had faith in Trail, and has emphasized it in a constructive policy." He then thanked his "real friends" and dismissed his enemies, "those who dislike progress, but who are quite willing to profit by the efforts of others." He closed philosophically, "the local newspaper reflects the spirit of the community and a sense of pride and loyalty should prompt co-operation with the ambition and efforts of the new publisher."[430] Elsewhere on his first editorial page, Willcox made a pitch for news. "Just give us the dope," he wrote, "and we will dress it up if you lack the time."[431] With that, four years of comparatively lively, informative, and fair-minded journalism began at the *Trail News*.

Later December editions included many items familiar to readers. School board reports, city council minutes, and "Local News" items were steady fare. Poultry shows were the best ever. An old miner died in his chair at the Victoria Hotel. Curling skips were chosen, with the CM&S's assistant manager S.G. Blaylock skipping rink 16. Blaylock was also elected president of the West Kootenay-Boundary Hockey League for the third time. A new photographic studio was announced. Another lawyer hung out his shingle. Six hotels had their licences renewed. Canadians contributed seventy cents per capita to the war effort in 1915. Trail's Dick Marshall, "Italian champion middleweight of Canada," fought to a draw against a Calgary prizefighter.[432] W.J. Bowser became premier, and former premier Sir Richard McBride became agent general of BC. Local mines showed a $1.3 million profit for 1914.

One thing that hadn't changed at the *News* was the call for recognition. "There is no enterprise that does so much for the corporation or the individual citizen as the newspaper," wrote Willcox. "It stands opposed to the town knocker, the town kicker, the town fanatic and the town drones. It stands for progress as against stagnation. It is ever ready to combat the schemes of visionaries and as ready to aid the construction plans of wise and levelheaded citizens."[433] There was also a renewed call for recognition of "Our Boys in Khaki." Willcox was thankful to Trail recruits for sending him notes on life in military training camp. Trail had a hundred phones, according to BC Telephone's *Telephone Talk*. And the hockey team was ready for the "puckchasing battles" of 1916.[434]

Willcox editorials sometimes shared a tongue-in-cheek sense of humour. "The *Creston Review* remarks that, coincident with the change in management of the *News*, Trail is putting on a night policeman. Well, well, well. But after all, we may need that bobby to watch the office safe, in which we keep our meal tickets. Yes, editors eat—sometimes."[435] And of course, there was the obligatory attention paid to local businesses. The CM&S's tenth annual report appeared, showing almost $800,000 in net profits. A Bank of Montreal branch opened. The dentist had arrived. The second Patriotic Fund appeal had begun. The front and editorial pages showed readers the courtesy of wishing them a Happy New Year. It was a gesture that had not been extended for many Decembers.

Smelter Soldiers, Measles, Red Reverend, "Douks and Doukesses" in 1916

As 1916 began, it was clear that the *News* was being transformed into a weekly with a personality, and a rather lively one. As a result, readership increased (20 per cent, Willcox claimed), and most noticeably so did advertising. Boring boiler-plate stories were almost gone. The first edition of 1916, all six pages of it, offered a packed front page. It was much of the same old news (sports, of course, with Blaylock's rink winning at curling), a new building, the latest mining news, metal stock quotations, and a note on the "Great Demand for Phones." And there were the usual silly news items: "As the men came from work at the Moyie mine one day recently they met three deer walking up the wage road. Dear, dear!"[436] Willcox provided an optimistic editorial on BC's mining prospects, but he also called on everyone to support their local church, lodge, or society. Be a booster for Trail, he counselled, and do your duty for King and Empire "for never was there a greater need nor a more righteous cause.... Do not be a shirker, be a worker."[437] CM&S general manager R.H. "Pat" Stewart, replacing Walter H. Aldridge, who had nego-tiated the smelter's purchase from F. Augustus Heinze, reported that 135 smelter employees were not among the shirkers but had enlisted, necessitating changes in staff positions.

By mid-January, apathy dominated the city elections with few voters turning up. Mayor Sidney Butler and his council were acclaimed. A public vote on build-ing a new park passed. Ottawa authorized Trail to establish a company of Home Guards. War coverage was limited to a report on a CM&S clerk that had enlisted. Cold weather, Red Cross donations, financial news, sports, and the choral society were all on the front page. The editorial page, now providing critical comment on issues affecting Trail, covered conscription (the *News* seemed to accept it as nec-essary), the absence of a local recruiting office, the need for a new sewer system, and Columbia River flooding. Mining news and zinc production history were on display as usual. Letters from Trail recruits filled almost a full page. A new fire hall alarm was promised. Trail was still tops in hockey. A squad of fifty soldiers was to be stationed at the smelter to "guard that important works in the future."[438] An-other squad was assigned to guard the Bonnington Falls power station. The now weekly report on the Patriotic Fund showed Trail's contributions at $20,000. Only Rossland was higher, at $25,000.

In late January, Reverend A.E. Smith was the "chief artillerist" demolishing the arguments of anti-prohibition proponents at a meeting in Trail. "The saloon men will not be entitled to compensation when their licenses are cancelled," he in-toned, "for, if these be compensated for, we must in justice compensate the widows and orphans because of the traffic, and those who have been deprived of education-al privileges, etc., for the same reason."[439] Smith, who had served as the Methodist minister in Nelson in 1913, would soon become one of Canada's leading Commu-nists. Willcox claimed the *News* was "this great family educator," and congratu-lated himself for it: "We started to improve the paper in such ways as our modest experience suggested, and it would seem that the people appreciate the effort."[440]

Winter sports, especially curling and hockey, filled the front page in February, even bumping to second place news that the Parliament Buildings in Ottawa had burned down. Again the editorial page was doing its job with items on an illegal deer killing, opportunities for prospectors, a promotion of the Rossland Winter Carnival, and local by-elections. Unlike earlier versions of the paper, Willcox seemed to give equal time to both parties. He practised the same non-partisanship during a by-election in Rossland. S.G. Blaylock was a lieutenant in the Trail Home Guards. In mid-February, an editorial urged the city to spend $20,000 on a new federal building. A second called for better fire safety and fire prevention.

In a momentary setback, Willcox was embarrassed when a hockey story was found to be "speciously filled with untruths." He explained the false story and his mistaken acceptance of it, adding, "When one man is doing the work of three or four in the editorial den, it is not surprising that some things escape his eagle eye."[441] He would be more watchful with hockey stories in the future, knowing that Trailites took their hockey seriously.

Previous *News* owner W.K. Esling, now engaged full-time in real estate, built an extension of the old Rex Theatre with the intention of renting it. Willcox later reported that Esling, "the largest owner of store buildings in Trail, and who last year invested about $30,000 here in this way, is already at work on improvements… representing about $1,000 in cost—with several possible tenants anxious to secure the same."[442] The *News* also observed that Esling "is starting work on a two story frame building adjoining Walker's store on Bay Avenue; on a small building for the custom house on Helena Street, opposite the opera house; and on another small building… near the Haglund blacksmith shop."[443] Clearly, Esling was earning his reputation as a hustler in his new field of interest.

As spring approached, Willcox lapsed into a boastful mood on his editorial page, suggesting that "the editor who understands his business and takes a pride in it, can see things more fairly and equitably than any other individual in the community."[444] Elsewhere, he claimed that "the gospel truth is that there was scarcely ever a broken down and unsuccessful lawyer, preacher, doctor, teacher or politician but that thinks he is divinely fitted to become a successful editor." Then in a moment tainted with hubris, he noted that an editor "really acquires more versatility, backbone, principle, ability and brains than any of those professions."[445] Another item sang the praises of the "home newspaper."[446]

Later Willcox offered a history of newspapers in the Kootenays, commenting that they "have kept a stiff upper lip and done yeomanry service in letting the outside world know of the wonderful mineral and other resources of this part of the Dominion." He noted that "In the daily field Kootenay-Boundary has been literally a newspaper graveyard, with champagne-appetite editors and publishers who possessed common, every day beer pocket-books—except when some one's leg was elongated, like a politician or a mining man wishing an 'organ'."[447]

When spring finally arrived, the *News* continued at eight pages. It reported a hundred measles cases in Trail, noted the Star Theatre was expanding to accommodate 400 patrons, and that another smelter worker, a crane operator, had been electrocuted. The Custom House rented space at Esling's building on Helena Street.

About $6,000 was sent to the Patriotic Fund. City council debated a new building and fire bylaw. Willcox again revealed that he was non-partisan when it came to party politics. "The Conservatives have their virtues and so have the Liberals and the Socialists," he suggested, "though none are [sic] sprouting wings as yet."[448]

There were 190 CM&S employees at war or in training. A remnant of the old anti-Asian view remained, such as with this "Local Matters" item: "It costs just $16 including costs to hit a chinaman [sic] in Trail. So George Smith found out before Magistrate [Noble] Binns."[449] And town booster poetry, now a staple item, had gone up a notch in quality: "Real towns are not made by men afraid/Lest somebody else gets ahead./When everyone works and nobody shirks,/You can raise a town from the dead."[450]

In spite of the war, and perhaps as a momentary reprieve from it, April brought renewed enthusiasm for baseball and football. A new tennis club had started. A delegation of women demanded and won a new sidewalk from city council. Council also floated debentures for a new fire hall. Trail's measles epidemic was subsiding. Zinc and lead production were up. Again, Willcox revealed his journalistic pride in being part of a newspaper community. For example, the *Enderby Press and Walker's Weekly*, where former *News* manager J.J. Clarke, now a Willcox employee, once worked, received the editor's nod of approval: "It is the salt of the earth in newspaperdom."[451] Another Trail soldier was wounded, and another was in a German prison. Six Austrians were interned at the Edgewood internment camp on the nearby Arrow Lakes.

In May, in what threatened to be serious labour troubles at the smelter, the company refused to give WFM Local 105's 1,200 members a fifty-cent raise. The company countered with an offer of twenty-five cents. It was voted down 500 to 17. While Willcox had dropped the "World Labor News" column, long a weekly feature in the Babington *News*, he still proved even-handed in covering labour disputes.

Again unlike the Esling-Babington *News*, Willcox more enthusiastically recognized Mother's Day with a salute to "one who did more for you than any other being on this earth."[452] About his job: "If the editor is for anything, the antis condemn him and vice versa. If he takes a stand he is trying to dictate to the community. If he doesn't take a stand he is a molly-coddle and a jellyfish. He is a crank, a reformer, a lunatic, a four-flusher, a crook, a disturber of the peace or just a plain idiot."[453]

Doukhobors, known for their pacifism, were commended for enlisting ninety members of the sect to serve overseas. "Even the devil should be given his due," Willcox commented.[454] He also seemed to display some sympathy for the sect. "The editor of this weekly luminary looked through his sanctum window the other day and saw a female Douk following the plow," he remarked. "It requires some spuds and roots for vegetarians to get enough to live and the Douks and Doukesses propose to have them."[455]

No doubt Willcox was in a melancholy mood when he reported the demise of the *Phoenix Pioneer*, the weekly he and Eber C. Smith had founded years earlier.

He noted that "the *Phoenix Pioneer* sang its own swan song—gave up the ghost and turned up its little toes to the daisies" after seventeen years.[456] Staying with this theme, he signalled his respect for Colonel Robert Lowery of the *Greenwood Ledge*, among the earliest of the region's pioneer editors. It "has never been raided by the sheriff," he quipped. "The colonel is still as trenchant as ever."[457]

Daylight Savings Time was introduced as summer arrived. Young boys were cautioned to stay away from cigarettes. A poem appeared about the reproductive capacity of the housefly. Another told of the soldiers' need for a smoke. Local automobiles and motorboats were on the increase. An editorial shamed local businesses for not matching the amount smelter workers had given to the Patriotic Fund. Fire hazards and fire prevention were among the editor's priorities. In a note of historical importance, Willcox reported that Trail's founding father, Colonel Eugene S. Topping, was ill in hospital at Vancouver. The enterprising Billy Esling opened the Aldridge Hotel, Trail's newest, offering turkey dinner in its restaurant. The hotel was named after former CM&S manager Walter H. Aldridge.

Ginger Goodwin, Labour Against Prohibition, Yes to Women's Vote, No to KKK

1917 smelter strike leader Albert "Ginger" Goodwin. Courtesy Cumberland Museum

Tracking labour movement activities, and probably signally increased public anxiety, Willcox reported WFM Local 105 members' acceptance of a fifteen-cent raise in addition to the twenty-five cents offered in May. The "From the Slag Dump" column reported that Local 105 recording secretary Peter J. Bolam was organizing about 200 smelter workers in Northport. He would eventually succeed, but on the down side, he faced a threat of deportation. An ad appeared under the heading "Workers, Attention," promoting a special meeting to support Albert "Ginger" Goodwin as the Socialist Party of Canada candidate in the coming provincial election.

About 700 voters heard from candidates, including Goodwin. "He spoke clearly and forcefully and did not mince his words," Willcox stated. "In his opinion the Conservatives fattened on the surplus, and he wished to know why they did not pass a compensation act that would be of benefit to the workingman while he was alive, rather than after he was dead or injured."[458] Goodwin appealed to the audience to vote socialist, delivering the same message at a Liberal Party rally "in his usual clear-cut manner, specially flaying the Liberals." Goodwin then concluded that "if the workers wanted a real change they should vote the Socialist ticket in September."[459] They apparently didn't and wouldn't, not this election anyway. At Goodwin's own Socialist party election rally, Local 105 leader James A. MacKinnon introduced the candidate, who spoke for an hour about the failure of the two mainstream parties to do anything for labour.

In August, the labour movement came out against the proposed Prohibition Act, arguing that "the measure is class legislation of the rankest type inasmuch as it allows that man of means to secure all the liquor he desires by importing it from outside points, but at the same time places a handicap on the workingman who can only afford to buy his beer by the glass."[460]

When school restarted in September, attendance had increased. The Methodists got a new parsonage. Red Cross volunteers heard an illustrated talk about the work of the Red Cross in Europe. Interestingly, Harry Blaylock, older brother of the CM&S's S.G. Blaylock, would become chief commissioner of the Canadian Red Cross overseas in April 1918.[461]

The Labour Day program was posted and to recognize it, Willcox wrote "Labor is one of the greatest assets of our national life." He added, "Without it all activities would cease." It was an unusual comment for the *News*. "Capital is essential, but labor is imperative," he continued, "and it is because of its vast importance and universal need that we are pleased to recognize the day set apart for its celebration."[462] The Labour Day parade and ball were big successes, with Goodwin and others stressing the value of unions.

An editorial again demonstrated Willcox's non-partisan approach: "If a paper, daily or weekly, is owned by a Socialist, Tory or Grit, said owner has a perfect right to conduct it as he pleases. But to be strictly fair he should carry a headline stating that it is a partisan sheet, and that what it prints about the other fellow should be considered in that light."[463]

By mid-September, the Liberals had taken power in Victoria. The official vote count: Goodwin 258, incumbent Conservative James H. Schofield 560, Liberal M.H. Sullivan 463. The prohibitionists won the referendum vote 612 to 606. Votes for women's suffrage tallied 803, against 416. Schofield remained the MLA despite the local labour movement's efforts to support Goodwin. Willcox predicted that women would win the vote as it should have been all along. Trail's sixth annual Fruit Fair was the usual hit, with the CM&S metal exhibit touted as a highlight.

Willcox offered some wisdom on the value of distractions like the Fruit Fair for coping with the difficulties of war: "There's a deal of homely philosophy in David Harum's saying that 'A reasonable amount of fleas is good for a dog, because it keeps him from thinkin' of being a dog'."[464] More inspirational poetry appeared and another case of infantile paralysis (polio) was reported. By month's end, the "Trail Boys in Khaki" column included several letters from German prison camps. "The Russians are said to be pressing the Teutons," said an editorial. "Why not have them dry cleaned at the same time?"

A lead editorial in October highlighted the need for homes for "wives and families living elsewhere, while the breadwinners are struggling under the serious handicap of having two sets of expenses as well as of losing intercourse with their families."[465] The "Note and Comment" column boasted that the *News* had doubled its circulation in the ten months that Willcox had been owner. The editor also bragged that he "had more than doubled the amount of reading matter carried" in "the oldest weekly in the Kootenays."[466]

In a prolonged dispute over street improvements, city council paid W.K. Esling $237.50 in damages for raising the grade on Spokane Street in front of his City Grocery building. Esling, in return, would need to raise his building to the new grade level. The Hollywood movie *The Birth of a Nation* made the front page, and five professors attested to its historical accuracy. Willcox called it "the most stupendous thing of its kind yet shown on the moving picture screen."[467] The film would encourage a revival of the Ku Klux Klan.

Rossland's WFM Local 38 and Trail's Local 105 supported the idea of a night school. Willcox agreed and advocated the teaching of technical skills and English to immigrants. "Work of Unions Brings Good Results," said a front-page news story on the December start-up of such a school.[468] Seventy-five students enrolled. Willcox could take credit for pressing the issue, but he gave much public credit to the unions.

An editorial celebrated Woodrow Wilson's victory in the American election. "The price of paper will now be pushed up another notch," Willcox chided, "so that he can write more notes while American citizens are murdered on the high seas or on the Mexican border."[469] John Kirkup, Rossland's first lawman, died, and Willcox paid tribute to him as "an outstanding character, where[,] as gold commissioner and governmental agent when that camp [Rossland] was one of the howling, booming kind, he preserved order and was a terror to evil doers."[470] The praise was not always shared.

In December, Crow's Nest coal miners, members of United Mine Workers of America Local 18, struck briefly to force an investigation of the cost-of-living situation. Willcox supported a raise for the miners. He hailed the Liberal premier's choice of William Sloan of Nanaimo as mines minister and Greenwood's Dr. D.L. McLean as education minister. As proof that the *News* was well read, Willcox noted that a set of false teeth had been returned as a result of a notice in the paper. Willcox was elected first vice-president of the weekly branch of the Canadian Press Association for BC. Blaylock was again on a rink of the curling club, but Willcox wasn't.

Later in the month, another poem from the front lines appeared, and "Casey at the Bat" and Robert Service's "The Shooting of Dan McGrew" took up considerable space. Their presence and that of a weekly selection of poetry suggested that Willcox had a literary side or that he needed to fill a hole where an ad failed to materialize. Of course, the paper continued to be jammed with those. Goodwin was elected secretary of Local 105, which announced a mass meeting to discuss the cost-of-living question. He didn't know it, but he was destined for martyrdom and would become an inspiration for future generations of trade unionists and labour activists.

Willcox sent Christmas greetings to his readers. So thrilled was Willcox over his acquisition of a new Linotype machine that he devoted a column to explaining it and giving his readers a short history of the machine. After noting a Grand Forks Doukhobor donation of $100 to the National Patriotic Fund, Willcox wanted the Doukhobors in Trail to contribute at least that much and more if they did not want to send men to war.

Another year of war was about to begin and Willcox was as well prepared to serve the city as he could be. But *News* readers hoping for more in-depth coverage of the war were probably disappointed with Willcox's brief front-page item headed "Late News of the War." Slightly more satisfying were the occasional frontline maps, essays from London observers, reports on the Red Cross's sock-knitting campaigns, and the home front's supplying of tobacco. Several letters of thanks from the front appeared along with casualty reports, tallies of Patriotic Fund contributions, fundraising dances, and lengthy articles on the smelter's production of lead, zinc, and other munitions materials.

Eight-page editions were now the norm at the Willcox *News*, and his new Linotype machine allowed the paper to decrease the point size of its columns. The front page was often clear of advertising—something that was unheard of under the previous owners—but with each edition the news hole seemed to narrow. Editorially, Willcox offered only the odd paragraph about the eminent defeat of the "Teutons" and Allied progress toward victory. Coverage in the Nelson and Rossland dailies made up for the absence of detailed updates in the Trail weekly. Although they probably arrived a day late, the coast dailies were another way to stay better informed. Despite Willcox's regular show of fairness, the Chinese were still treated unfairly in the *News*.

Sports coverage may have fallen off dramatically, but movie coverage had increased. The Star rented big Hollywood blockbusters starring Charlie Chaplin, William S. Hart, Douglas Fairbanks, Mary Pickford and Sarah Bernhardt. This was a Trailite's regular and affordable chance to enjoy a night out, but it was hardly an escape from the war, since many films depicted fictionalized battles in Europe. Willcox never wasted a column inch of space even if he had to fill it with wartime poems of patriotism and boosterism. Whether he was comforting the afflicted was another question.

Col. Topping and Mrs. S.G. Blaylock Die, CM&S's Warren Arrives in 1917

Hockey season opened the first week of January 1917. Willcox posted the Governor General's New Year's greeting on his front page. The rest of the page was filled with financial news, social notes, and a weather report. An editorial looked ahead to 1917 as another year of growth and expansion for Trail. The public was praised for showing more interest in the coming municipal election in which Mayor Sidney Butler was re-elected for a third term. CM&S announced a net profit of $996,496.35. The twentieth annual curling bonspiel was held. A Willcox editorial criticized Liberal

Premier H.C. Brewster, a salmon canner and former printer's devil, for not living up to his election promises, particularly the one ending patronage.

Mrs. S.G. Blaylock died from a blood clot on the heart or brain in late January. Also dead was Colonel Topping, 73, the "father of Trail." Willcox also announced the death of Buffalo Bill Cody—perhaps a fitting addition given that Topping was a Wild West figure in his own right. The annual masquerade carnival was a success. Willcox bragged that readers were "getting more reading matter of special and general interest than ever before."[471] He published a history of the smelter as a national institution. War news was almost absent, although an inspirational poem about the khaki uniform and the maple leaf symbol appeared.

Goodwin was back in the *News*, attending the BC Federation of Labour convention in Revelstoke where he was elected the first president of the newly formed Trail Trades and Labour Council (TTLC). Affiliates included the steel workers, WFM Local 105, carpenters, machinists, barbers, restaurant workers and linemen. Willcox promoted war loan certificates, offered praise for some Liberal cabinet appointments, and filed an engineer's report recommending more water for Trail. A Topping obituary appeared listing his accomplishments.

In mid-February, a religious education conference was held in Trail. Local 105's F.W. Bartle and Goodwin were among the officiators of a union Valentine's Day dance. Willcox wished the Brewster government well, but cautioned against imposing too heavy a tax burden on the mining industry. A second editorial blasted Germany and assured readers that the Allies would win the war, now 936 days old. The push for more water continued and a new bylaw would generate another $50,000 for that purpose.

A Trail man escaped from a German prison. Next to that story was an account of the Armenian Massacre. East Trail would get a new school. Trail would get a new theatre. Women won the right to vote as of March 1. CM&S offered a twenty-five-cent-a-day war bonus to all employees. A new opera house was announced. Star Theatre owner N.M. Trafton denied rumours that he was of German heritage. The latest Red Cross sock drive for soldiers was honoured with a poem.

By the end of March, war news had expanded to two columns. Night school classes were going well. The police had sent stray dogs "to the canine hunting grounds by the cold lead route."[472] A whist party merited front-page coverage. Another Trail soldier received the Military Medal for Bravery for rescuing the wounded. The revolutionary government in Russia had imprisoned the former czar, Nicholas II. A reprint from the *Kamloops Sentinel-Standard* complained that Chinese merchants have "not only monopolized the laundry business, domestic help and other jobs of more or less servile nature, but are now entering upon general mercantile pursuits."[473]

The US finally declared war on Germany in early April. A group of independent Doukhobors had gone to Oregon to establish a colony.[474] Council rejected a request to keep pigs in the city. The ever-helpful Willcox advised readers to "talk plainly, briefly, naturally. Say what you mean, mean what you say, and don't use big words."[475] Two short editorials advised Trail citizens to grow spuds to assist the

Production and Thrift Campaign. Willcox urged the government to buy advertising to tell people how to do it. Also newsworthy that spring, new CM&S general manager J.J. Warren's family moved to Trail.

In a reprint from *Chamber's Journal*, entitled "Some Fallacies About Editors," Willcox raps his readers for thinking of an editor as a "distracted man" who is perpetually lacking news to fill the hole.[476] Soldiers wrote to thank Trailites for their Christmas boxes, and Willcox called on them to contribute more to help disabled soldiers. Meanwhile, news came that two more Trail soldiers had been wounded. Sock knitters reached their goal of 1,012 pairs. Editorials reminded readers that the end of the war was near and lamented that twenty BC newspapers "have given up the ghost."[477]

In one of his first actions as CM&S managing director, J.J. Warren told his 3,000 employees in late April that the company would not grant a fifty-cent increase, and that he rejected the installation of a dues checkoff system allowing the union to have members' union dues deducted from their paycheques. Warren wanted to deal with separate committees of workers from each workplace regardless of whether they were members of the union or not.[478] It was a precursor to Blaylock's Workmen's Co-operative Committee (WCC) system to come. The company-financed union would keep the union at bay for another twenty-five years.

Several more Trail names appeared on the war casualty list, including two fatalities. Local 105 president B. Simpson joined the Royal Flying Corps and was replaced by long-time local trade unionist John A. MacKinnon. Premier Brewster doubled his own salary, and Willcox said he was probably worth it. Readers were advised to kill flies and save lives. Esling was reportedly seen in Alberta attending to his real estate business interests there.

In May, CM&S offered to increase salaries using a production bonus system that would see salaries increase based on the stock market value of lead. The workers voted 262 to 200 for the proposal. There was rebellion in the BC Liberal fold with several MLAs displeased with Brewster. Willcox sounded a warning but said Brewster was doing a good job. Tax increases were coming, including a poll tax. Canada's war machine had enlisted 6.25 per cent of the population. Willcox, in an unattributed item on the problem of the returned soldier, wrote: "A good many people are clamouring for 'land for the returned soldier,' when 90 per cent of them do not want land."[479] He capped his comment with nativist fervour: "They would like, though, to help the returned soldier dispense with the services of the yellows, blacks, browns and the riff-raff and bobtailed of Asia and Europe. Make Canada an English-speaking country—absolutely. Teach English in the schools and only English, and the problem of the returned soldier will solve itself."

Some miners, particularly coal producers in the Crow's Nest, rejected the CM&S's earlier 25 cent offer of a wage bonus in mid-May. Others were holding out for 30 cents, although the *News* was in favour of the federal government ending the strike. Willcox wrote editorials about Allied attacks on German U-boats, registering women voters, the need for a city water-sprinkling system, the importance of auto insurance and the threat of wood ticks.

More war poems "are enough to make any man fight," Willcox stated.[480] It was not clear if he meant the poems encouraged enlistment or that they simply wanted to escape from them. Another child drowned in Trail Creek. *Intolerance*, D.W. Griffiths's 1916 film made in response to the controversy around the racism in his *The Birth of a Nation*, was coming to the Star. Three more Trail men enlisted and a former construction superintendent for CM&S was killed in action. About 800 new names, mostly female, were added to the Trail voters' list. A provincial department of labour was in the works. The *News* published a descriptive letter from a wounded Trail soldier to his mother. This one and others were a personal way for Trail families to keep up with the war.

Ginger Goodwin and other executive members of the Trail Trades and Labour Council appeared before city council to demand a fair wage scale be inserted in all city contracts. An editorial claimed the previous BC Conservative government under Richard McBride "practically let the railway promoters have their own way in this province."[481] The Grits also took their licks from Willcox, who said Premier Brewster had not lived up to his election promises. CM&S assistant manager Blaylock addressed the international mining convention in Nelson, describing the current state of production at the smelter with its workforce of 1,300 men. If women were also employed as war workers, as they would be in the Second World War, he did not mention them. Fifteen-cent movie tickets were to be taxed two cents. The *New York Tribune* paid tribute to the Canadians who fought at Vimy Ridge.

Willcox posted the CM&S quarterly shareholders dividend of $261.91 in June. It came at an inopportune moment for company negotiators since the workers were demanding a pay increase. With a coalition government in Ottawa, passage of a conscription bill seemed a certainty to Willcox. He also wanted Ottawa to invoke war measures to end the coal strike. Former Rossland resident Mrs. E.S.H. Winn, wife of the head of the workers' compensation board, had been arrested in Victoria for manslaughter in the motor vehicle killing of a pedestrian.

Willcox editorialized about the "Publishing of up-to-date war news," noting that weeklies are "handicapped by lack of room, mechanical equipment, wire service, finances, etc."[482] The Canadian soldiers' taking of Vimy Ridge was described as almost a miracle, with several Trail soldiers wounded there. Willcox agreed with union leaders that the government should conscript wealth as well as men. A cigar factory was coming to Trail. Two Trail men joined the US Navy. Willcox supported selective conscription and blasted Quebec's slackers. German bombings of London killed or wounded 500 with no military advantage. Esling dismantled the Columbia Hotel in Rossland and moved it to Bay Avenue in Trail replete with the sign.

Later in June, city council endorsed conscription unanimously. An order-in-council appointed a commissioner to deal with the coal strike. About 400 of Trail's union members met to discuss anti-conscription views and to consider a BC Federation of Labour resolution allowing for a general strike on the issue. Another smelter worker was electrocuted and a zinc plant worker was crushed to death. A Trail man noted "the novel experiences of coast people during the street carmen's strike."[483] A short item described the importance of molybdenum (steel hardening metal).

Tadanac was the new name for Smelter Hill. Local 105 elected John A. MacKinnon president and Goodwin secretary. F.W. Bartle remained treasurer. Willcox again supported compulsory military service: "None of us wish to learn the goose-step—and the passing of this bill will make it all the more certain that no free-born British subject will ever do so."[484] Willcox, as he often did, expressed frustration at those who would advise him on how best to run the *News*: "Here,' said the editor, 'are a number of directions from outsiders as to the best way to run a newspaper. See that they are all carried out.' And the office boy, gathering them all into a waste basket, did so."[485]

A new concentrator, including an oil flotation process, was installed at the smelter to handle zinc ore from the Sullivan Mine in Kimberley. The CM&S had bought the mine in 1913. Trail merchants issued a front-page statement arguing against further price cuts, providing a list of goods with their wholesale and retail prices. The statement, sent to Local 105 secretary Goodwin, read in part: "We have done our very best to sell merchandise at the lowest possible prices consistent with the service we render."[486]

Woman Film Censor, Vimy Ridge, Meatless Tuesdays, the 1917 Smelter Strike

Willcox praised the BC government for appointing a woman movie censor. He also lauded the end of the coal strike and the reopening of the Crow's Nest mines with workers getting a 22.5 per cent increase. And in the needy editor department, Willcox recalled the days when subscriptions were "paid in chickens, eggs, ham, wood, wool, apples, potatoes, butter or any other article raised on the farm." He suggested it may again "become popular with the rural press" and would be "a good sign when a man wants his weekly paper bad enough to be willing to bring in a bag of potatoes, goobers [peanuts], or other things with which to reimburse the needy editor."[487]

In mid-July, bloodhounds could not find a Rossland woman who had mysteriously disappeared. Doing his civic duty, Willcox called on Mayor Fred G. Morin to fix the water shortage problem. A Trail Red Cross nurse was injured in a German torpedo attack. Lauriente's store advertised twenty pairs of free overalls for union workers. Willcox wanted an explanation for "why a strictly party organ cannot see anything that is worthy in the acts of the opposition."[488] It was ironic, since the Esling-Babington *News* was a solidly Conservative organ that gave no quarter to the Opposition.

The Trail Opera House Company opened the new Liberty Theatre. Willcox compared the trench-digging machine that was in town to construct the new sewage system to the trench diggers in France. He gave the Russians a cheerful hurrah for "giving the Austro-Germans the horripilations."[489] He also warned motorists not to exceed the 15 mph speed limit. A reprint from the *Wall Street Journal* noted that a Doukhobor had died fighting for Canada at Vimy Ridge.

Trail workers got a lecture on the workings of the workers' compensation act. Goodwin chaired the event. Compensation board member H.B. Gilmour visited

Liberty Theatre exterior. Courtesy Greg Nesteroff Collection

the *News* office and pointed to four office safety concerns that Willcox pledged to fix. Local 105 contributed $524 to the widow of a smelter worker who was electrocuted in the roasters. Trail commemorated the war's third anniversary.

A Willcox editorial advised readers to eat less, noting that food controllers, that is, ration officers, were here. He also recounted a *Saturday Evening Post* story about two Canadian soldiers who had escaped from a German prison at Geissen. One of them was a Trail man. Willcox was steadfast in pushing for a sprinkling cart for Trail, and his quest was ably assisted by temperatures that soared in July as they often do in the Kootenays. It helped his case that forest fires threatened the city.

When Trail was hit with a "baptism by fire," as Willcox put it, the city was "Saved By a Miracle."[490] The fire hit the Catholic Church hardest, with $22,500 in damages. Willcox asked if Trail would now support city council to put fire protection in place. He and other editors before and after him were all preoccupied with the threat of fire. Starting with W.F. Thompson, several had lost their livelihoods due to fires. In his book on mining camps around Trail, historian Garnet Basque described the conflagrations that engulfed places like Phoenix, Cascade, Brooklyn and elsewhere. Sometimes the local newspaper was saved, but often it was razed with the rest of the town.[491]

A reprint argued that the three-month Crow's Nest coal strike had cost $8 million in lost wages and production. Former BC premier Sir Richard McBride died in London. A letter from a wounded Halifax soldier asked if the labour movement had forsaken them by voting against conscription. Meatless Tuesdays and Fridays had started. More than 600 Canadian members of the International Typographical Union were in the trenches and 50 had died there. Willcox saw it as evidence that the labour movement supported the war to the end.

Hotels observed beefless Tuesdays in early September. Ore being shipped to the smelter from local mines was down about 95,000 tons, sending jitters through the local economy. Willcox warned that Germany was far from defeated. War poems appeared in most editions, but few were from local poetasters. One exception was Margaret Black of the Baptist Manse at Trail who submitted one called "Brothers, to Arms." A new movie theatre was operating called the People's Preference Theatre. What Willcox called "probably the most successful Labor Day celebrations ever held in the Kootenays" drew a thousand people.[492]

Willcox boosted the seventh Trail Fall Fair and noted the growing "Win-the-War" movement that puts "winning the war above winning a political contest."[493] Local MLA James H. Schofield's son, Jim, wrote to describe capturing a German machine gun. A former Trail man won two war medals. Musicians in Trail were organizing a union. Willcox insisted that "If there is any reason why the Doukhobors should be exempted from taxation, we have failed to notice it."[494] He also kicked off a fund to buy a motor launch for Allan G. Horsfield, a severely injured soldier (loss of one eye and other injuries). The fund had reached $455.04 by the time it closed.

BC prohibition took effect on October 1. The new law allowed hotel bars to sell soft drinks and 2.5 per cent beer. A McKim Advertising Agency directory showed that the *Trail News* was among 924 weekly newspapers publishing in Canada. Class A conscripts were needed under the terms of the Military Service Act. Semi-monthly paydays began and Willcox credited the Brewster government with the popular innovation. An automobile club was organized with sixty charter members. *The Battle of the Somme* was playing at the Liberty. *The Birth of a Nation* was still at the Star. *Neptune's Daughter* was at the People's Performance Theatre.

In mid-October, the government exempted smelter employees ages 20–34 from military service. Managing director Warren explained that "the works of this company are really a munitions plant, and that those engaged in said works are really serving their country and aiding in the prosecution of the war just as much as if they were armed and in the trenches."[495] A coalition, or Union, government was formed in Ottawa. Another smelter worker was electrocuted. Trail formed a branch of the Imperial Order Daughters of the Empire (IODE). Willcox announced that a new Victory Loan would be released. A letter from a Trail soldier asked what was to become of the returning soldier. Mine operators wanted the federal government to support them through loans.

Blaylock was the Trail branch Win-the-War League president. In early November, he chaired a convention of about fifty people in Nelson that chose Conservative MP Robert F. Green to nominate a Kootenay representative to the new coalition government in Ottawa. Blaylock made a speech on the lead ore situation. Esling was named chair of the Rossland Victory Loan committee.

Smeltermen were paying into the Patriotic Fund through an automatic wage checkoff sent directly to the Bank of Montreal. Blaylock was accused of making money on the scheme, prompting him to respond "that insinuations had repeatedly come to his ear that the company was making money out of the fund, and that he was there to hear any man make such a statement and that he would proceed to knock him down if he did."[496] A man working on the Trail sewer system died in a cave-in.

In mid-November, the smelter's 1,500 workers—machinists, boilermakers, carpenters, electricians, plumbers, pipefitters and general day labourers—"laid down their tools and walked out to enforce a universal eight-hour day."[497] The walkout idled the smelter for the first time in more than twenty years.[498] Blaylock refused to negotiate with the Trail Trades and Labour Council (TTLC), arguing that the company already had an agreement in place with Local 105. The local denied that the walkout was connected to protesting conscription. The *News* estimated that the local had about a thousand members and there were another 200 union affiliates to the TTLC. The strike vote was 352 to 43, making a total of 395. Willcox noted that WFM international president Charles Moyer had called on workers not to strike while the war was still on. In another editorial, he said it was "unfortunate" that the union could not reach an agreement. "No question of wages was involved, but one of eight hours instead of nine for those not already working eight hours."[499] It was a softer approach to a labour dispute than readers had come to expect.

The strike, the first since the smelter began in 1895, reached a stalemate in late November with Blaylock correcting an account in the *News*. "I have heard that some of the union officials are saying that they have permitted certain men to remain in the plant so as to keep it in such condition that when a settlement was reached the men would be able to go back to work in a body," he told Willcox. "The position is entirely different. A number of our shift bosses are on duty in the plant. When I found that they were being molested by some of the Union pickets—one of them an Austrian—I told the officials that this action was wrong and should cease, and that these men should not be made more uncomfortable than necessary. To this the Union Committee agreed."[500] An editorial hoped that a settlement could be found and estimated that the strike would cost the Kootenays $500,000 and affect as many as 20,000 workers across the country.

Meanwhile, the Trail Dancing Club held a strike benefit dance and gave $142 to the union. City council instructed its solicitor to sue the *Vancouver Province* for libel because of a "lurid story" under the headline, "Flatly Refuse to Obey Law at Trail—Terms of Military Service Act Flagrantly Disobeyed by 1,500 Smeltermen—Make Bonfire of Victory Loan Literature and Refuse to Subscribe." The *News* reported that council believed "the workingmen of Trail and the city itself were done a grave injustice by the unwarranted publication of such rot and nonsense."[501] Board of Trade president Noble Binns wired Premier Brewster to condemn the *Province*'s false statements about the strike being motivated by conscription: "The men are presenting themselves as fast as the tribunal can handle them."[502] The TTLC issued the following statement: "The strike is being conducted under the Trades and Labour Council of Trail, for it embraces all the Unions that are working at the smelter. All the other arrangements as to wages and hours have been taken up through the Mill & Smeltermen's Union [Local 105], yet for this measure it brings in the various unions existing at Trail, which are trying to establish this condition [eight hours]."[503]

Willcox reported on the Board of Trade meeting with the CM&S, stating that J.J. Warren had refused to discuss the shorter hours issue. Like Blaylock, he argued that an agreement was in place. The *Victoria Colonist* editor refused to divulge the name of the journalist who wrote the article considered defamatory against Trail. Willcox published a mild editorial hoping that a settlement to the strike "will bring a cheerful yuletide to over 20,000 people hereabouts."[504]

In December, the federal government assigned W.H. Armstrong "to look into and if possible settle the strike."[505] Another former Trail man was awarded the Military Cross. Willcox noted that the "Teutons" held a peace conference with the "Bolsheviki element," and he praised President Woodrow Wilson's efforts. "As yuletide draws near there is every reason for optimism,"[506] Willcox counselled. He also offered these words of wisdom: "Some people think that Billy Sunday [the evangelist] should be given a medal for saving more souls than any man in America. Others, however, are in favor of giving the medal to Henry Ford, on the grounds that he has been responsible for shaking hell out of more people than any man living. Apparently it is a toss up between them."[507] A drawing of a woman about to cast her vote in the federal election was titled "To Mothers, Wives and Sisters."[508] A Trail nurse was going to the frontlines in France. Trail had 1,300 voters on the electors' list. The city's $40,000 sewer system was about to open.

A mass meeting voted to end the strike after thirty-six days.[509] Goodwin contacted smelter management to ask if the men could return to work immediately. The *News* calculated that the strike had cost $216,000 in lost wages. Blaylock and Warren insisted that they had an agreement to the end of the war, but the men denied that such an agreement existed. A letter from Mine Mill international president Charles H. Moyer said "We find that the Trail Trades and Labour Council had no authority under the laws of the American Federation of Labour, or those of our own international, either to carry on negotiations with the Consolidated company re working conditions, hours, etc. or to call a strike."[510] Moyer then stated that the CM&S had "repeatedly requested that the matters in dispute be taken up through the Mill and Smeltermen's union. The failure of the union to grant these requests constitute a violation... of our constitution."[511] Moyer deemed the strike "unlawful" and said "we hereby declare the plant of the Consolidated company at Trail fair."[512] (Note that the WFM had changed its name to the International Union of Mine, Mill and Smelter Workers in 1916, possibly to soften its image as a radical union.)

Willcox's editorial called it a decision of "sensible men" and argued that "the entire trouble might have been avoided." He did not explain how.[513] A second editorial lauded the victory of the Union government in the election. Willcox advised the new government "to see that sedition is stamped out so completely in the Dominion that its pro-German or pacifist head will not dare be shown anywhere in Canada."[514] The *News* claimed that because the smelter had fulfilled its orders as the strike began, there would not be as many workers needed.[515]

The strike diminished Local 105 and inspired Blaylock to create a new anti-strike weapon called the Workmen's Co-operative Committee. Smelter workers

Rossland women's hockey team, ca. 1900, illustrates how the Kootenays cherished their sports, especially in winter. Courtesy Rossland Museum and Discovery Centre

would continue to report for military service as the war cut Europe to ribbons. The smelter would resume operations in the New Year with Willcox in full support of its ore processing rate increases and in defiance of a proposed mining tax. A new mayor and a new provincial premier were installed. Trailites were still observing meatless days and liquor advertising filled the *News* in a last grab for cash as prohibition set in. Curling and women's hockey supplied a distraction from the war as did the Star and Liberty Theatres. Under Willcox, the *News* appeared to be thriving.

5–TRAIL NEWS (1918–1919)

WAR'S END, GLOBAL FLU AND LABOUR MARTYRDOM

The *News* Reports on Sorrow and Prosperity in the Smelter City

No one, including *Trail News* editor W.B. Willcox, could know that the end of the "War to End All Wars" was still almost a year away at the start of 1918. The smelting business was picking up after last year's strike, and Willcox avidly supported the CM&S in its complaint about a proposed mining tax. Nobody could foresee a worldwide plague that would kill 50 million people, some of them Trailites. And only the most astute observers of labour relations in Canada—in Trail they would include the CM&S's S.G. Blaylock—would be aware of a radical political movement called the One Big Union that was blowing across Western Canada.

By early 1918, Willcox no doubt shared Blaylock's sensitivity to socialist union battles and had chosen to move cautiously in Blaylock's direction when such threats arose. By then he had found his place among the weekly newspaper literati of the day, including journalistic stars like Colonel R.T. Lowery of the *Greenwood Ledge* and Patrick O'Farrell, an Irish-American freelance writer who once worked for copper king F. Augustus Heinze. O'Farrell earned Willcox plaudits for "using his pen to get right after the pro-Germans in our midst, the Bolshevikis, IWW's [Industrial Workers of the World], and others of that calibre."[516]

Early in the year, Willcox lamented the passing of the "good old days of newspaperdom" when he cribbed this note from the *Vancouver Sun*: "The modern country editor is a helpless coot compared to the one who used to do all the reporting, set up the stuff straight from his head, lock up the paper and borrow money to pay the boy that helped him from the man who came around to collect a bill."[517] The *News* editor also relished local rivalries that were part of the "old days." He regularly fought with

W.B. Willcox bought the News from W.K. Esling in 1915. He is shown here under an umbrella that served as the *Spokane Daily Chronicle* newsroom after a fire destroyed its office. Courtesy *Spokesman Review* Photo Archives

J.J. Clark and Elmer D. Hall took over the *Trail News* in 1917. Hall bought an earlier model of this Linotype (typesetting) machine used by the *Kaslo Kootenaian* in the 1940s. Courtesy Kootenay Lake Historical Society

Kaslo Kootenaian editor H.W. Power over the issue of mining tax increases or ore processing costs. When Power purchased a "silent drama business," Willcox commented sarcastically on how much extra time Power had. "Doubtless, when he is not operating the finest linotype in the Kootenays, writing brainy editorials, setting ads, lambasting the Consolidated company, making up the paper, running the large press, doing job work, sweeping out the office, dunning delinquent subscribers, and a few dozen other things common to newspaper offices, he requires something to keep him out of mischief. Here's hoping he may make bales of kale in his moving picture house."[518]

In this way, Willcox was giving his readers a glimpse of the similar weekly grind he faced to get out the *News*—a rare look inside the workings of the paper. He clearly related to Power's situation as well as that of a "down east editor" who commented on the life of a small-town newspaper editor: "Ever sit at a typewriter and... give the proper space to the life of a departed citizen, laud the beauty and grace of a bride, see that every organization has its name mentioned, give the names of all the new officials of any order, announce the events which are planned... write everything which everybody wants you to write about, and withal make no enemies? Then you're partly fitted to be an editor of a small-town newspaper."[519]

Willcox's lament extended to the quality of freelancers and he was clear about what he wanted from them: "In sending news, contributors should write plainly with ink or typewriter: do not use indelible pencil and NEVER write on both sides of a sheet unless you wish the typographical artist to endanger his future by lurid remarks on the side."[520] He would repeat the instruction many times over in the next year and a half of his editorship. Editors that followed him would do the same.

The smelter had been closed since mid-November due to the 1917 strike and it now reopened, employing more than 1,000 workers, many of them immigrants. As always, the company enjoyed regular boosts from editor Willcox as ore shipments began to increase. The CM&S showed a net profit of $1,076,828.50 for 1917.[521] But the year did not start auspiciously for Giovanni Catalano, sixteen, who drowned in a Pachuca tank in the zinc plant.[522] More fatalities were to come, with the coroner ruling most of them accidents.

Willcox encouraged Trailites to continue giving to the Patriotic Fund. In mid-February, the Red Cross women's auxiliary reported sending 340 pairs of knitted socks to the front as well as $177.10 and a quantity of tobacco.[523] Trail gave almost $100,000 to the fund that spring; of this amount, smelter workers donated almost $85,000.[524] A prisoners of war tea and dance added more funds. The *News* also encouraged Trailites to raise pigs in their backyards to furnish soldiers with more pork. Meanwhile, beefless and porkless Tuesdays were still required on the home front. The editor strongly supported a food conservation program, and Trail soon appointed its own food controller.

Although the war was three years old in mid-February, sixty-two Trail men were reportedly called up to the Princess Patricia Canadian Light Infantry (Princess Pats) and other military regiments under the Military Service Act.[525] But at least one recruit soon went AWOL. Local jeweller Noble Binns, who also presided over the Trail Board of Trade, with Willcox serving on the publicity committee, chaired the local exemption tribunal. It rejected the appeal of 1917 smelter strike leader Albert "Ginger" Goodwin despite medical evidence that he was unfit for active duty. *News* readers got snippets of the war through front-page photographs of trench combat and air dogfights. A news dispatch from Europe claimed the German government had funded the Bolsheviks.[526]

Brief reports also appeared in the form of letters home. A wounded soldier hoped the war would soon be over because "he feels he has spent the best part of life in France, teaching Germans better manners."[527] Herbert Jackson wrote to a "Miss Weir" describing the horrors of the London air raids.[528] Trail police chief Benjamin Downes had forty-seven aliens reporting to him.[529] Former Trail clarinet player, George W. Maddams, was now in custody after trying to evade military service.[530]

Wartime poetry also found its place in the *News*. Rudyard Kipling, Robert Service and J.W. Bengough, a well-known Canadian political cartoonist, were regulars. Even birth control activist Dr. Margaret E. Sanger tried her hand at verse. Typical was prospector Sandy Mac's "For Home and Country": "Oh men of Canada arise,/As men in days of yore,/And fight for hearts and home, boys/As you never fought before."[531] More action-oriented verse also appeared, such as Australian Lieutenant Leslie Bumpus's "Passing By": "Passing by! Passing by!/Wiv a little whistlin' sigh,/Nearly got you that time, sonny,/Just a little bit too high."[532] Sadly,

Willcox reported that Lieutenant-Colonel John McCrae, Canadian author of the celebrated poem "In Flanders Fields," had died of pneumonia on January 28. He was forty-five.

Some Trailites had cheered the adoption of the Prohibition Act in BC on October 1, 1917; others were arrested for violating it. The bill, not rescinded until 1921, led to a flood of *News* advertising revenue as liquor producers rushed to make final sales. Women were advised to "exhibit day by day and hour by hour the same courage a man shows upon the field of battle."[533] And a reprinted item from the *Wall Street Journal* warned Trailites that "Socialism Is Failure."[534] Perhaps it alluded to the Russian Revolution the previous October. It did not refer to a comment on socialist MLA James H. Hawthornthwaite, who visited the Kootenays to promote his bill calling for a general eight-hour day for all employees. The legislature rejected it, but it had some support from local MLA James H. Schofield. Later in the year, Hawthornthwaite called on the government to borrow $125 million to build homes for returning soldiers and to take over sawmills and canneries to give them jobs.

Hit the Hun, Swat the Fly, "Fightin' Sons-of-Guns" and Poetry Galore in 1918

After the strike, smelter workers began to return from Spokane and other locations in the US, building the Trail workforce back up to pre-strike levels. Willcox's editorials expressed concern over the sagging demand for metals and its impact on the smelter. He also praised the CM&S office workers who "donned overalls and went to work unloading cars of ore, coal, coke, etc."[535] The *News* editor saw this work in a positive light. Many smelter workers would not likely have shared his view. Willcox was effusive in his praise of the CPR's pamphlet "Fightin' Sons-of-Guns" about "the boys of the Maple Leaf" doing battle in France.[536]

Early in the year, Fred G. Morin, a smelter master carpenter, officially became Trail's new mayor. He had been acting mayor since the previous fall. A night school provided workers with English and arithmetic lessons. Trailites, shocked by the massive Halifax explosion in December 1917, donated $500 to a relief fund. Local curling and girls' hockey rivalries entertained the public as did hot competition in a church league.

Trail had the largest number of telephones in the Kootenays, with 250 as of December 1, 1917.[537] It was another indicator of the smelter city's steady progress. Both the Star and Liberty Theatres continued to feature silent movies like the million-dollar film *Daughter of the Gods*, starring Annette Kellerman, the world's "greatest woman swimmer."[538] The kiddies could see *Aladdin and The Wonderful Lamp*, starring Francis Carpenter. The Liberty also featured Irish, Scottish and English songs and dances as well as a minstrel show from Northport, Washington, that included "black faced artists."[539]

Movies were a critical aspect of wartime social life in the city, so Mayor Morin and city council took it seriously when a dispute arose regarding the live music that patrons of the local theatres expected with their silent pictures. The band had stopped playing, and theatre manager N.M. Trafton blamed Local 713 of the

American Federation of Musicians. Trafton said the union was demanding too much money. Union secretary Jas. Pasta said Trafton was consistently cutting wages and thus forcing the movies to go musicless. The *News* provided the battleground for the fight, which was settled a few weeks later.

Advertising was more plentiful than ever as business thrived in the smelter city. The Trail Mercantile Co., for example, advertised work gloves at 65 cents, work shoes at $4.50, butter at 50 cents a pound, flour at $3 a sack, and potatoes at $2 per CWT (hundredweight).[540] However, a new income tax introduced on January 2 would add a severe burden to the mining industry, Willcox argued. A new $8,000 Catholic Church building replaced the one lost to fire in August 1917. Willcox was supportive of good Christian businesses and he promoted popular American evangelist Billy Sunday, a conservative. But he was not so kind to ethnic minorities, such as Chinese immigrants and Doukhobors.

Of the Chinese, for example, he stated "They may be thrifty and steady workers, and they may be reliable, but few can honestly say that, all things considered, they are a desirable addition to our population."[541] In Willcox's view, "Coolie labor" was not wanted.[542] He was no kinder to the Doukhobor religious sect. When it was suggested that "The Douks" should return to Russia, Willcox enthusiastically supported the move.[543] When the sect refused to pay a $5 poll tax to the Patriotic Fund, the editor pounced: "The fact is that every blessed Douk in Canada should be tickled to death to pay the poll tax while he is exempted from the Military Service Act."[544] He also published racist comments about an African American preacher down in Washington State who was kicked in the stomach and "had a revelation."[545] Nor did Willcox discourage racist advertising in reference to the Chinese workers in the kitchen at the Tadanac Cafe.[546]

In the spring, Premier Harlan C. Brewster, a Freemason who owned a cannery, died suddenly of pneumonia, and farmer John Oliver replaced him. Willcox called the new premier "a man of independent thought and action and of the highest standard of citizenship."[547] As noted, Willcox always supported the Kootenay corporate power structure, and the editorial support continued until the end of his run as editor and to the end of the weekly's lifetime.

War coverage in spring 1918 noted that 100 Trail men were drafted and on their way to war, a reminder that bodies as well as other war materials were still being shipped to Europe. Columns like "Echoes from the War" and "Slants on the Great War" helped readers visualize the war's carnage and fed a visceral hatred for the "Hun." Statistics added to the horror with the US Food and Drug Administration stating "about 4,750,000 persons have died of starvation in Europe since the war began, while about 4,250,000 have been killed by fighting."[548] But it was columns like "Trail Boys in Khaki" and the frequent flow of letters from the European front and German prison camps that brought home the gruesome reality of the European conflict.

In a typical letter, Private Harold Weller, one of the original volunteers from Trail, "returned last night minus an eye and with shrapnel wounds."[549] Bombardier E.G. Payne, "the first man who rushed to the colors" when war was declared, visited his family in Trail. He "lost no time in responding to the call when the Mad Dog of Europe started things in August, three years ago," the *News* noted.[550] In May, readers learned that D. Bilsom Merry had escaped from a German prison camp. He would arrive home later in the summer and would soon receive a letter from the king and queen, commending his service to the Crown. Sergeant William Butorac announced that he had received the Military Medal for Bravery. Herbert S. Smith, former president of Mine-Mill Local 105, wrote to thank the Smeltermen's War Fund. Former Local 105 president James Lawrie also chose to "don khaki." Readers also got much bad news. For example, William A. Luff, another former smelter worker, was killed in action in France. Herb Smith landed in hospital with a nervous breakdown.

Willcox relied on letters of thanks to lift local spirits. The tireless Red Cross knitting team and the Smelter Hill Knitting Club efforts were effusively thanked. Still, there was no respite from the constant official encouragement to economize at home to aid the war effort. One reminder: "Kind and kareful Kanadian kooks, so an alliterative expert reminds us, kan keep killing kaiserism in their kitchens by ekonomising."[551] A small ad reminded Trailites to "Eat Less Bread" and weekly advice came from the Canada Food Board. Its ads urged "Our Allies Must Be Fed" or to "Fight With Food." The Trail food controller advised homemakers on how not to waste food and how to feed a family of five on a budget. Also monitored was the fat count in local dairy products.

By April, the Trail Red Cross had shipped fifteen cases of shirts, pajamas, socks, towels, sheets and other items to the front. Cigarettes were also shipped and were much appreciated by local boys. Tobacco consumption was on the rise at home as well, perhaps due to more women smoking, but that did not stifle the export of smokes to the front. Corporal Jack Turner chose a poem to thank Trailites and others who sent cigarettes to the trenches:

> When the cold is making ice cream
> of the marrow in your bones,
> When you're shaking like a jelly
> and your feet are dead as stones,
> When your clothes and boots and blankets,
> and your rifle and your kit,
> Are soaked from Hell to Breakfast,
> and the dugout where you sit
> Is leaking like a basket,
> and upon the muddy floor
> The water lies in filthy pools,
> six inches deep or more;
> Tho' life seems cold and mis'rable
> and all the world is wet,
> You'll always get thro' somehow
> if you've got a cigarette.[552]

With prohibition still on the books until 1921, liquor may also have been a secretive way to forget the war or at least dull its impact. A local brewery tried to take advantage of the situation and was charged in Magistrate Noble Binns's court with selling beer over the 2.5 per cent alcohol content limit. Binns was kept occupied with other crimes as well, including illegal gambling, bigamy and at least one charge under the Wives' Desertion Act. And Willcox covered the case of Lee Fook, alias Lee Sam, who faced four charges of false pretenses.

Photographs were now more prominent and provided another way the *News* could share a sense of life at the front. In one, British tanks are seen moving into attack formation. In others, air dog fights are depicted. Still others show military targets and troop movements. Another photo showed German soldiers who "lost the use of their eyes by having their own devil's plaything—gas—which they had directed against the French—turn on them by a sudden shifting of the winds."[553] Most prominent among the portraits were those of Allied commanders and politicians. French General Ferdinand Foch and British General Sir Alexander Haig, in full dress uniform, were seen in many editions of the paper. Occasionally prominent society women were also pictured. For example, Mrs. Chalmer Watson, MD, appeared when she was appointed controller of the Woman's Army Auxiliary Corps in Britain, and Viscountess Grimston, a British Red Cross worker, won a place among the few women (other than those in movie ads) whose photograph appeared in the *News*.

War poetry was not always welcome at the *News*, perhaps because there was so much of it. "One of the awful results of this war is the crop of war poets that has made itself heard and felt," carped one item.[554] "'I must thank you for saving my life,' said a returned soldier to a verse writer. 'I carried your book of verses in my breast pocket; a bullet hit it, but it couldn't get beyond the fifth verse'."[555] The *News* staff must have reached a new plateau of anger with this response to poetry submissions:

> They say that our work is essential,
> That printers are much in demand.
> So that what people think
> Can be printed in ink
> And distributed all through the land.
> But, gee, when I glance at the copy
> —The manuscript kind I abhor;
> I just lose my goat,
> Make a grab for my coat,
> And yell 'Please, mister, send me to war!'[556]

Nevertheless, Willcox published great heaps of poetaster submissions, much of which fed the public thirst for the imagery of war. For example, Corp. John W. Thompson wrote the following:

Oh, crush the aggressor and smite the oppressor,
Far force his foul footsteps from France's fair shore,
Till the home desolator, the shrine desecrator,
The tyrant shall ravish the world never more.[557]

The entry of the US into the war brought forth a poem that won the National Arts Club prize. Newspapers said it "sets the pulses leaping." One stanza urged victory for the Allies: "To France—with every race and breed/That hates oppression's brutal creed."[558] The call from the front for more socks inspired Doris F.A. Saville to write:

Socks, Socks, Socks,
Like a whole brigade of clocks,
Sounds the clicking of the knitting,
Steady sticking is Hun-hitting.[559]

Trailites also regularly checked the *News* for tallies of donations to the Patriotic Fund. In one spring report, Trail gave $411 to the fund, while the Smeltermen's Fund gathered $1,200. The Junior Red Cross raised money as did the YMCA's Red Triangle Fund. Thousands of BC families were assisted in this way as they struggled to survive family war deaths and shortages on the home front. By July, Trail had given another $1,595 to the fund, $1,200 of it from the Smeltermen's War Fund.

As an added diversion, the *News* promoted the annual "Swat the Fly" campaign, advising that "one killed now means ten trillion million that we'll not have later."[560] A store in the Gulch took advantage of the food board's declaring ice cream a food and opened a first-class ice cream parlour, but the board's dictates did not always improve morale. For example, it "made it unlawful for any person in Canada to use for private consumption French pastries, cakes or biscuits with icing or cane sugar."[561] Even candy got the axe.

Social activities abounded at various service clubs. Trail's Odd Fellows and Rebekahs (the women's division of the Odd Fellows), for example, paraded in celebration of the order's ninety-ninth anniversary. The Daughters of the Empire and the Knights of Pythias had regular dances in Trail as did the churches, unions and groups like the Great War Veteran's Association. Judging from the *News*, virtually everyone found the twenty-five cents required to see a film.

Labour's Martyr, Red Cross Socks, "White Man's Canada" and a Killer Flu

By the summer, special police constables were on the hunt for conscription evaders. This included, most suspiciously, Albert "Ginger" Goodwin, leader of the 1917 strike. In late April, Willcox warned that thirty-five Trail men could have their service exemptions cancelled as "the terrible German drive in Picardy, with its holocaust of lives… is cementing all parties and factions to the strenuous task that is still before the world of righteousness and humanity."[562]

As mentioned, Goodwin had been judged unfit for immediate military service in an earlier examination. But in May, the military tribunal rejected the letters of three doctors diagnosing Goodwin with "chronic stomach problems."[563] The Vancouver Trades and Labour Council refused to endorse Goodwin's request for exemption, but Local 105 did come to his aid. The union's acting secretary, Peter J. Bolam, endorsed the request. But Goodwin had already left town in search of a secret refuge.

Goodwin's case was followed closely in Trail, but the *News* was hardly well outfitted to cover the story. At its best, a feature news story detailed what happened to Goodwin when police caught up with him in June. The *News* reported that Dominion Police had "Exchanged Shots With Trail Man" and offered a description of the raid on the Vancouver Island camp where Goodwin had been hiding. "Evidence was secured in the effects which the police gathered together showing that Albert Goodwin is among them, and he is believed to be the leader of the gang," the *News* report continued. "How many men are with Goodwin is not known, but the supplies captured indicate that the gang had prepared for a long stay. It is certain, too, that they were well armed.... Five Dominion and provincial police joined in the chase."[564]

In early August, Goodwin was shot dead and became a national labour martyr. Canada's first general strike took place in his memory. The *News* reported on the trial of Dominion constable Daniel Campbell, the man who killed him. The ruling was "justifiable homicide" on a charge of manslaughter. Sidebars to the main story were headlined "Evaders Coming In," "Appeals to Socialists" and "Socialists Want to Know."[565] Willcox shed no tears for labour's martyr:

> Goodwin deserves no sympathy nor do those who think as he does. Canada is at war and has called its young men to the colors. He was one of them, and his persistent evasion of his duty brought the natural consequence. Thousands have gone willingly and gladly and many have paid the price. Albert Goodwin paid it, not in the line of duty, but because he would not conform to what we are all subject to and threatened an officer. He was a bright man and could have made a name for himself.[566]

The jury of public opinion is still out more than a hundred years later.[567]

With Trail's population at 4,500 and growing, there was plenty of local news to share with the 2,000 workers now employed at the smelter. The *News* circulation had more than doubled to 1,000 subscribers. To serve their needs and desires, little escaped Willcox's notice, and he supplied reports on virtually everyone's movements that spring and summer. Among the items: his daughter Elizabeth's school grades, a threatened strike at the Northport smelter, and city council's plans to build 3,210 lineal feet of sewers (local contractor Victor Bianco would win the bid). Willcox had long crusaded for a sprinkler wagon to keep the dust down on Trail streets. It was finally on its way.

Even a slight mishap merited coverage in the weekly. For example: "Last Sunday afternoon, while riding her horse from her home in Patterson back to Trail, Miss Rachael Newsman, one of the teachers in the Trail public school, was thrown from the animal and badly bruised."[568] She would soon recover. Willcox seldom included much more about women than the knitting news or the usual run of married couple jokes. But he did praise Mrs. Ralph Smith, "the only petticoated member in the BC legislature, [who] attends strictly to her knitting all the time, and presents a good example to some of her colleagues."[569]

In his many appeals for the payment of subscription arrears, Willcox shared his philosophy that the price of a subscription rewarded the editor who "congratulates a man on his marriage, that announces the birth of his children, tells where the neighbors spent the Sabbath, tells him of whipping his wife, warns him of tricksters and fakirs, points him out as a wretch and a scoundrel when he has to go to jail, and bears the great burden of grief and sympathy of the entire community for a whole week when he dies."[570]

No Kootenay editor could claim those rewards more than Col. Robert T. Lowery, and Willcox might have rightly attributed the following comment to the *Greenwood Ledge* editor: "There is more joy in a printing office over one subscriber who pays in advance and abuses the editor on every occasion, than over ninety and nine who borrow the paper and sing its praises without contributing a solitary cent to keep it out of the poorhouse."[571] Willcox also enlisted the opinion of the London newspaper publisher Lord Northcliffe: "What they want, he says, is the home paper, the local, which tells who was at the church social, who has been married, and which team won the game."[572] Willcox willingly assented.

Racist attitudes were well represented in the *News* with jokes using terms that today are considered unacceptable: "A colored [*sic*] drill sergeant is reported as saying to his squad: 'Now when I gives de word of comman', Eyes right! I wants to hear every [redacted] eyeball click."[573] In a later edition, this appeared: "TNT—Travel, [redacted], Travel."[574] Like most of his predecessors, Willcox grew up in the US and was schooled in the post-Civil War period. Black Americans rarely came to Trail, but the local culture had long been poisoned with racist views from south of the border. Of course, there was much homegrown racism as well, particularly against Asians. In one example: "Two Chinese restaurant keepers at Revelstoke were last week fined $5 and costs for each having a white girl in their employ."[575] This latter case was in response to 1919 provincial legislation prohibiting Chinese business owners from employing white women, ostensibly to "protect" them.

Willcox lent full support to Kootenay MP Robert F. Green when he called for an end to alien labour and support for a "white Canada."[576] In his editorial on importing Asian labour, Willcox made it clear where he stood on the issue: "If we want to keep this a white man's Canada we must be careful how we open the door to the yellow race."[577]

Also like his predecessors, Willcox was a smelter city booster. The weekly's banner declared Trail to be the metallurgical mecca of Canada, and Willcox published articles promoting that image. Comments on the mining and smelting in-

New Denver Ledge office in 1898, with legendary editor Robert Lowery (centre) who received regular praise in the Trail weekly for his caustic wit and social criticism. Courtesy Janice Wilkin

dustry from CM&S managing director J.J. Warren and assistant managing director S.G. Blaylock were often featured. When markets brightened, as they did for zinc that May, the *News* reported the favourable tidings.

Despite his fawning comments, Willcox reported on a local farmer's suit against the company: "The case has created no small amount of interest locally, the plaintiff endeavoring to show that his loss of crops, chiefly hay, last year, was due to smoke damage, while the defendant claimed that a large part of it was due to the unusually dry year that prevailed in 1917."[578] The company was ordered to pay $2,170, but escaped any lectures about shirked environmental responsibility in the *News*.

In July, more of Trail's enlisted sons came home, but the war continued to take more lives. Cadet Roy Weir, who died at an air training camp near Toronto, got a military funeral at the Liberty Theatre. J.E. Riley, formerly private secretary to the CM&S's J.J. Warren, was now safe at Witley, England. Machine gunner Lieutenant Walter D. Truswell wrote to his mother "about a narrow escape he had in the great German drive in March and April." He had to swim the Somme River to save his life. "There was nothing for it but to swim," the *News* reported, "and his experience when a boy in swimming in the swift Columbia River at Trail stood him in good stead and probably saved his life."[579]

Later that summer, the Great War Veterans and Returned Soldiers Aid Committee (later the GWVA and eventually the Canadian Legion) announced plans for a parade and public reception in celebration of the return of local boys Bilson Merry and Wesley Weir. Former *News* staffer Frank Pike had become an instructor in the wireless division of the Royal Air Force in Ontario. The GWVA welcomed

Lieutenant-Colonel Rowland Bourke, who visited his sister in Trail. In August, he was awarded the Distinguished Service Order for bravery. Also in August, Dan Shields, twenty-three, of Trail, made the supreme sacrifice somewhere in France.

That fall, CM&S's assistant manager S.G. Blaylock learned that his brother, Colonel Harry Blaylock, was made a Commander of the British Empire in recognition of his Red Cross services. In September, smelter worker William Barnes was killed in action. In November, Corporal R. James, another smelter worker, was also killed in action. Bert Sibbald wrote home to say he'd won a military medal. Clearly the war was not over for Trail even though Armistice Day was around the corner.

Autumn brought another kind of war as well; the *News* called it the disease that "Bears the Name of 'Spanish' and is Rapidly Spreading."[580] By October 25, there were twenty cases of the deadly flu in Trail, schools were closed and big gatherings forbidden as the city took precautions to hold back the pandemic. Nelson and Rossland reported several hundred cases, with Rossland possibly "in worse plight than any other city or town in Canada" according to population. The Nelson mayor would succumb to it, as would Rossland's police chief.[581] Already the mistruths had started to spread: "Many people in Trail are of the opinion that the prevalence of smelter smoke here will help materially to keep down the spread of influenza in this place."[582] Misguided doctors told people that smoking was good for fighting the flu.[583]

In early November, Mayor Morin said masks were required and advised that "as many as 25 per cent of the smelter workforce were sick."[584] Willcox quipped that "Flu masks are as common in Trail these days as huckleberries in summer time, and the doctors say they are the real thing too. There is no option now about wearing them."[585] In fact, flu masks were showing up in great variety. Some were homemade and others were factory bought. The *News* helpfully provided lists of what to do in case of flu. "How to Keep From Getting the Influenza" offered the all-too-familiar list the world now knows by heart from Covid-19 experience. The article "What to Do if You Have Influenza" counselled people to observe nine don'ts. Number 2: "Keep away from other people. Do not kiss anyone."[586] As the pandemic geared up, and the death toll mounted, help was on the way in the form of Zell Hunt, a phrenologist and physiognomist who "gets the questions from the mind by telepathy and the answers by veritable inspiration." For two bucks a pop, he would "help you in health, love and business."[587]

In the midst of the pandemic, the war was still going on and, as noted, Trailites were continuing to learn of their war dead. Now, as forty-three BC towns closed down, they faced another life-threatening enemy, one that they could not see. Former *News* owner W.K. Esling had donated the use of his Aldridge Hotel as an auxiliary hospital as Trail recorded hundreds of flu cases and fifteen deaths.[588] Meanwhile, Willcox told readers to "not be afraid."[589] He further counselled that the losses had settled so far at about 1 to 2 per cent of Trail's population. Rossland ran from 3 to 4 per cent. It was cold comfort as the disease raged into a full-fledged epidemic, killing 2,014 in BC in three months.

In mid-November, the *News* reported total cases of 600 with thirty-seven deaths. "Case No. 1—Last night in Trail a delirious man, sick wife and two small children were taken care of by a girl eight years old who had a fever of 102. YOU were snug in your bed."[590] A flu diet kitchen had been set up to help stricken families. Rossland suffered another flu-related loss when the daily *Rossland Miner* was reduced to a weekly. By the end of November, the *News* was reporting some improvement on the flu front with only seven more deaths that week. Smelter workers could return to work, but only after being certified by a medical officer. Normal was not quite there yet.

In mid-December, five new deaths were reported, three the week before. The financial cost to the city was $2,127.49, but the human cost was much higher. As Willcox stated, "Trail has lost more lives in four or five weeks from influenza than were killed from this place in over four years of the war."[591] By the end of December, no new flu cases were reported. Trail's schools opened for the first time since October 21. Perhaps the end was near, although flu deaths were still going unreported.

Throughout the war, the *News* had escalated its attacks on the Doukhobors. Rumours of their return to Russia were circulated in the weekly, despite sect leader Peter Verigin's insistence that they were staying in Canada—as evidenced by the purchase of 10,000 acres of land in Saskatchewan in May.[592] When fire destroyed the Doukhobor pipe factory and planing mills at Brilliant that month, Willcox showed no sympathy. Damage was estimated at $20,000.[593]

In June, when the Board of Trade approved a meeting with the BC Telephone company on "the matter of the possibility of awarding the contract for the new phone building in Trail to the Doukhobor society," Willcox hoped that "it would not be done."[594] When the "Douks," ever industrious, won a contract to produce strawberry jam for army use, Willcox treated it with disdain.[595] When the sect objected to compulsory manpower registration for everyone over sixteen years old, Willcox commented that "the Douks have had exemptions enough most people think, and it is pleasant to know that for once they were forced by law to do just as the rest of the community did."[596]

Willcox pressed the reading public to register in a government manpower survey, so when news came that Doukhobors were refusing to give their names, rejected ownership of property, and were otherwise "singing and chanting" as they were taken to jail, the weekly frowned upon their unruly behaviour.[597] When the sect bought the Peters ranch, they were "invading the Rossland section… [where] about sixty of them are now at work taking the hay crop off the place. They will utilize it for stockraising." That same August week, "a number of raspberry growers at Hatzic have sold the crop to the Doukhobors for seven cents a pound on the bushes. The Doukhobor women are picking the berries and the lords of Doukhobor are picking the profits."[598]

Nude protests over official harassment were dubbed Adam and Eve parades. Doukhobor youth were closely watched and, if charged with an offence, the *News* pounced on the event. Willcox persisted in exposing Doukhobors as unassimilable aliens, and he was cheered on by the Board of Trade. It, in turn, agreed to boycott

Doukhobor services, and the Trail Reconstruction Board lobbied for their deportation. For Willcox and future editors, the Doukhobor wars would continue long past 1918.

Deport the "Douks," Wear a Mask, Fruit Fair, Chautauquas, and War's Aftermath

By the spring of 1919, Willcox was still escalating his war against the Doukhobors with a report that two more Trail veterans' associations were calling for their deportation.[599] When the sect inserted an article in the *Nelson News* outlining measures they were willing to take to help returning soldiers, Willcox gave no quarter, noting that the GWVA wanted to give its land to the soldiers, "as they did not do any fighting."[600] Perhaps the most damning of all Willcox's attempts to oust the Doukhobors was his penchant for criticizing their industriousness. He joined the chorus of nativist calls to deport them, citing examples of their lawlessness. But worse, he caught them out as competitors in the Trail building industry.

"The Douks have either secured or are about to secure contracts for the erection of several new houses here," Willcox reported. "Invariably their figures [cost estimates] are far below those of any ordinary contractor, no matter who he may be... and they only pay a wage of overalls and a diet of vegetables to their numerous workmen." He then pilloried their communal approach to living and operating their businesses. Attempting to cover both sides of a bad argument, he noted "the man who is building does not exactly relish paying from $500 to $1,000 more for his house than the Douks would charge. This does not take into consideration the quality of work done by the Douks, the hours they labor, or the long drawn out time required to complete a job." The Doukhobors were hooped either way; they could do quality work at lower prices but offended the local competition... and Willcox.

To offer some relief from the war's unrelenting bad news, and a momentary breather for the Doukhobors, Willcox provided much space, paid and free, to the local movie houses. Douglas Fairbanks, Fatty Arbuckle, Ethel Barrymore, Tom Mix and Charlie Chaplin were often on screen that spring. In June, the now-forgotten Dorothy Dalton starred in *The Flame of the Yukon* at the Star. William Farnum, equally unknown today, starred in *A Tale of Two Cities* at the Liberty. The *News* described Dalton's character as "a woman as lawless and free of love as Meribee's Carmen."[601] *The Birth of a Nation* still attracted Trail moviegoers every few months, fomenting racism anew and filling space in the *News*.

War poetry was still regularly on offer. For example, Willcox republished "In Flanders Fields" that June, along with three accompanying poems written in memory of "Flanders" author Lieutenant-Colonel John McCrae. The annual Trail Fruit Fair was a major distraction that the *News* covered from planning stage to prize-giving ceremony. Willcox lauded the fair as "broad and liberal and educational in its tendency and [it] cultivates a healthy competition."[602] The weekly also reported on local chautauquas, noting "a number of interior towns this summer are enjoying the educational and instructive advantages" of the popular cultural events.[603]

In July, the *News* joked that "a peace advocate is a ninny who opens his ears to what the Huns say and shuts his eyes to what they do."[604] But the big news came at the end of the month when CM&S assistant manager S.G. Blaylock dazzled the local press with a speech to the international mining convention in Revelstoke. After praising the smelter workforce's wartime performance, Blaylock reflected on the 1917 strike. "This strike was brought on by a few radicals and was never desired by the majority of the men," he said. "This was proved by the fact that the more thoughtful men broke the strike by themselves and forced the leaders to call it off."[605] Borrowing from the *Kamloops Standard-Sentinel*, Willcox added this note: "Mr. Blaylock made a name for himself in the reading of that paper and cleared up to a very large extent the unfortunate atmosphere that has prevailed in this province during the past six months."[606]

In early August, about 1,000 Trailites celebrated the fourth anniversary of the war, pledging to carry on the fight to victory. Women had often been saluted for their knitting and food skills. Now the *News* highlighted their role in the airplane spruce production industry at three Northern Pacific Logging Company camps on the Queen Charlotte Islands (now Haida Gwaii). They were "women waitresses," and the "innovation" has met the full satisfaction of the men and the management.[607]

With more Trailites buying automobiles, a motoring club formed, and Willcox joined with his own vehicle. The *News* began to sport travel features extolling local scenes of natural beauty as viewed from the driver's seat. In one case, Willcox, apparently agreeing, quoted the *Macleod News* editor as follows: "One old lady was very disturbed over the editor being able to drive an auto around. We would like to inform such people that it's not because we can really afford a car, but just for the simple reason this life is so damned short that we believe in having a good time while we can, not hoarding up our money."[608]

As motoring became more popular, Willcox supported calls for improved roads and more of them. A year later, Trail would receive $34,040 from the province for that purpose. The *News* was also keen to see improvements to local schools and provided much space to Principal George Hindle of Trail High School. Among other things, Hindle called for more public parks. A secret *News* columnist named "The Sphinx" joined in the calls for public improvements, stressing a public park and library in several columns. The weekly added some edge by publishing comments from "The Vaporizer" in support of the Sphinx's community improvement campaign.

In October, Willcox pursued his private war against Bolshevism and the IWW, reporting the following news: "A.S. Embree, who succeeded [William "Big Bill"] Haywood as leader of the IWW, has been arrested in Chicago under the Espionage Act. He is held under $10,000 bonds, and is now being tried." Of interest to Trail readers, Embree had worked as a printer for the *Grand Forks Gazette*, the *Phoenix Pioneer* and the *Boundary Creek Times*. Filling out the profile, Willcox noted that he "has a college education and is a socialist."[609]

In its November 15 edition, the *News* announced that the war had ended that Monday. The CM&S managers sent a notice to employees, warning that "No employes who have been absent since November 1st will be permitted to return to work unless they can show a quarantine clearance."[610] Local stores responded with sales announcements. Trail Mercantile Company advertised Bovril at $1, Johnston's Fluid Beef at $1.25, and Fancy Alberta Eggs at 65 cents a dozen. Later in the year, the Mercantile also offered men's worsted trousers for as low as $5.50. Mills' clothing store advertised "union suits" and "the best underwear." White's promoted boots for women and growing girls, regular $4.00, on sale at $2.95; men's ties, 39 cents; and boy's boots, $4.50. Soon they would buy full-page ads directed at male consumers: "Mr. Man, How Is This? Men's Blue Stripe Bib Overalls all sizes, Union Label 98c."[611]

Three weeks after the Armistice, the *News* provided the grim statistics of the war. "Canadians Fought in Twenty Battles in War—Had a Total of 418,918 Soldiers Who Were Shipped Overseas—50,000 Men of the Dominion Are Sleeping in France or Other Foreign Lands—211,000 Casualties."[612] In December, Trailites could read about the experience of war in a German prison camp in a book about Trail soldier Private Marvin [*sic* Mervin] H. Simmons. It was called *Three Times and Out: A Canadian Boy's Experience in Germany*. Canadian women's rights activist Nellie McClung wrote it. Houghton Mifflin published it.

Willcox continued to do his wartime duty on the home front. In a series of articles titled "How to Pronounce Them—War News Names Made Easy," the *News* provided readers with a handy guide to the many French names they were reading in war reports. It was a way to name where their sons had fought and possibly perished. He also warned against buying German-made goods, claiming they were the products of international socialism and "should be looked upon with just as much suspicion as the articles of trade and commerce with which we were more or less familiar in pre-war days."[613]

Baiting socialism had always been a favourite game for Willcox. In assessing prospects for 1919, the editor made it clear that "anything that has even a suspicion of the Bolsheviki tag should be shunned."[614] He continued his rant with support for co-operation: "There is no room for Bolshevism on the North American continent, and the sure way to avoid that sore on the body politic is for each and all to spur himself to do his best."[615]

Smelter Soldiers Come Home, More Flu Death, Bolshevikis and Red Flags in 1919

New Year's 1919 brought the return of more of Trail's boys in khaki and spurred plans for the commemoration of the final victory. Willcox suggested a clubhouse for the veterans. There was talk of a pay raise for them. Curling season had begun, and Willcox centred out the Blaylock rink. The CM&S assistant manager was also a news item as he had remarried in Calgary at the end of 1918. There was no mention of the local Anglican Church being unwilling to marry Blaylock to Kathleen Riddle because church rules did not permit someone to marry his deceased wife's sister. The public spotlight would increasingly be on Blaylock as the man who would hire many returning soldiers.

In early January, the *News* reported fifteen new flu cases, but said they were all light. While some concerned themselves with the "The Mystery of the Flu… [which] Still Refuses to Yield Up Its Secret of Germs," others turned to verse for some fun with the pandemic.[616]

> Are you thirsty when you eat?
> It's the Flu!
> Are you shaky on your feet?
> It's the Flu!
> If you feel a little ill,
> Send right off for Dr. Pill.
> He will say, despite his skill:
> It's the Flu![617]

The CM&S's thirteenth annual report showed a net profit of $867,259.48 and declared that "During the war [the] company furnished the Imperial Munitions Board with 22,356 tons of spelter [zinc], 39,606 tons of lead and 6,831 tons of copper."[618] Willcox allowed as how company managers "have made mistakes; otherwise they would be growing wings," but the CM&S's record is exemplary.[619] Blaylock also had new prospects on the horizon, for J.J. Warren was soon made president of the company, leaving open the managing director's job. Blaylock would now be in command and he had in mind a major change in labour relations at the smelter.

Readers had been given a hint about those changes the previous December in a *News* report headlined "Men and Management Discuss Co-operation." Now, as general manager, Blaylock would oversee the creation of what would become the Workmen's Co-operative Committee. The new co-operative pact was mentioned again at the end of January with a note that improvement had been shown. By 1920, Blaylock's brainchild, his shield against another workplace disruption, was set to be the only worker representative on smelter hill for the next twenty-five years.

Blaylock saw the new plan as a way to avoid future strikes, and in devising it, he revealed no love lost for radical unions. "Labor was extremely restless owing to the ever-increasing cost of necessaries and to the continued agitation of a number of men with strong IWW tendencies who endeavored by every possible means to promote sabotage, misunderstanding and discontent," he stated in his explanation of what caused the 1917 strike. "Every means possible was adopted to avoid a breach with the men, but finally demands were made in such a manner and in such direct repudiation of a definite agreement recently negotiated that they could not be conceded."[620]

The New Year also saw the reopening of the Star Theatre after a two-month hiatus. Management promised to cater "to the working men and their families, securing [the] best picture attractions possible to offer at 25 cent prices."[621] Hockey season was also coming, and McPherson's advertised Lightning Hitch Hockey

Shoes. Ladies' curling was also in the offing. Fransen's Barber Shop in Crow & Sullivan's billiard parlour wanted Trailites to "give him a trial."[622] The annual masquerade skating carnival would be a success, trout season would open May 1, and ballroom and fancy dancing lessons were being offered to the young people. The Mounties were coming to Trail, and the new Castlegar ferry would shorten the trip to Nelson.

By the end of January, Trail had up to twenty-five new flu cases, but it seemed the disease might be subsiding. The bug that was flying about was less virulent, said the *News*, although young people might be more susceptible. Some deaths were still being noted, including some high-profile cases. S.G. Blaylock's mother was among them. By late March, a ban on dancing would be lifted "as the flu has flown."[623] Or had it merely flown to the nearby Boundary Country, including Grand Forks, where signs of the pandemic were still evident?

Meanwhile, the threat of a Seattle General Strike in late January got former Spokane man Willcox's back up. He argued that now is not the right time for workers to demand higher wages: "It is time for level heads among the workers to assert themselves and keep their equilibrium."[624] He lashed out again at the "wreckers," observing "in other times they worked secretly, ratlike, undermining the social and economic fabric. Today they mass in armies and call themselves Bolsheviki and Industrial Workers of the World."[625]

Willcox continued his rant on Bolshevism in February, stating that Russia's Bolsheviki doctrine had "brought Russia down from one of the greatest food producing countries on the globe to a condition of starvation."[626] Willcox shared anti-Bolshevik rhetoric from elsewhere as well. A *Calgary Herald* article, referring to the labour conference in March that led to the founding of the One Big Union, came down hard on "a resolution of sympathy for Russian Bolshevism and German Spartacanism."[627]

He saved some invective for Romeo Albo, an Italian man who had lived in Trail for a time and had worked with Ginger Goodwin during the 1917 strike. "So long as labor organizations follow the leadership of such fellows as Albo, just so long will they be discredited, be their objects ever so worthy," Willcox argued. "During his operations in Trail Albo submitted articles for publication in the *News* but they were declined. Now that he is caught with inflammatory literature in his possession as well as a book on the manufacture of bombs, he will probably pose as a martyr to the cause of labor."[628]

The Seattle strike, which occurred February 6 to 11, and in which 60,000 workers took to the streets, attracted no sympathy in the *News*.[629] "Sympathetic strikes do not seem to secure much sympathy as a rule, in the long run. Making the innocent suffer is not popular with the people at large."[630] Willcox was fully supportive of US troops and sailors wielding machine guns against the strikers and praised Seattle Mayor Ole Hanson, who "took a firm stand and would countenance no IWW or Bolshevik methods."[631] Much later, Willcox ran a photograph of Hanson, naming him a hero for crushing the strike.

It seemed odd that Willcox also chose to run a photograph of Russian revolutionary Leon Trotsky on his front page in mid-February. In a final blow against general strikes, the *News* published this passionate denouncement from the *Vancouver Sun*: "A general strike is a civil war on the sick and helpless, on the innocent and defenseless population. The weapons of that kind of warfare are hunger and suffering, deprivation and injustice." The strikers had stated openly that "one purpose of the proposed general strike is to demonstrate labor's solidarity. It is a poor kind of solidarity which makes war on victims who cannot hit back," the *Sun* argued. The *Sun* called the strikers "a criminal menace to the public" and issued a demand to "Stop the ranting and deport the ranters."[632]

The Seattle strike and later Western labour conference were red flags to Willcox. When the conference's OBU plan reached Trail through Joe Naylor, a BC Federation of Labour vice-president and friend of Ginger Goodwin, Willcox gleefully reported the meeting's cancellation. It was called off "as the hundred odd returned soldiers in Trail, some of whom had left an eye in France or a leg or an arm in Flanders or were incapacitated or disabled for life, had no relish whatever to even permit a man who had voted in Calgary for the things they had fought against, to advocate from a public platform in Trail." Willcox concluded that "they were strong for unionism but not for the Russian or German brand."[633] Later he finished his rant: "With that delectable pair of cutthroat ideas [Bolshevism and Spartacanism] they couple the one big union plan, to appeal to labor, thinking thus to hoodwink the average worker."[634] To his delight, a poem had crossed his desk entitled "Bol-she-veek," and it supported using the name as a slur but shunned the same idea with names like "wop" and "dago."[635]

In May, the OBU was back in Trail. This time it was John Potter from Fernie's United Mine Workers Local 18 who carried the torch. Peter J. Bolam, the former Local 105 secretary, introduced him. Potter gave a detailed thirty-minute talk on the OBU and "proved to be quite clever on the platform, but did not give many straight out and out replies to queries that were put to him," read the report.[636]

Poetry appeared again that spring, albeit less frequently, and sometimes the verses had a workplace theme. In "Safety Rules," a poem borrowed from *Safety Engineering*, the message was a welcome change from war propaganda:

> A little care, a little thought,
> Preserve the lives of men;
> So back up 'Bill' and take a think
> Of Safety now and then.[637]

It also showed a renewed awareness of the dangers of the smelter workplace and a reminder that there were still frequent fatalities occurring up the hill.

Some hoped BC prohibition would soon be on the wane, much to the glee of those who had paid almost $1,000 in fines for violations of the Prohibition Act. Ironically, Prohibition Commissioner Walter C. Findlay got caught selling liquor illegally and went to jail. Other higher-ups were also implicated, but Findlay refused to name names.[638] More evangelistic meetings were coming as were "Harvey's

Greater Minstrels and Creole Beauty Pageant." East Trail got its first street lights. Dr. John Nay, the local health officer, enforced a flu-induced ban on dancing. A Great War memorial was being planned for Trail. City council was about to increase the dog tax.

Predictably, negative articles on Doukhobors did not abate in 1919. One example was from the editor of the *Grand Forks Gazette,* who wrote that the sect was a "distinct menace to Canadians who are already established."[639] Another stressed the need for deportation, with Sergeant Major Jimmie Robinson, "the first man from Canada to win the Distinguished Conduct Medal in this war," strengthening the call to oust the pacifists.[640] A League of Nations to end all wars was being discussed by the Allies. The Paris Peace Conference was dividing up the spoils in what would become the Treaty of Versailles.

Willcox gave the six-week Winnipeg General Strike, May 15 to June 26, front-page coverage, depicting the prairie city as "in the throes of the greatest labor struggle of all her history."[641] But he had no sympathy for it. For him, it was a grave error and he searched for supporting views.[642] "At such times the malcontent, the IWW and the bolsheviki come right to the front—they capitalize every possible unrest, real or fancied," he fumed. "Unfortunately, they find many converts, men who ordinarily would never think of taking up such standards. They believe in using force and preach six hours per day at a dollar per hour for common labor. In short a spot of utopia."[643]

Willcox's anti-union posture got more support when Mine-Mill international president Charles Moyer revoked Trail Local 105's charter.[644] Moyer's withdrawal of international support for the 1917 strike had sounded the strike's death knell. Now he nailed the coffin shut. Willcox also enlisted support from J.W. Hays, secretary-treasurer of the International Typographical Union, who told his 66,000 members not to sacrifice the benefits they now enjoyed to the "fallacy" of the OBU.[645]

Despite his hard line against radical unions, some of Willcox's colleagues at the Canadian Press Association clearly saw a newspaper's role differently. "The press must relieve itself of the suspicion that it is merely the mouthpiece of capitalism," said CPA president J.W. Taylor. "The papers should stand by the working man when he is right. It is not merely enough to say that he is entitled to a living wage. If he is capable of earning more than that under fair conditions, then he should get more."[646]

Willcox treated the CPA advice diffidently. Near a photograph of John D. Rockefeller, the world's richest man, the editor intoned that "organized labor will not allow itself to become associated in any way with Bolshevism," adding "labor men should draw a clear line between themselves and the advocates of the European revolution.... The employer and employe are allies. The Bolshevist is their common enemy."[647] As his parting shot at radical unions and Bolsheviks, he pointed to the Winnipeg General Strike as an example "of what lengths things will go to unless well balanced men steer the ship of labor. Labor must be recognized and must be dealt with—and it must on an equitable basis. But the desired end cannot and will not be accomplished by revolutionary methods."[648]

At the end of May, Willcox ended any speculation back in January that the weekly might convert to daily publication. "With this issue of the *Trail News* the present editor and manager turns over the paper to J.J. Clarke and Elmer D. Hall, who have been identified with the *News* for several years, and who will have charge of the business on and after June 1st," he announced. "After nearly four years of strenuous work we have felt the need of an extended rest and change."[649] On June 1, 1919, Clarke and Hall set to work shaping the weekly into the publication they wanted it to be.[650]

The sale prompted the *New Denver Ledge* to comment that "Beach will probably go to Spokane and bow in his good Canadian money upon fruit farms or something else that he knows nothing about." Putting aside the jocular teasing, the weekly added, "He has been a noted figure in BC journalism for many years, and his old friends do not like to see him shoot across the line in order to hide his bankroll under the folds of Old Glory."[651] Meanwhile another era was about to begin for the *News*. Whether it would bring with it the smelter city's first daily newspaper, the new owners were not letting on just yet.

6–TRAIL NEWS (1919–1921)
FROM PRINTER'S DEVIL TO EDITOR-IN-CHIEF

Another Yankee Holds the *News*'s Pro-Business, Anti-Radical line

Elmer D. Hall seemed to represent the classic image of the pioneer newspaperman when he took the reins of the *Trail News* in mid-1919 from Walter Beach Willcox, a former employer, colleague and friend. Hall and co-owner J.J. Clarke had served many years as newspapermen tramping across the Kootenay region. Hall brought the broader experience and had perhaps made the greater investment, for he alone would appear in the masthead. Under the front-page banner, he boasted that the *News* was "Published in the Electro-Chemical Metallurgical Mecca of Canada." Now he would be challenged to outdo Willcox in promoting the smelter city and keeping Trailites informed.

Trail had passed through many hard years before Hall sat down in the editor's chair. The First World War had brought death and sadness to many residents. The impact of the 1917 smelter strike also lingered in the early years of the Hall *News*. Readers had suffered the devastation of the 1918 flu. The Russian Revolution two years earlier influenced political views in the community, and Hall's editorial page seldom ceased to criticize that historical event. As he embraced his new editorship, he followed in his predecessor's footsteps in reserving his sharpest commentary against

Final *Trail News* editor Elmer D. Hall in his printshop, date unknown. Courtesy Hall Printing Company

Bolshevism. But Hall did not stray far from his bread-and-butter areas of coverage.

Police court transcripts, city council meeting summaries, school exam grades, movies, dances, whist games, sports and weather forecasts all received regular coverage and often on the front page. To help ease the pain of war, and assist the readjustment to peacetime, the region's movie houses, including Trail's Liberty and Star Theatres, continued featuring all the big silent stars of the day. War-induced anxiety also fostered an interest in miracle cures with paid advertisements and testimonials steadily encouraging people to buy Tanlac, a weight reduction compound. Many other supposed cures were to follow as ready sources of relief—and ad income.

Hall also emulated previous editors in participating in the local sports and cultural scene. For a time, he ran the local baseball team, for example, and he "knew who was who in the community."[652] He also directed an orchestra in Trail, which is where he and co-owner J.J. Clarke, once well known in Britain for his ability as a saxophonist, may have shared enthusiasm for the local music scene. Vaudeville concert advertisements sometimes mimmicked African-American accents, distastefully poking fun at people of colour.

Hall was born on September 24, 1875, in Kansas City, Missouri, the son of machinist and newspaper proprietor Jesse Riley Hall and Mary Jane (Mollie) Baker. Elmer moved to Washington State with his parents sometime between 1881 and 1885, probably first to Whatcom. There he followed in his father's footsteps,

The Trail Italian Band was popular in early Trail. *News* editor J.J. Clarke, an accomplished saxophonist, paid close attention to local musical events. Courtesy Trail Historical Society

working first as a machinist, then moving into the newspaper business.[653] He married Nebraska-born Mabel Mrkvicka on December 28, 1901, in Seattle.[654] It was a good match, for Mabel worked alongside Elmer in the newspaper business for the next twenty-five years. After Mabel died, he remarried twice more, first to Sarah Beckerton, and then to Mabel's younger sister, Pearl Antoinette Mrkvicka.[655]

His newspaper career was well underway when he was barely twenty. In the late 1890s, he worked on the *Cascade Record* with Willcox.[656] He also worked for *News* founder W.F. Thompson, possibly after he had moved to Alaska, calling him "a fine fellow and an agreeable employer."[657] In 1901, he was manager of the *Grand Forks News*, "a weekly journal that shall be the pride of the community."[658] In 1908, he founded the *Herald* in Bossburg, Washington, where he also owned a butcher shop and grocery store. When the newspaper burned down later that year under mysterious circumstances, Hall went in search of fresh newspapering territory.[659]

In 1909, Hall remained in Bossburg "where he expects to go into the fruit raising business."[660] Apparently, the Hall family settled there for several years, but in 1917, the first issue of the *Republic Journal* appeared, with Hall as its manager. Stated the *Orient Journal*: "He will undoubtedly give the people of Republic a weekly of which they may feel proud."[661]

Later in 1917, Hall began publishing the short-lived *Northport Times*.[662] It was "well gotten up in every way," noted the rival *Northport News*. "Mr. Hall is a young man, an excellent printer, a fair writer and a good 'mixer'."[663] By May 1918, Hall had crossed the Canadian border again and hired on as a Linotype operator at Willcox's *Trail News*.[664] The following June, he bought the weekly, with Clarke as his silent partner.

Like his predecessors, Hall was keen to generate revenue from printing contracts, subscription sales and advertising revenue. His political views ranged from an early flirtation with the Republican Party to one with the Canadian Conservatives. "Elmer was behind [that is, supported] the organization of the union movement," noted a booklet on his printing company.[665] However, as this review of his years at the *News* revealed, Hall was often supportive of Blaylock and the company and often shunned unions like the radical One Big Union (OBU) and the Industrial Workers of the World (IWW).

Suffragettes, the OBU, Blaylock's Buick, Zane Grey, and Blackface in 1919

On June 6, about a week after Hall took possession of the paper, he appeared as manager in the first post-Willcox edition. His first editorial laid out his intentions. "It will be the earnest endeavor of the new management to maintain the present high standard of the paper," Hall promised, "and [I] can assure the business public of Trail that the continuance of the liberal patronage as accorded our predecessor will be fully appreciated." Laying out their credentials, Hall stated that he had twenty years' printing experience and that Clarke had been *News* manager for four years under Billy Esling. For the previous two years, he "has been linotype man and foreman of the News," he added. The editorial assured readers that the paper

Downtown Trail, showing Post Office, Opera House and BC Telephone office.
Courtesy Rossland Museum and Discovery Centre

would be "independent in politics" and will "devote its energies to the upbuilding of Trail and vicinity."[666]

In the June 6 edition, Hall reported on a union meeting held that week, revealing that an effort was being made to revive the old smeltermen's union. Three speakers were liberally quoted. Soon, however, it became clear that the new union was part of the OBU, a new workers' organization that was more revolutionary in tone than the previous union, the Western Federation of Miners. Hall soon viewed it as an enemy despite one organizer claiming the OBU was against child labour and for the "political and economic freedom of women."[667]

William Potter claimed that a Trail businessman had falsely accused him of wanting to cause a strike: "The only business I am here for is to organize for the One Big Union which will eliminate strikes."[668] Former smeltermen's union president Herbert S. Smith, now returned from war service, was in attendance, as was William A. Burns, executive member of the International Union of Mine, Mill and Smelter Workers. Hall was not impressed, offering as a counterpoint the anti-radical views of Charles Perry Taylor, secretary of the Washington State Federation of Labor, illustrating both Hall's anti-OBU politics and his American roots.

Nor did Hall sympathize with the women's suffrage movement. "Sylvia Pankhurst has been arrested again," he crowed of the British left-wing activist. Then he got nasty. "That girl is a brat. During her earlier years she was accustomed to hearing her mother [suffragette leader Emmeline Pankhurst] rave, and she got the habit. The mother is said to have seen a light and to be leading a better life, but Sylvia is sot in the ways of wickedness," Hall continued.[669] Then he went over the top: "A national society for the suppression of pests ought to be organized in

England and sprinkle this obstreperous maid with insect powder."[670] There was more negative commentary to come about women's role in society with Hall regularly using the "Clipped and Censored" column for jokes and epithets often at the expense of women, racial and ethnic minorities.

The second edition of the Hall *News* announced the founding of a Navy League for Trail. A local football (soccer) league was formed with a largely British following. And a branch of the United Farmers of BC was organized. In "Local Happenings," a new Bank of Montreal building and a new post office were on the horizon, wooden sidewalks were being built in Trail East (as distinct from the separate community of East Trail), the Liberty Theatre had a new manager who promised a new coat of paint, the ferry in Castlegar was welcomed, and the CM&S's S.G. Blaylock bought a brand new five-passenger Buick McLaughlin car.[671]

More teachers were hired and paid $900–$1,800 a year. Hall added a "Safety Rules" section that began with a poem: "There was a man in our town,/And he was wond'rous wise./He wore his safety goggles/When the chips might hit his eyes."[672] The columnist known as "The Sphinx" spelled out the good things in life: "It is the little things like the toothache and babies, corns, and freckles, electric light bills we forget to pay, spring onions and postage stamps, grey hairs and bald spots, bootlaces and missing buttons… that make life one grand sweet song."[673]

With the war just ended, and soldiers returning home to find life wanting, such homilies and lectures on the importance of frugality must have grated on some readers. Hall's anti-immigrant editorials surely exasperated non-nativist readers. "It is passing strange that American and Canadian laboring men should seek for their leaders and spokesmen men who are not citizens and who, in most cases, speak only broken English," he suggested. "If these loud mouthed foreigners were deported it might follow that some men who respect their flag and country would take their places to the everlasting good of all concerned."[674] A majority of Trail's citizens were in fact first- and second-generation immigrants. Ironically, new Canadians seemed a fair target to Hall, himself an immigrant.

Though the war had ended, the *News* continued to promote the purchase of Victory Loan bonds as a wise investment. Hall also offered advice on avoiding financial fakers. With more Trail soldiers arriving home, advertising picked up with the Star and Liberty Theatres buying substantial space. Especially popular were the cowboy star William S. Hart, Madame Olga Petrova, "The Panther Woman," and a seemingly endless stream of others. City Grocery advertised toasted wheat flakes at 10 cents a package. Hunt Bros. & Kennedy advertised novels by Zane Grey, Jack London and Mary Roberts Rinehart, known then as America's Agatha Christie. Men's garters were on sale for 35 and 50 cents at Trail Mercantile as well as straw hats at $1.25–$2 and boaters at $2.50 and $3. A. Mills & Son offered Panama hats for $5–$6.50. These local businesses and others supported the *News* throughout its existence.

As spring rolled toward summer, the weekly noted that former editor Willcox visited the Inland Empire capital of Spokane in June, possibly in preparation for a career move. Former *News* staff member Mike Bohle also went to Spokane to join the *Chronicle* staff. Former Trail mayor Fred G. Morin was also moving to

Spokane, the nearest metropolis south of the border.

A "concert" was offered at the Methodist church featuring "Black Face Artists." In the paper, editor Hall offered his characteristically offensive view on modern minstrelsy and its origins in Black America.[675]

The *News* reported that Oleo margarine was banned again, land was available to returning soldiers, the CM&S had donated to the Salvation Army doughnut hut, and a deadly US poison called "Lewisite" could wipe out a major city. Dog owners were informed that they would need to pay a $5 tax on their "bow wows" if they did not wish to see them "transported to the realm of happy hunters."[676] The new football league enjoyed a $75 donation from the CM&S to purchase gold medals.

In an early editorial gesture, Hall ran ads advising the public that "When Forests Burn, Taxes Increase." He was to become a regular advocate of fire safety, urging better fire-fighting equipment: "No city can hope to attain prominence that does not protect itself from destruction."[677] Remembering his days in Phoenix, also vulnerable to fire, he provided a history of the Granby mine closure there, but offered little sympathy for the out-of-work miners, noting "people who delve for riches in mother earth must expect to take the bitter with the sweet."[678]

In late July, Hall covered the city's peace celebration, calling it "One of Greatest in History of City—Kaiser Taken to Scaffold and Executed Publicly."[679] The mock execution showed that memories of the war were still fresh. In fact, Dominion Day 1919 was a salute to war veterans with a Returned Soldiers' Aid Committee organizing a reception. It was also an opportunity to see the first game of the new Trail Football League. The Salvation Army sponsored a Sunday picnic. Mrs. A.E. Gooderham explained why Britain rules the waves.

Hall hailed the long-awaited peace agreement, blaming German procrastination for the delay. He praised city council, noting that "with good water and sewer systems, cement walks, electric lights and substantial fire equipment Trail will rank among the best little cities in British Columbia."[680] Hall also reported that a Nakusp woman got the Mons Star, a British campaign medal, for service as a nursing assistant in the British Expeditionary Force.

Normally, Hall would comment favourably on his competitors, but his tone changed when it came to union-owned papers like the *Fernie District Ledger*, an avid supporter of the OBU. "With the suppression of the Winnipeg Labor News and the arrest of the editors, our local agitator is beginning to show signs of cold feet. He has been just as busy as the Winnipeg men in trying to tie up the whole country."[681] In early July, Philip M. Christophers, president of District 18 of the United Mine Workers of America, brought a charge of slander against the rival *Fernie Free Press* editor J.R. Wallace. The jury sided with Wallace.[682]

In late summer, Hall reported "the editor of the *Fernie District Ledger* says the editor of the *Fernie Free Press* is 'skunklike' in his methods. The *Free Press* editor says his contemporary is a 'guttersnipe' and reminds him that he had to 'eat crow' for previous utterances—such is life in the coal belt."[683] By early September, Hall would report with seeming glee that the union-owned *Ledger* was in trouble, saying it was time to let the "white elephant" die.[684] In "Why don't newspapers tell the truth?," he argued that "the truth is that they exist for the sole purpose of telling the truth." This apparently did not include the *Ledger*.[685] It was dead by the end of August.

Drowning deaths in the Columbia River were accorded front-page treatment. War dead continued to be listed. Local service clubs like the Knights of Pythias were regularly covered. The miracle substance Tanlac held its space. It was touted repeatedly in what were probably paid testimonials. Several other magic potions were said to be cure-alls; some were hailed as particularly effective against flu infections. Hall afforded much space to N.M. Trafton, manager of the Star Theatre, who expounded eruditely on the movies and their stars. It was a good exchange, with Trafton supplying the *News* with copy and guaranteeing weekly revenue from movie ads. The Bank of Hamilton opened a branch in the city that spring, joining the Bank of Montreal and the Bank of Commerce. The trio of banks attested to Trail becoming a growing monied town.

In mid-July, Hall again found reason to criticize unions. Labour leader Romeo Albo, who had been labelled a radical in an earlier Willcox editorial, was arrested under a new Immigration Act and would soon be deported.[686] In other news, the editor cheered J.J. Warren's promotion to the CM&S presidency after four years as managing director. Bolshevism, as mentioned, often fueled Hall's editorial invective, but socialism was also favourite grist for his mill. Hall hinted that socialists were really as greedy as everyone else.

Also in July, he announced "the News will be issued daily just as soon as conditions justify such a move.… The time has not yet arrived, but we will be here when it comes."[687] Indeed, it would come. But there was much preparation before that day arrived when the *News* would leave the ranks of the weekly family of country newspapers. As reported in the *McKim Advertising Directory* that summer, fifty-five new weeklies had appeared in that family.[688]

In early August, the Baptist church held a Sunday picnic and a piano tuner would arrive, perhaps another sign that the city was maturing. Also promising was the twenty-five-cent-a-day wage increase the CM&S granted for smelter workers. But with post-war costs still high, it might not have seemed such a huge wage hike. Still, it was probably the first real improvement Blaylock could credit to his Workmen's Co-operative Committee, the company-run workers' representative.

In a foreshadowing of future problems, Hall reported that the CM&S "will endeavor to establish [the] fact that smoke is not altogether [a] hindrance to crop production."[689] Area farmers disagreed and would eventually make it known in a court of law. Hall would ultimately side with the company in pursuing his role as chief CM&S booster. Expressing much civic pride, he suggested "outsiders will please excuse us if we seem a little cocky."[690]

The pride was further fostered with Hall's endorsement of the new Trail Amateur Athletic Association, a rapidly growing mainstay of the weekly's future sports coverage. He also cheered city council's decision to spend $10,000 on cement sidewalks, prompting him to comment "Trail is gradually getting out of its swaddling clothes."[691] It would improve even more if the city ordered a fire truck, Hall suggested, later noting "if the smoke from forest fires gets any thicker residents of Trail will have to wear gas masks."[692]

When S.G. Blaylock became general manager in mid-August 1919, Hall saluted the "genial manager" and praised the company's $500 scholarship to the son of any employee.[693] Daughters were not to be favoured with this substantial company assistance to education.

Ford, Carnegie, Roosevelt, *The 39 Steps*, Smelter Fumes, Bolshevism, and Tanlac

International news was limited in the early Hall *News* and he often highlighted American stories. For example, he reported that Henry Ford was awarded six cents in a suit against the *Chicago Tribune* for calling him an anarchist. Ford didn't challenge the fact that he kept his son out of the army using his financial influence to do so. Nor did he argue the fact that he "favored distribution of certain pro-German or alleged pro-German literature or propaganda and was generally very un-American both in some of his acts as well as words."[694]

Elsewhere, Hall supported the US invasion of Mexico, noted the death of steel magnate and philanthropist Andrew Carnegie, celebrated the centenary of steam inventor James Watt's birth and quoted a New York doctor who claimed "Influenza and pneumonia are no more to be feared than a boil on the back of the neck."[695] Many knew better in the smelter city.

On the domestic front that summer, Hall reported progress in soldier settlement at Creston and, in his developing anti-radical style, he complained that some metal trades workers were a "bunch of trouble makers."[696] New BC government decisions set a minimum wage of $14 a week for women eighteen years and older, allowed office workers to receive a minimum weekly wage of $15, and forbade the employment of women under eighteen. Such factual reports did not fit with Hall's view that all women belonged in the home.

For the literary set that autumn, a review of John Buchan's novel *The 39 Steps* appeared. Buchan would later serve as Lord Tweedsmuir, Canada's Governor General. The new "Housekeepers' Column" offered recipes for ginger beer, rhubarb catsup and piccalili, a kind of tomato salsa. Sugar shortages would persist into the fall as would distasteful jokes about Black Americans.

The Hall *News* was using the same source of fillers the weekly had always relied on, and much of it included bad jokes, reams of doggerel poetry, World Series baseball winners, gruesome accidental deaths and profiles of famous people, usually Americans. Hall announced in early September that the paper was moving to ten pages due to a surge in advertising. He later noted that the paper was twenty-five years old "and we are not ashamed of it."[697]

As he would often do, the "manager," as he was called in the masthead, added a comment on "country newspapers." They belong "to the people of the territory they cover," he quoted from an Oregon weekly. "The people have a right to use the columns for the dissemination of news and the editor is, and acts in[,] the capacity of custodian. The profits, of course, go to the editor; but they are not enough to base any argument on—so the people can in truth and in fact regard the country paper as their own."[698]

Hall included some advice for news reporters: "Avoid all petty contentions. Don't try to use the newspaper to get even with someone for whom you have no fancy. A good reporter is absolutely impersonal." The non-partisan rule did not seem to apply to Bolshevism. Even local theatre manager N.M. Trafton got into the act with a disclaimer about the film *Bolshevism on Trial*: "In offering to the Trail public what is indisputably the greatest picture of the greatest problem of modern times we wish everyone to first be sanguinely aware that we are providing you with this picture strictly in the sense of an attraction and not with any intent of political influence."[699]

Hall was delighted to learn that the Mounties had rounded up several anarchists at Vancouver, and he was decidedly on the CM&S's side in a dispute that had erupted at Kimberley where about 300 workers had struck for the first time. They demanded a dollar a day increase, arguing that the company was paying the lowest wages of any mine in BC. Blaylock refused to grant the wage increase, saying that the price of lead would not warrant it. The *News* speculated that the dispute would last a long time, that many of the miners had already moved to jobs in Fernie or into the bush, and that the CM&S had stockpiled enough ore to allow the company to fight the strike into the winter.[700] No settlement was reached until the end of the year and only then with assistance from a federal labour department official.[701]

With the school year in full swing, Hall turned to the ninth annual Trail Fruit Fair where Trail's Great War Veterans' Association displayed many war souvenirs, including a German officer's sword tassel. S.G. Blaylock annually entered the fair's vegetable and fruit-growing competitions and, as in past years, he won in several categories, including marrow, muskmelon, tomatoes and pickling. At the same time, the Rebekahs, the women's division of the Odd Fellows service club, held a whist drive. Rossland's Eagles planned a grand ball. And the Temperance Union held its regular monthly meeting.

The Prince of Wales was on tour in Canada in the fall of 1919, but passed over Trail in favour of a brief rail stop at Castlegar. Nevertheless, about 300 Trail students met him, gave the "Trail yell," and sang for the prince. The *News* said they did the smelter city proud. "The Prince of Wales must be a union pressman," said a later humorous clip. "He makes a good impression wherever he goes."[702]

The Duke and Duchess of Devonshire visited Trail in mid-October when the city gave the vice-regal couple a full reception at a packed Liberty Theatre. At the opera house, the crowd gathered to hear the duke's lengthy speech, and "hundreds of people lined the street and sidewalks."[703] The duke was named Canada's Governor General in 1916.

While the 1918 flu epidemic seemed over, Rossland, Fernie and other Kootenay towns feared it would return that winter. That didn't stop sports fans from attending what *News* reporter Owen Lennon described as "a [soccer] match replete with thrilling moments." The Trail team was hoping to trounce Fernie, but redemption from an earlier defeat was only partially satisfied when the game ended in a tie.[704]

Hall continued defending the CM&S, taking the company's side over a Supreme Court of Canada lawsuit for crop damages that drew attention to a nagging problem. In 1918, Alfred Endersby, a rancher residing near Rossland, had recovered damages in a judgment of the BC Supreme Court against CM&S. Endersby was awarded "$2,170 and costs for damages done to his crops, timber and fruit trees by smelter smoke."[705] Other such suits would follow.

In December, one of the eight Winnipeg General Strike leaders, out on bail awaiting trial, spoke in Trail. Hall covered his speech, made to a large audience at the Star Theatre and again at the Knights of Columbus (KC) Hall in Rossland. It was unusual not to see a negative *News* editorial on the strike, but Hall made up for it in later editions, with renewed attacks on the One Big Union, whose leaders "are pariahs of the labor world." Immigrants might have felt slighted when he concluded that "a labor movement backed by alien enemies, unwise leaders and the rag tag and bob tail of the laboring men may cause a lot of unnecessary trouble, but it cannot succeed."[706]

A guest editorial added some fiery new rhetoric: "An ominous word at low breath is passing over the country," wrote Hall. "It is the whisper of the radical in the ear of the ignorant. And the word is Revolution. Half demons, half despot, the red radicals are to sally forth in the still of the night and with concerted guerilla tactics proclaim the reign of the Bolshevik in America."[707] He made a slightly less denigrating comment about unions reprinted from the *Baltimore Enterprise*: "Local loafers are now talking of forming a union and joining in a strike sympathetic with the Bolsheviks. It is to be hoped they will strike and quit loafing."[708] A second guest editorial from the *Enterprise* laughingly called the IWW the "Insidious workers of the world." Hall got in some licks as well. "A great many IWW and other outlaws are fleeing from the wrath of an outraged government like animals before a prairie fire and the Canadian and Mexican borders are their objectives."[709]

A basketball club was formed that winter. City council would prohibit teamsters from driving on the sidewalks. The *News* said BC had eighteen stills in 1918 and seventy in 1919. "Safety Rules" offered "Ten Rules for Foremen." These included the following: Be fair. Make few promises. Don't waste anger. Don't hold spite. The plant was still operating in Kimberley despite the strike. Teachers would get a raise to $1,500 a year as of January 1, 1920. The CPR's fleet of ocean liners now were regularly featured. And in a typical attempt to support local business, Hall advised Trailites to avoid buying from peddlers.

As 1919 came to a close, the *News* announced that Trail had surpassed its Victory Loan quota with 821 contributors subscribing $219,550. The Great War Veterans' Association took the Doukhobors to task, charging that leader Peter "Lordly" Verigin disavowed letters accusing the sect of not fully participating in the war. Trail dined but did not wine BC's attorney general, J.B. De Farris, and its public works minister, Dr. King. S.G. Blaylock spoke to a resolution to fix the Trail-Nelson road. Nero Lerro, who once lived in Trail, was to be deported as part of a round-up of local Wobblies (IWW).

The New Year's Eve Annual Ball at the armory featured Eddie Hall's Jazz

Orchestra. Hall complained that the much-loved reverend Father Pat's grave was being neglected. Poetry was back in the *News* with this ditty called "Trotsky":

> Come, all you brother Bolsheviks
> And wisdom hear from Trotsky;
> I'll show you how to stop this row
> And put all troubles in the potsky.[710]

It "has been tried out and proved impracticable even under the most favorable circumstances," Hall added, "yet there are those in British Columbia who would bring Canada to the level of Russia if in their power so to do."

Hall wasn't quite finished and suggested that "there are too many strikes and too much strike talk and not enough work; too much howling about high prices and not enough common sense economy and hustle, and too many loud mouthed agitators working their jaws instead of their hands."[711] He then turned on the Fernie coal miners' OBU local. "Poor old Fernie. Well may she be called the 'Calamity City'," he joked. "There is either a strike at Fernie or one just brewing, and it is said that life there is just one damn thing after another."[712]

Meanwhile, the CM&S would soon post its third-highest production levels, with almost $8 million in gold, silver, lead and zinc. Curling season opened with talk of a rink being built at the back of the Fruit Fair building. City elections were on the horizon. All seemed well in the smelter city as Trailites prepared to enjoy a green Christmas. Hall pursued his campaign against radical unions. Annual hockey fever was setting in. And paid testimonials persisted in promoting the miracle product Tanlac.

Joe Hill, Phoenix a Ghost Town, Smoke Eaters, Dempsey, and Father Pat in 1920

At the start of 1920, Francis Edmund Dockerill was acclaimed mayor. Wartime sugar rationing was still operative, prompting Hall to call for a "sugar armistice." Trail's Methodist Church hockey team defeated Rossland's United Church team 2–1 in an "orgy" of sports activities. S.G. Blaylock was elected president of the new Kootenay District Hockey League. Music lovers enjoyed "the colored singers at the Star."[713] Mary Pickford thrilled audiences in *Capt. Kidd, Jr.* at the Liberty, and Ruth Roland starred in a serial called *The Tiger's Tail*, with its "All female stars!"

A. Mills & Son featured men's spring caps for as low as $2.50. The Mercantile offered Japanese mandarin oranges at $1.25 a box, a pound of Canadian cheese at 40 cents, and sauerkraut at 25 cents. Two bakeries would compete for the bread business. The Housekeepers Column gave a report on workplace safety from "Miss Ida Tarbell." Perhaps unknown to the editor, Tarbell had distinguished herself as a muckraking journalist exposing corporate corruption in the US. Her investigative reporting contributed to the breakup of Standard Oil as a monopoly trust.

In many ways, it was business as usual for Elmer D. Hall as he entered his first New Year at the helm of the town's only newspaper. On the second day of 1920, he supported the ravaging of immigrant worker communities in the US. "The last ten days in the United States has [*sic*] seen the greatest rounding up of anarchists ever staged on the North American continent," he wrote, revealing that "thousands of the most active 'reds' were gathered in by the strong arm of an outraged nation in all parts of the country." Among those arrested were "the leaders of the movements called 'communists,' 'communist labor,' IWW and kindred anarchistic societies."[714]

The Palmer Raids, named for US Attorney General A. Mitchell Palmer, were conducted against immigrants, particularly Italians. Among Palmer's raiders was J. Edgar Hoover, who would carve out a future career for himself as director of the new Federal Bureau of Investigation. The resulting Red Scare wrought fear in North American Italian communities, including the one in Trail.

In mid-January, a poem expressed similar views. "Of anarchists we're weary," wrote Walt Mason, "Of all the kindred freaks,/of agitators beery who jar us with their shrieks;/and so we've started shipping the lot across the sea,/and they may do their yipping in Russia, which is free."[715] An article about the sedition trial of a Wobbly leader brought a different poem to the pages of the *News*. This time, a sarcastic poem apparently meant to denigrate the radical union recalled the spirit of Joe Hill, the IWW songster who had died by firing squad five years earlier in Idaho.

> Onward, Christian soldiers, rip and tear and smite,
> Let the gentle Jesus bless your dynamite;
> Splinter skulls with shrapnel, fertilize the sod.
> Folks who do not speak your tongue deserve the curse of God.
> Smash the doors of every home, pretty maidens seize,
> Use your might and sacred right to treat them as you please.[716]

By the end of January, what historians would later call the "Western Labour Revolt" seemed in full swing and Hall informed his readers of the uselessness of strikes "as a cure for the discontent of toilers."[717] He assured them the strife would not last long. "The OBU of Trail tried to promulgate a strike on the first of the week," he wrote, "but it evidently lacked both pep and numbers."[718] The threat had also arrived at Trail's back door just across the border with Northport smelter workers demanding better wages and preparing to strike for them. "When laboring men learn that the agitators are their worst enemies they will have learned a great lesson," Hall advised. "Loud mouths and glib tongues are seldom capable of sound reasoning."[719]

Blaylock, possibly sensing that discontent was close to home, gave "all employees of the company" a fifty-cent raise.[720] Hall hailed the wage increase, calculating that it would add $15 to every smelter worker's monthly paycheque. "In these days of turmoil, flu, strikes, rumors of strikes, lockouts and walkouts, high prices and highballs, every little bit helps."[721] But the threat of strikes was less a concern than the return of the flu, reportedly spreading in Kamloops. A measles epidemic had hit Nelson. Trailites were urged to get vaccinated for smallpox, and more miracle cures, including buckthorn bark, were popping up in *News* ads. Citizens were advised to avoid crowds.

The weekly now served its 1,000 subscribers under a new slogan that read "Published in Canada's Greatest Smelting Center." Judging from Police Chief Benjamin Downes's report, though, *News* readers could have imagined Trail as the BC Interior's crime capital. At least ninety-four crimes were committed in 1919. Some were violent: conspiracy to defile a woman and violations of the Offensive Weapon Act. Police also reported that fifteen dogs were destroyed in 1919 and seventy-one enemy aliens were reporting to police. Offenders could not be blessed by the departed clergyman Father Pat, but he was commemorated in a miner's poem:

> He wore the Church of England brand
> But didn't bank on creeds;
> His way to hearts was not with words,
> But helpful, lovin' deeds.[722]

The intensity of possible labour conflict must have suggested to Hall that his readers needed some respite, and he turned inward for it with this joke. "Subeditor—Nothing doing in the news line today. Editor—All right. Put a pair of trousers on the office cat, photograph him, and we'll run a special on the oldest living man in town."[723] He also asked readers not to "grumble if your paper is not up to the high standards of your ideals," adding sassily, "charitably remember that no editor is capable of getting out as good a paper as you could yourself."[724]

With spring around the corner, Hall awaited its harbinger, a robin. Alas, it snowed soon after the first sighting. The inclement weather didn't stop the local football team from opening its season, and a new baseball association named Hall as its representative. He would stress player obedience. It was also a time for Hall to partake of what would become a favourite editorial topic: advising young girls on proper moral behaviour. Wandering the streets after 5:00 p.m. was a definite no-no.

Another favourite editorial topic, and one that Hall viewed with a critical eye, was city hall, which he called "a disgrace to the town." Furthermore, "the fire department is a joke."[725] On a less critical note, Hall reported that the CM&S had declared a shareholder dividend. He also praised the company for announcing its housing scheme for married employees, who could borrow a maximum of $2,000 to build their own home. Also in the news, CM&S general manager Blaylock had a new daughter, but lost his mother. His father, Rev. Thomas Blaylock, had died in 1912.

Hall was not happy with readers' submissions to the paper, and he told them so. "Please hand us in news items when they are fresh," he scolded. "We prefer not to publish a birth after the child is weaned; a marriage after the honeymoon is over; or the death of a man after his widow is married again."[726] Hall also chastised readers for misunderstanding the role of their local newspaper: "It is not the purpose of the Trail News to disseminate scandal in any form, neither do we conduct this paper for the purpose of advancing anyone's political ambitions, or promulgating anyone's social prestige." In what would pass as editorial policy, he added "we do not believe in publishing all the fool communications sent in, for the very good reason that every other man you meet has either an actual or imaginary grievance which he thinks the whole world should know about."

Hall cleared up all misconceptions about the paper's role, saying "we have steadfastly refused to grind political axes for anyone." In a further clarification of the paper's role, he said "we are strong advocates of harmony—even the ravings of agitators, both imported and home grown, have failed to stampede us."[727] With that, he proudly calculated that circulation had increased by a third, adding, "country weeklies are pre-eminently the home papers of newspaperdom. They are not hurriedly scanned while men travel to business, then left to brakemen to gather up. They go directly to homes where their reading is a duty as well as a pleasure."[728]

As mentioned earlier, politics and radical unionism were fair editorial targets and Hall spared no criticism. Even the movies he recommended complied with his anti-radical posture. In *The World Aflame*, showing at the Star Theatre, readers learned about a man who "broke the strike but not the strikers—he deported the bolshevist strike-makers and gave labor a sample of true American leadership."[729] When Roger Bray, a leader of the Winnipeg General Strike, was sentenced to six months in prison, the editor quipped "it seems that Mr. Bray brayed once too often."[730] A photo of "Nikola Lenine, Bolshevist Premier" appeared in the same edition. A few weeks later, the *News* agreed with the *Kaslo Kootenaian* that it is "good advice to those workers who have fallen for the propaganda which has been handed out by the OBU."[731]

In May, about seventy Trail veterans celebrated the anniversary of the Battle of Ypres. A feature article celebrated Kate Carmack, the First Nations woman who apparently made the first gold discovery in the Klondike at Bonanza Creek, Yukon. Readers learned that a Chinese Masonic Lodge had been established, with about forty members living in Trail. Trail police court heard cases, including chickens running at large, a stabbing and a prohibition offence. About 10,000 acres of surrendered Doukhobor land near Kamsack, Saskatchewan, had been given to soldier settlers. And due to the high price of flour, two loaves of bread would now cost 25 cents instead of 20 cents.

Although summer was beckoning, hockey was still being played, with the Smoke Eaters beating Nelson 14–4. The *News* sports reporter waxed flowery: "Nelson has come, been defeated and have wended their way homeward, and their remains but joy, pure and [unreadable] in the hearts of the Smoke Eaters."[732] The mining town of Phoenix, about 160 kilometres west of Trail, was soon to be a ghost town.[733] The Orangemen's Orange Lodge opened with sixteen members. Labour department statistics showed that 378,047 workers in Canada belonged to unions in 2,847 locals, many of them affiliated to US unions.

Later in June, a letter from Blaylock's Workmen's Co-operative Committee complained that the OBU in Trail had created "a great deal of opposition" during negotiations with doctors for a workers' compensation package.[734] Hall also reported on Mine Mill union leader H.S. McLuskey's speech advocating tripartite co-operation and further discrediting the OBU. In a full-blown assassination of the radical union, the Mine Mill man charged its adherents with dual unionism and compared it with earlier radical movements such as the Knights of Labor and Eugene V. Debs's American Railway Union, both radical unions in the 1890s. That fall, Hall enlisted the help of W.H. Hoop, a "Recognized Authority on Trade Unionism," who opined "the wreckers paid and will do for some time for monkeying with the OBU. It has but one plank in reality and that is revolution."[735] John M. O'Neill, another Mine Mill leader, also slammed the OBU as another IWW.

Hall got editorial support from the *Kaslo Kootenaian* when the weekly blasted the OBU for striking to reinstate a worker at the Bluebell Mine in Riondel on Kootenay Lake. Bobby Barrow led the walkout. "While both Bobby Barrow and Tom Roberts apparently manage to live off the hard earnings of their fellow workers, it is inconceivable that anyone would give them credit for the ability to run an industrial concern employing 20 men. How they manage to work the workers without working themselves is a mystery."[736]

For Hall, radical unions like the OBU and IWW were part of the Communist threat. In "Capitalism," he ranted against critics of the system. "It is easy to bundle up all one's wrongs, mark it 'Capitalism' and let it go at that," the article intoned. "That is how Lenine [*sic*] and Trotzky [*sic*] so well succeeded with their nefarious plans, though they are not such fools as to believe all they preach. They at least are intelligent men."[737]

Whether Hall saw government control of liquor sales as part of that threat is not clear, but by July he was lashing out at the Moderation League, an anti-prohibition group that advocated government control of liquor distribution. It, he said, was "nothing more or less than an attempt of the distillers and brewers to stabilize their industry by placing the booze business in the hands of the government."[738]

The Christy Brothers Circus was in town that summer and, though it no doubt thrilled the kids, Hall complained that it took money out of the community. Fruit Fair planning was underway, and Blaylock's Workmen's Co-operative Committee was in charge of Labour Day festivities. Soon the Dramatic Order of the Knights of Khorassan, more familiarly known as the Dokkies, "swooped down on the oasis of Trail for the purpose of initiating about 25 hapless tyros into the mysteries of the order, and increasing by that number the membership of Shem El Nessim Temple, No. 172, of Nelson."[739]

If all the social activity created stress, Trailites could turn to Tanlac and Vinol, another questionable remedy advertised in the *News*. Health faddists could also buy the Wonder Health Restorer: "God gave herbs to relieve suffering." Joining them was Dr. Le Frere's Parisian Complexion Cream to quickly remove black heads, pimples, enlarged pores, crows' feet and wrinkles.

It was also a sad time for Hall. He lamented the demise of the once-thriving town of Phoenix, where he and former *News* owner W.B. Willcox had started the *Phoenix Pioneer* "in the young days of the camp." The first paper was printed on a Washington hand press, he recalled, but later "we bought an old Country Campbell cylinder press and the installation of that old cylinder press nearly cost the writer his life."

He provided the following gruesome details: "While the mud in front of the Pioneer office was estimated to be only four feet deep, the team hauling the drum of the press, failed to find a comfortably [*sic*] footing even with their hind legs and were fast disappearing from view when assistance arrived, and with much rope, and a lot of profanity, the horses were brought to the surface, resuscitated and finally placed on firm ground." After that breathless account, the editor noted that "getting the big cylinder out of the mud and into the office is a subject we do not like to dwell upon."[740] Hall also lamented the retirement due to bad health of Col. Robert T. Lowery, *Greenwood Ledge* editor, "dean of Kootenay and Boundary newspaper men and one of the most interesting writers in the west.... 'Pop' will be missed."[741] In late May, the "paragrapher" without peer had "passed beyond the grave."[742]

Hall was in better spirits in October when he boasted about his achievements at the *News*. As he put it, "the whirigig [*sic*] of time has reeled off a quarter of a century since the News made its first appearance and its subscription list is greater now than ever." He felt "pardonable pride in the fact that the News is read in nearly every home in Trail."[743] The paper's twenty-three "newsboys" had sold 688 copies that week, and the post office had mailed another 242 copies. By his calculation, "our thousand circulation in the city, based on a 'three to one' reading public, which is the average figure given by actuaries of big business and by recognized newspaper agencies throughout the world, gives the Trail News 3000 regular weekly readers."[744]

In late November, he added a touch of modesty, agreeing that "we cannot make such extravagant claims as some of our contemporaries," but he staked his rightful place among them. "Up until the latter part of 1915, the Trail News was a small five-col folio, while this issue of the News (the largest in its history) contains 12 pages six columns to the page," he boasted. Street sales were "probably greater than that of any other country weekly in Canada," offering as evidence "newsboys' records that show the paper's growth probably not equalled by any other country publication in the Dominion."[745] There would be future battles with those newsboys, but for now, Hall would use them to support his boasts.

The CM&S was again named in an arbitration hearing over fume damage to local crops and Hall was back to supporting the company over the farmers. He would also raise his editorial sword against the anti-temperance campaigners of the Moderation League. Hall would be on the losing side of both those battles, the former when the company was eventually fined for pollution and the latter when a plebiscite showed the public supported the league's position. The fine was off in the future, but Hall had this to say about the plebiscite: "Students of modern history know that women cannot be depended upon to vote for prohibition."[746] And they did not! The Methodists, with a sizeable following in Trail, sensed the coming "wet" era. Clearly Hall had appointed himself the conscience of the city and the arbitrator of its morals; prohibition was thus a significant target for him.

Blaylock made the news again when he volunteered to serve as a starter at a local sports event. As Hall facetiously explained, "Starter Blaylock evidently had a bolsheviki pistol—It worked only part of the time."[747] James H. Schofield was re-elected as the Conservative MLA for Trail and announced that he would also run for re-election as mayor. Former *News* owner William K. Esling won the Rossland electoral district in a recount to become the MLA. It was the beginning of his long political career as a Conservative.

Hall's *News* Finds Its Mojo, Local Sports and City Politics in 1921

In early 1921, Hall, announced that the paper "carries the greatest amount of advertising ever."[748] As usual, the *News* reported on city council meetings, endorsing council's ban on selling tuberculosis-infected meat. Again, it fit with Hall's concern about the community's health. Police court, always a good source of news, included prosecutions for gambling, indecent assault, grievous bodily harm, and selling cigarettes to children. As had become its habit, the *News* gave service clubs, including the Elks, Odd Fellows, Rebekahs, Daughters of the Empire and the Knights of Pythias, front-page coverage along with church news. Hall advocated large church services that would encourage "the comingling of all the people... to develop a fine spirit of friendliness, which is hardly more than perceptible at present."[749] The Presbyterian church obviously agreed, since the congregation was planning to build a new church that year. Support for evangelic religious activities also steadily picked up as another enduring *News* topic.

In other news, F.E. Dockerill remained mayor. Miracle cure Tanlac was now joined by Buckley's Cough Syrup, which declared "The 'Flu' Dare Not Return."[750] BC's population had reached 700,000, according to an unnamed source. Facts did not necessarily need to be verified in the Hall weekly although he counted on their veracity by subscribing to several news "Exchanges" or cribbing from other local newspapers.

When fire struck the old Star Theatre building and "threatened the whole town," Hall was livid: "Let's do something before the town burns down."[751] He also pressed council to adapt means to suppress the dust that summer. He was following Willcox's lead on the issue. And Trail faced other problems that spring when Blaylock filed notice to incorporate Tadanac as a separate municipality. Soon the battle would be on, with Trail city council concerned about the loss of tax revenue.

In April, CM&S reported a net profit of $291,349.83, with Blaylock praising the men for "developing great efficiencies."[752] The "Ore Shipments" column indicated the good or bad health of smelter business. In a single-industry town like Trail, such information was valuable to job seekers and those who were looking for signals of an economic downturn that would send them in search of new jobs. For example, it was obvious good news for Trail that zinc production had quadrupled in Canada since 1916.

Coverage of unions also continued apace in 1921, with ten strikes reported in BC from the previous November. Later the paper would report 285 strikes and lockouts Canada-wide, 18 of them in BC. Hall keenly celebrated the "OBU Dying Out at Copper Mountain."[753] He also reported that unionism was "strangling Britain," and heartily congratulated Washington State for declaring the IWW an "outlaw organization."[754] Unions opposed immigration, fearing a loss of jobs, but employers' associations supported it, perhaps as a source of cheaper labour.

Also still newsworthy were the movements of Chinese Trailites. For example, Hall reported that local Chinese Freemasons held a joint celebration with the Chinese Protective Society. As summer approached, he defended the paper's frequent publication of news about bootlegging, gambling and other crimes. "We are simply following a charitable impulse," he explained. "We are not believers in sensationalism. Yellow journalism does not appeal to us. We do not believe in playing up scandal for the sake of bringing the paper into prominence or some of our enemies into disrepute."[755] The purity of heart might someday lapse, but for now the *News* remained a family-friendly organ.

On the cultural front, Trailites continued to get their thrice-weekly dose of Hollywood, but only at the Liberty, the sole source of movie ad revenue since the Star building, built in 1896, closed its doors. Cecil B. DeMille's *Why Change Your Wife?* and D.W. Griffiths's *Broken Blossoms* were on the marquee. Perennial favourites, William S. Hart and Douglas Fairbanks, were joined by Wallace Reid and Mary Pickford. Fatty Arbuckle, yet to face trial for murder, also appeared regularly on the Liberty screen. Will Rodgers was *Cupid the Cow Puncher* on the same bill with Lionel Barrymore. Edgar Rice Burroughs's Tarzan movies were all the rage.

Robbie Burns Day was an annual event that the Trail Caledonian Society heavily promoted with Hall's help whenever Trail celebrated the memory of "Scotland's favorite son, her 'ploughboy poet'."[756] Unfortunately, much of what passed as poetry in the *News* was bad. An example:

> Mary had a Thomas cat
> It warbled like Caruso;
> A neighbor swung a baseball bat
> Now Thomas doesn't do so.[757]

Sport was not so much a theme at the paper as it was a passion that now included curling, with the *News* covering the season-opening bonspiel. "Local pucksters" beat Nelson 12–1 in an ongoing battle for the Daily News Cup. Sports fans could also enjoy a rough and tumble game of lacrosse, Canada's other national sport, but it could get a bit too rough for Hall. He complained loudly about a Nelson player who was a "big dirty bully" and accused the Nelson team of "cheap, rough sportsmanship."[758] Later he would state that "lacrosse to live must be clean." Trail's arch sports rival Nelson would eventually agree to play clean. He allowed that it was a fast game, but insisted that Trail rules "do not permit one player to maliciously injure another."[759] In boxing, on the other hand, world heavyweight champion Jack Dempsey could do whatever he chose to in the big ring and off.

The town's intellectual set would continue to read about church and high school debates. One such debate posed the question "Should leniency be shown the Germans?" Clearly the war was still a real presence in the city more than two years after it had ended.[760] The younger crowd could "trip the light fantastic" until the wee hours at Swartz Hall or attend a performance of *What Happened to Jones* performed by local thespians. The annual chautauqua, the travelling tent shows that flourished in the US and Canada from 1917 to 1935, started to appear in *News* ads.[761] As another reminder of the variety of talent that would come to town, the Liberty Theatre offered Victor and his Piano Accordion. As if that wasn't enough to keep the town busy in its leisure hours, the *News* said there was a "crying need for some sort of a community recreation hall."[762]

Another ongoing theme, socialism, was never off Hall's editorial agenda and was frequently the object of humour. "'Father', said the small boy, 'what is a social-ist?' 'A Socialist, my son, is a person who doesn't care much what kind of a govern-ment he gets so long as it is something else'."[763] In late spring, Wobbly leader "Big Bill" Haywood reappeared in the *News*. Word had it that he was fed up with the Soviet Union, where he had found refuge from US courts, and he planned to give himself up and serve his twenty-year sentence in Leavenworth penitentiary. Ap-parently, Hall suggested, "prison in the USA is preferable to freedom in Russia—or perhaps the outlook for eats is better."[764]

Another well-worn *News* theme was Hall's banter about those who criticized the paper. "If you ever feel like kicking because the paper costs four cents, just remember, please, how many folks and how much time it takes to prepare four cents worth of news," Hall carped.[765] In "Our Stenog Gets Peeved," a female staff member wrote that she hated short skirts in accordance with Hall's strict moral code regarding women.

Hall later protected his editorial freedom, explaining that his comments "are not intended to be considered as carrying with them any suggestion of finality," but merely to "stimulate thought."[766] It was a response to a sharply worded letter to the editor from Mayor Dockerill, who said the editor did not "fully inform yourself before attacking a public servant."[767] Hall had laced into the town's superintendent for what he presumed was slack behaviour.

The end of summer seemed to fire Hall's engines regarding the OBU, for he slammed Tom Roberts and five of his colleagues for striking in the Slocan min-ing district. The article called Roberts "a four-flushed organizer, and a gas-inflated demagogue" and branded the strike the "saddest fizzle."[768] He didn't stop there, but turned his guns on the provincial and federal politicians, who "are misfits and con-sume the time of the legislature with fool questions and idiotic suggestions."[769] He again had the town superintendent in his sights when he proposed a business man-ager for the city, so "we would know who to blame for our reckless expenditures."[770]

Not quite out of ammo, he told the Doukhobor farmers to go back to Russia. Still feeling feisty, Hall declared that two-thirds of Trail's population of 4,500 were *News* readers, hailed Kaslo's Robert F. Green as the first senator appointed from the Kootenays, and reported that the CM&S Company Store "Finds Snake in Bananas." Another civic election had taken place. And another self-serving poem arrived:

My father says the paper he reads ain't put up right.
He finds a lot of fault, he does, perusin' it all night.
He says there ain't a single thing in it worth while to read,
And that it doesn't print the kind of stuff the people need.
He tosses it aside and says it's strictly on the bum—
But you ought to hear him holler when the paper doesn't come.[771]

As school doors reopened in September, Hall kept "City Dads" (city council) on guard with a detailed analysis of how they spent municipal taxes. He promoted Labour Day, now called sports day, perhaps because few unions were involved in organizing it. It was a banner year, the *News* reported, with the day's events attracting up to 5,000 people. When they weren't in class, the older kids enjoyed Douglas Fairbanks as Zorro at the Liberty. Adults could see Marion Davies, girlfriend of newspaper magnate William Randolph Hearst (later scathingly depicted in Orson Welles's *Citizen Kane*) in *The Restless Sex*.

Trail boxer Luther Gordon made the front page, with Hall promising readers that "he is depending on his right hand wallop to bring home the bacon."[772] Hall also reflected on the weekly's past. "The Trail News is twenty-six years old this week," he wrote, noting that the paper "was one of the first business houses in the city, and has always been abreast of the times. Its columns have always chronicled the doings of the people, of this and surrounding districts, and its fyles [sic] form the most comprehensive history… that it is humanly possible to obtain."[773]

Near the end of 1921, Hall focused on one of his perennial bugbears—reader disrespect, but he saved some kind words for the local amateur theatre group that had scored a success with *All of a Sudden Peggy* at the Liberty Theatre. He shared a get-rich-quick story about an Asian miner named Ah Foo who had made a mint mining platinum in northern BC. He was saddened when a young smelter worker named John Murray died ("Drops Dead on Sidewalk") and Thomas Gilliland, thirty-seven, perished in an ore bin at the CM&S concentrator.

At year's end, Hall announced that the provincial legislature failed to pass a bill to enshrine an eight-hour work day. He reserved some of his fire for local politicians. "Bulls, blunders and general mismanagement on improvement work can be directly charged to this council," he snorted.[774] He greeted the coming New Year with a so-sorry note to the Russian-born anarchist Emma Goldman, or "Red Emma" as she was known, and her "old paramour," [Alexander] Berkman, who now want "to return to the states" after being deported to Russia two years earlier.[775]

That wrapped up Hall's second full year as *News* boss. He seemed ready to roll toward a third, intent on afflicting the comfortable and comforting the afflicted, as an old journalism adage put it. How much he and his cohorts at the weekly would do either would reveal itself as the paper matured in its role as chronicler and conscience of the smelter city. Was this the year, Hall would decide to go daily? It was a dream that had been around since the first days of the *Trail Creek News*, but it had always eluded owners from W.F. Thompson to W.B. Willcox. But Hall was cagey about the possibility. He had been ever watchful of the local press and he was cautious about taking giant steps. Now, might Trail get its chance? Perhaps 1922 would lay the groundwork for the long-contemplated leap.

John Barleycorn, Bolsheviks, Smelter Pollution and Eskimo Pie in 1922

Editor Elmer D. Hall hailed the New Year in his January 6, 1922, edition, complaining that it was a noisy one. Arthur J. Martin would soon be the new mayor, and Hall would praise him for running one of the "snappiest" council meetings in memory. The editor got help with his city council watchdog role from a Mrs. Margaret C. McNair who wrote to ask if it was fair for council to keep appointing the same person to so many public paid posts. But council's performance was only one of several big issues that lay ahead for Hall in his third year as the printer's-devil-in-charge. One of them, the proposed incorporation of Tadanac, would test his CM&S loyalty, pitting him against long-time *News* owner William K. Esling, his former boss. Another issue presaged a bigger fight over smelter pollution. Much was in store as the *News* entered its twenty-seventh year.

Elmer D. Hall. Courtesy Hall Printing Company

As usual, mundane events mixed with more critical ones as the year progressed. Readers learned, for example, that CM&S general manager S.G. Blaylock had had a severe sinus attack. National Fish Day was coming on February 1, and everyone was "requested to eat fish."[776] Eskimo pie, the chocolate-covered ice cream bar that had been invented the previous year in the US, was selling for 10 cents at MacKinnon's. Trail housewives, not always accorded equal treatment in the *News*, were advised that they could reduce their meat bill without sacrificing meal quality. They could now smoke, "but the old-fashioned way of scratching a match still remains a strictly masculine privilege."[777] Hall was "flabergasted [*sic*]" to learn that Trail's population was down to 3,015 from 4,500, according to the new census.[778] Clearly the circulation figures he cited in 1921 would need adjusting.

Humdrum gave way to genuine passion in the sports arena for, as we've seen before, Trail was first and foremost a sports town, starting with hockey. The local team would beat Nelson in West Kootenay League hockey competition, the "pucksters" playing "one of the most exciting games played in Trail for years." Such coverage marked an improvement in sports writing at the *News,* with some of the best and liveliest reportage: "It took ten minutes overtime to do it and if anyone at the game didn't get their full fifty cents worth of thrills they must have been both deaf and blind."[779] The Trail team was on its way to winning the McBride Cup and Nelson Daily News Cup that year.[780] Other winter sports received equally vibrant, some would say overzealous, treatment. A Trail Country Club for golfers had formed, with CM&S general manager S.G. Blaylock as vice-president.

Gloria Swanson and Tom Mix joined the cavalcade of movie stars to cross the Liberty Theatre screen in 1922. And million-dollar comedian Fatty Arbuckle would be found not guilty of a manslaughter charge in the death of actress Virginia Rappe. He claimed he was broke, and the trial publicity ruined him. It was a perfect story for a daily in the world of sensational headlines. If an evening at the movies provided no distraction, readers could always consult a pen-pal expert. Young men could correspond with "French girls and others" who are "refined, charming and wish to correspond for amusement or marriage if suited."[781]

Readers learned of a young Italian man's death in another smelter accident that spring. The Trail City Band played before an enthusiastic audience at the Liberty, and Hall earlier noted the "enthusiastic manner in which the band is always greeted in Trail."[782] Travel features now appeared frequently on inside pages. Many of them were promotions for the CPR's tourism service on land and sea. Also making regular appearances were stories from antiquity. Hall was as keen as ever to give readers a sense of historical Egypt. He also printed boilerplate features on the Aztecs, Chinese, and the ancient city of Ur.

Many of the same news criteria and editorial themes would prevail in the coming months. Odd Fellows, Pythians, Elks and Moose would install new officers and the *News* was sure to report the names on its front page. They were, after all, business associates of the editor, and they supplied his bread and butter through advertising. Hall would also continue his losing battle to boost prohibition in "John Barleycorn Fast Losing Grip" and to support harsh prison sentences for drug peddlers and bootleggers. Wobbly leader "Big Bill" Haywood, "who "narrowly escaped the hangman's noose twenty-five years ago," was still hot copy for Hall.[783] The One Big Union remained a target of Hall's anti-radicalism. Nor did he have any sympathy for local farmers' continued concerns about smelter fumes destroying their crops.

Defunct *News* rivals were reported as "reposing in the journalistic boneyard."[784] Hall, never too humble, printed a visiting *Vancouver Province* editor's remark that "the News in former days did not compare with the paper now being issued."[785] The *Province*'s rival, the *Sun,* took a drubbing for apparent inaccuracy in political reporting: "We fail to see where there is anything to be gained by wilfully distorting facts, twisting interviews, magnifying little things of doubtful authenticity, and eternally prodding the premier and his cabinet."[786] He also repeated his oft-noted scolding to readers about the editor not being responsible for opinions expressed in letters to the editor: "Nearly everyone who has arrived at maturity knows this to be a fact, but occasionally we run across a reader who is either lacking in reasoning ability or judgment and assumes otherwise."[787]

In April, the CM&S annual report showed a balance sheet total of $21,317,471.17. Blaylock credited his Workmen's Co-operative Committee, which had "eliminated friction and has greatly increased the general efficiency of the plant."[788] The WCC would also have the desired effect of curtailing union organizing activity for the next two decades. Hall pledged support for a war memorial building.

In May, readers got their first hint that Hall was moving toward a bigger and better *News* when a front-page headline, supported with an illustration, declared "Trail News Installs Modern Linotype." Hall gushed that he would give "our constituents" the news "without fear or favor... helping our readers to a better realization of the finer things of everyday existence."[789] With the new Model 14 Linotype installed, Hall was ready to meet those needs. This was clearly a turning point for the paper. Hall now possessed the tools to secure more lucrative printing contracts and eventually begin daily publication.

As new technology came on stream, readers were asked to "pass lightly over any of the trivial discrepancies which may appear in this number, remembering that we have sacrificed something to our desire to render service to our patrons at any cost to ourselves."[790] The following week, Hall announced that "After a supreme effort on the part of the staff of the News, augmented by draymen, general machinists, carpenters, joiners, millwrights and blacksmiths, the Trail News is now safely and comfortably housed in its new home on Cedar Avenue."[791]

All the changes might have gone largely unnoticed, but not the arrival of a bell in honour of the saintly Father Pat, the West Kootenay region's pioneer clergyman. Also serving as a distraction was the coming of the chautauqua, the annual tent show that developed "the community spirit."[792] Still another distraction was a film at the Liberty based on Canadian Ralph Connor's novel, *Cameron of the Royal Mounted*. Moviegoers doubtless welcomed the news in June that CM&S had granted bonuses for efficiency "to encourage care and discourage waste."[793]

The first murmurings of political discord in the smelter city came in midsummer when the Board of Trade endorsed the incorporation of Tadanac as a separate municipality. Hall jumped into the fray, arguing in favour of the new town within a town. Not everyone shared his view. Indeed, former *News* proprietor William K. Esling, now a member of the legislative assembly, was among "a few disgruntled natives." Hall adamantly supported the incorporation, and he urged Trailites to tell the government to accept the proposal without "forcing Tadanac to increase her population in order to become incorporated."[794] Blaylock, who led the incorporation drive, had methodically spelled out the new boundaries, the proposed taxes, and offered reassurances that Trail would not lose on the deal.

City council would soon capitulate and Blaylock would get his town. In fact, it wasn't until F.E. "Buddy" DeVito became mayor in the 1960s that Tadanac rejoined Trail after a public fight. But in 1922, Hall used his editorials to back the proposed new boundaries, and he and Esling locked horns about it publicly. He chose a bizarre backdoor route of attack. Why would Esling turn against the CM&S when for twenty years "he received a fair price for the work he performed for the smelter"?

In reviewing past *News* business records, Hall hit harder on the financial end, exposing "Mr. Esling advocating heavy duty on lead and other measures which might have had a great bearing on the prosperity of Trail and the smelter in particular." Not usually given to vitriolic personal attacks, Hall was unbridled in his criticism. "Mr. Esling accused the writer the other evening because we endorsed the incorporation of Tadanac," his tirade began. "Everyone present knew Mr. Esling was on the defensive, and he was wild in his desire to pull against the tide and permitted himself to utter statements that in his saner moments he would have thought twice before uttering." It was a direct shot across the bow followed by this *coup de grâce*: "any man who has the welfare of the town at heart will agree with us."[795] Hall used a second editorial to press BC's premier to accept Tadanac's incorporation and assured local businesses that it posed no threat to them. The "crux of the whole problem," Hall later stated, "was that Trail stood to lose $24,000 in annual taxes."[796] It would become an issue the following spring when Blaylock pressed harder for incorporation.

In late July, Hall announced that the *News* would soon install the only "automatic press" outside Vancouver.[797] It was another sign that a change in frequency could be imminent. Another poem best expressed Hall's determination:

> The paper is rotten, the paper is dead
> "It's a helluva rag," so everyone said.
> Its news is all stale and its jokes are punk
> "Its looks are disgraceful, its copy is bunk."
> They slammed it and knocked it and cursed it all day,
> No words could express what they wished to say;
> They composed in its honor a grim hymn of hate
> Yet oh, how they howled when the paper was late.[798]

In what might have been another crack at Esling, Hall offered this thought: "You never know where a politician stands, but you can always tell where he lies." He followed it up with a second thought that might also have been aimed at Esling: "The best advice we can give any citizen of Trail is to so live that you won't have to ask to have it be kept out of the paper."[799]

On September 1, 1922, Hall delivered on an earlier promise. "The Trail News will install tomorrow the only automatically fed press in the province of British Columbia outside of the coast cities," he boasted. "This press will, no doubt, prove a labor-saver and, along with our other modern machines, places us in the front rank among the country offices of British Columbia."[800] After a quarter-century as a weekly, the *News* seemed poised to become the smelter city's first daily newspaper of record. It was a dream Elmer D. Hall must have dreamt since his early days on the staff of the Esling *News*.

Smelter workers got a raise in October subject to market forces. Some Chinese smugglers were arrested in Vancouver in November, further fuelling anti-Chinese nativism. Hall pressed for better roads, "not the kind of bottomless sand constructed affairs which we have enjoyed, lo, these many years."[801] Turning to education, the editor advocated an end to homework, an "idiotic practice." He also demanded an electric fire siren instead of the current "turkey bell."[802] Another sports controversy blew up when Hall called anonymous letter writers "cowards" in a spat over a Nelson lacrosse player. "He even was afraid to use pen and ink, but brought his typewriter into play," Hall raged. "Of course the typewriter he was using couldn't spell, neither could it punctuate, but the ignoramus using it was none the wiser."[803]

In his final stand of the year, Hall again supported the CM&S in its dispute with several farmers regarding the smelter fumes problem. "People are losing patience with the 'smoke farmers'," he argued, "and the sympathy that was once theirs is fast fading away."[804] In the next edition, he said the farmers' claim that smelter fumes had damaged crops was a "wild desire to 'farm the smelter'." Assuming he spoke for the town, he added, Trailites "are just beginning to realize the hue and cry over smoke damage to crops is greatly exaggerated… and even if the damages were one hundred times greater than at present, they would still remain in favor of the smelter and mines['] millions of dollars every year."[805] To reinforce his argument, he published an article by E.A. Haggen stating that poor cultivation practices were the problem, not smelter fumes. It seemed the farmers were to blame for their own misery.

Esling was back in the news when he charged that the province was "robbed" in the Pacific Great Eastern Railway (PGE) "fiasco." The provincial government had purchased the railway in 1918, and it remains the publicly owned BC Rail today. Esling's comment provided another opportunity for Hall to take an editorial punch at his old boss: "Mr. Esling made a good deal of play in regard to it and intimated that he knows a great deal. Then when he was called to the stand to give evidence under oath as to what he knew, he refused to say a word."[806] Esling wasn't the only Victoria politician to feel the sting of Hall's lash: "The little gas bags have been having the time of their lives" with "idle prattle and acrimonious debate on subjects not worthy of notice."[807]

Perhaps the reason for such anger stemmed from Hall's objection to the Retail Stamp Act, which required merchants to place a stamp on every payment of $100 or more. The Retail Merchants' Association supported his opposition. Local politicians did not escape his wrath either. With the annual civic elections coming, he took a year-end swipe at Mayor A.J. Martin and his council. It had not "left any permanent monuments to mark their tenure of office from the ordinary," he wrote.[808] One reason: they did not advance Hall's cause of a fire protection system. It was a complete switch from the editor's positive comments at the start of 1922.

The bad weather forced a hockey game cancellation in late December, disappointing "Local Hockeyists." When the weather improved, "Trail Tigers Get Their Claws Cut." The Nelson Cubs did the cutting in a match that saw the home team's rivals "too quick for Jungle Opponents in Slashing Match (5–2)."[809] Moviegoers would flock to see heart throb Rudolph Valentino and Strongheart, the Wonder Dog at the Liberty. And *Lorna Doone* was on its way to the big screen. Anyone who did not relish cooking a New Year's Eve dinner could enjoy one at the Star Cafe, where the menu included eastern oysters on the half shell, Consomme Princesse, boiled salmon with anchovy sauce, and deep-dish apple pie with whipped cream for dessert.

Hall clearly was in a fighting mood as the year ended. If his mood didn't change, he would need a daily to vent his growing anger and better support his many civic causes. Despite Hall's criticisms, Mayor Martin would be re-elected in 1923. Tadanac would separate from Trail. The smelter city would still have a hockey team that could beat Nelson, and there was a solid outlook for the lead and zinc market. Hall was ready for the future as he waited for Trail to catch up.

Politics, Free Enterprise, Miracle Cures and Heads-Up Hockey in 1923

The IWW and OBU were still seen as active threats to civic and workplace peace in 1923.[810] Socialism and Big Bill Haywood, "one of the world's most rabid socialists," still found plenty of space on the editorial page and in the news columns. Miracle drugs continued to attract space, both paid and editorial, throughout the year. Tanlac, Adlerika, Carnoll and Vick's VapoRub were regulars. Also in competition was Halcyon Lithia bottled water, the latest cure-all for what ails the liver, kidneys and skin.

In sports, boxing had become a year-round interest. The *News* covered the fight game from all angles, including one instance where Hall sought financial aid for the destitute spouse of former heavyweight champion Bob Fitzsimmons, citing what he considered excessive aid to immigrant minorities. "There seems an abundance for the heathen Chinee and the East Indian," Hall complained, while Mrs. Fitzsimmons lived in poverty while helping "wayward girls and other down-and-outers."[811] Hockey rivalry again surfaced between Trail and Nelson. The weekly charged that Nelson was guilty of unsportsmanlike play, stressing that the *News* preferred that the game be "played in a fast, scientific, and strictly gentlemanly manner without a hint of rowdyism."[812]

CM&S's Blaylock was a trustee governing play for baseball's McBride Cup. Changes to the rules included the insistence that all players be amateurs. The question would later arise in connection with the Nelson team. The *News* noted that "Captain Dick Drew of the City team led his band of bludgeon wielders to victory Sunday afternoon in a see-saw game of the Tadanac nine, score 13–7."[813] And the rivalry could get vicious.

Some women were also sports enthusiasts, but they rarely appeared in the *News* except when it seemed a novelty. "Several ladies have broken into the curling game," it was reported in an early 1923 "Happenings" column, but not on the sports page.[814] Hall was less interested in sports women. As he had stated many times before, he wanted all women to stay at home and savour the pleasures of motherhood. A new column, "Modern Golf" by W.J. and Frank Thompson, might have been added for Blaylock and the executive set. Lacrosse aficionados formed a club to appeal to fans of Canada's other national sport. Trailites wanting a break from the smelter smoke were enticed to "Spend a Holiday at Kaslo, BC, the Switzerland of America" where you could "eat your fill of Kaslo cherries—the world's best."[815]

With a city election in the offing, Hall advised local electors to choose wisely among the "aldermanic timber."[816] Businessmen, particularly *News* advertisers, were uppermost in Hall's mind and he pursued his clientele with rigour and determination, even sponsoring a "Trade at Home Campaign" in repeated editions of the weekly. The biggest business of all—the Canadian Pacific Railway, owner of the smelter, garnered several column inches a week. Featured were profiles of company executives, especially E.W. Beatty, the first Canadian-born president of the company. When CM&S announced a new mill at Sullivan Mine in Kimberley that year, Hall said BC should feel gratified by the company's resource development projects.

Civic boosterism and engendering pride in the smelter city were featured. In that vein, Hall continued to spearhead public concern about the lack of fire protection. Even a faulty fire hydrant could arouse his invective. But, as in 1922, his support did not extend to farmers who continued to complain that smelter fumes had destroyed their crops. Hall happily concurred with a Kaslo farmer's view that smelter smoke was a useful "germicide" worth considering.[817] Immigration also stayed on the editorial page. Hall was against "unrestricted immigration," citing results of army tests on foreign-born soldiers: "More than one-third were found to be of such low intelligence that they were graded in occupation lower than the common laborer."[818]

In fraternal society news, the Dramatic Order of the Knights of Khorassan or Dokkies, founded in 1894, was newsworthy mostly because of their extravagant festivals and parades. They were connected to the Knights of Pythias in the way Shriners were to freemasonry. Mormons also got their chance. Mrs. Marion Williams of Utah was pictured in Mormon Temple Robes before addressing an "anti-Mormon mass meeting at the Presbyterian church." It included her experience with polygamy, "the most exciting story ever told."[819]

Health issues had also become regular items on the editorial page and in the features section of the paper. Early in 1923, local health officers set a quarantine due to the prevalence of scarlet fever. Hall supported more stringent observance of Trail's quarantine laws, but he would later side with a growing anti-vaccination movement regarding other health threats. Hall's *News* also championed the fight against drug trafficking, bootlegging and smuggling. But when his editorials were not battling for his causes, he could sink into what seemed a melancholy mood, often chastising young people or working women.

At the movies, Pola Negri was often on the marquee. That spring, Mark Twain's *The Prince and the Pauper* arrived. Canadian-born screen darling Mary Pickford continued to grace the silent screen as "America's Sweetheart." Marion Davies also found her spot. Later in the summer, France would announce that it had suppressed D.W. Griffiths's *The Birth of a Nation* because of its racism.

Trailites could also enjoy a new billiard table, comforted by a bylaw assuring that the pool hall was visible from the street and held limited business hours. But that did not satisfy Hall's moralistic opposition: "So long as these places are permitted to operate, just so long will men of idle hours hearken to the tinkle of 'chips that pass in the night'."[820] It was not the last editorial on the evils of gambling.

Later in the year, the Trail Amateur Dramatic Society would perform the comedy *Green Stockings,* and the Pythian Sisters would offer *Fads and Fancies.* Motoring would join the long list of local pastimes, with ads promoting Studebakers, Buicks and Maxwells. Trailites could vicariously travel the frontier backwoods with Pauline Johnson, featuring her poetry and a recitation of her writing at the Liberty that spring.

In April, Hall hailed the arrival of the Trail Memorial Hall and a technical high school. Support for better education had become a hallmark of his editorship. He believed "the community[,] which has learned to place the proper and adequate emphasis on the need and the value of education[,] has taken several steps in the direction of progress."[821] Ironically, given this view, he began publishing Slats' Diary, an ungrammatical attempt at humour that seemed to make fun of peoples' inadequate speaking abilities.[822]

The Workmen's Co-operative Committee system had been operating for three years in place of a certified union, and that suited CM&S manager Blaylock. In his spring annual report, he noted "great credit is due to the men who have served on these committees."[823] Those workers still hopeful of rekindling a local branch of the One Big Union might have disagreed. For others, memories of the 1917 strike still rankled.

Trail was to get cement sidewalks that summer in keeping with a goal of Hall's campaign to foster civic pride. "A citizen should be as ashamed to cast refuse into his street as to spit on his parlor rug at home," he lectured.[824] The annual "Swat the Fly" campaign was also designed to keep things neat and tidy. Even graveyards could come under attack. "Let us think about the living, flowers, trees and men," he argued. "The world would be better if every graveyard were made into a park and a playground."[825] With the money now apparently secured, Trail could get a new municipal hall and the *News* was part of the battle to secure it.

Citizens' health continued to be of concern, and to that end, Hall counselled readers as follows: "Man drinks strong, black coffee, and that clogs the valves; he drinks moonshine liquor and that strips the gears; he gulps down lemonade, ginger ale, pop, iced tea and what not and then wonders why the boilers do not generate heat." He concluded, "If you should take a donkey and put him through a like performance he would be dead in a month."[826] Also a public health concern was the distribution of dirty or below standard milk. City council dealt with it at the offending dairies.[827]

The promised discussion about Tadanac's bid to become a separate municipality heated up again. As mentioned earlier, the small community of company managers' homes on CM&S property overlooking Trail wanted to go it alone. First, a notice about extending its territory into parts of Trail appeared. Then came the subsequent legal notices, and by late May, a third notice seemed to end the matter; Tadanac would separate. But the issue of property taxes remained unsettled and would soon test city council's resolve.

Editorial innovations for 1923 included "The Strength of the Small," a new column by American commentator and Unitarian clergyman Richard Lloyd Jones, and "Home Sweet Home," a cartoon strip by Terry Gilkison.[828] Other cartoons would follow; all would reflect Hall's values regarding the household, women's role as homemakers, and well-disciplined children. Spring seemed to fuel his efforts to instruct young girls on suitable marriage partners: "No girl regrets losing a hero who was a common, cheap, tin-horn sport and she had better be a kitchen queen for dad and mother all her life than a broke-hearted drudge of a slave for such a brainless brat a single day."[829] Women were often portrayed as mindless household drudges who think little of the world's troubles, but in this backhanded compliment he argued that "they are taking care of the real questions of life—domestic politics and the eternal war against the high cost of living. God bless 'em."[830]

There was more. On choosing a mate, Hall had this to say: "He snores, plays, prays, fights, votes, cries, laughs, eats, smokes and cusses. He cheats a little. Girls, take your choice of color and take your chances with a specimen of this animal we call 'man'."[831] He chose poetry to reinforce his advice:

> If he earns your praise, bestow it;
> If you like him, let him know it;
>   Let the words of true encouragement be said;
> Do not wait till life is over
> And he's beneath the clover,
> For he cannot read his tombstone
>   when he's dead.[832]

It wasn't only girls and women who received the editor's unsolicited advice. Young men, too, needed his counsel. Regarding the best route to success, he told them it was "time to stop worrying and buckle down to your job."[833] For working-class youth "who are climbing the ladder of achievement without the polish of advanced education," comes this thought: "Lord, whoever told them a fellow likes a girl who is bold and forward! No fresh flapper for me, no siree!"[834] And this old homily: "Back of every successful man you will find a sensible woman."[835]

Keeping youth on the correct path stayed on the editorial page in June, with Hall advising school graduates not to drink whisky. They were further advised to be honest, respect the opinions of others, and accept an obligation to mother. For educated girls and their parents he offered a short lecture: "Why shouldn't this girl graduate for a time believe in the entire goodness of the world; believe in perpetual sunshine! The band plays jazz for her now; her pulses quicken, and she is happy. It is well. Why should she know that further down the path there are no flowers, the bands no longer play and the clouds often shut out the sun?"[836] Such comments were no doubt addressed to his own family. He also had advice for homemakers. The ban on Oleo margarine was a mistake, Hall told them, for "good oleo is infinitely better than bad butter."[837]

At mid-year, the Volstead Act in the US won Hall's strong support as did other prohibition measures, although profits from government control of liquor sales were benefitting Trail's schools and hospitals. The issue could be greeted with humour on occasion: "Chasing rum-runners seems to be the regular thing, but who ever took rum without a chaser!"[838] Forest fire prevention also remained a concern, with Hall noting the loss of millions of dollars in fire destruction. His concern for workers was never ambitious, but he did cheer when women began to earn a minimum wage of $14 a day in manufacturing and $15.50 in fish canning.[839]

Moody again, he scoffed at the happy days of yore, praising the conveniences of modern life. Then he seemed to contradict himself with a lament for the disappearing "old-fashioned family life."[840] Later he did so again. "What has become of the simple life of our grandsires?" he asked his readers. "Where are the folk dances and games on the lawn? These things have been crowded out of the village life by the automobile and the saxophone."[841] In July, he was back on his civic pride bandwagon: "I owe my city my full measure of civic loyalty."[842] Judging from past editorials, members of the Moderation League were disloyal, for Hall blamed the business lobby group that supported government control of liquor sales for the increase in bootlegging.

Summer brought forth horror stories like the news about the forty Chicago girls who were victims of a white slave ring and unusual events like the Caledonian Society's celebration of its first anniversary haggis feast. Summer was also a time for Hall to reflect on the state of newspapering. "A wisely conducted newspaper is like a banquet," he wrote. "Help yourself to whatever you wish, but do not condemn the entire spread because pickles and onions may be included."[843] Another editorial explained the process of writing as it pertained to a favourite Hall cause. "When the cost of school extension seems particularly heavy," he wrote, "efforts are made to have it appear as if the local editor were unmindful of the public interest in forever boosting for new avenues of learning. But let us lift the professional curtains so that you may see there is usually helpful thought behind the writing of an editorial."[844] A poem was meant to assist in newsgathering:

> If you have a bit of news—
> Send it in;
> Or a joke that will amuse—
> Send it in;
> A story that is true
> An incident that's new—
> We want to hear from you—
> Send it in—
> If it's only worth the while
> Never mind about your style—
> Send it in.[845]

Seldom did Hall offer readers a peek inside the workings of the paper. Now he provided a humorous, self-deprecating look. It opens with the editor berating a young worker, a printer's devil, about using bad language. "Young men, don't swear," he scolded. "There is no occasion for it outside of a printing office, where it is useful, when the paper is behind time. It also comes in handy in proof-reading and is 'indispensable' when the ink works badly and the press begins to 'buck'." And finally: "It is sometimes brought into use when the foreman's mad; and it has been known to entirely remove the tired feeling of the editor when he looks over the paper after it has been printed. Outside the printing office it is a foolish habit."[846]

The editor moved on to new problems at the end of summer. He was disturbed at the loss of the local Red Cross branch and the district nurse. "Really, we are funny folks," he observed. "We can spent $110,000 per year for booze, but we can't find $1,800 a year for something that affects the health and well-being of the children of Trail." It was followed by a scolding: "Trail, shame on you!"[847] Hall promoted various summer events but shunned attendees who "drink all the beer and eat all the hotdogs and occupy the chairs all afternoon."[848]

Hall also took another swipe at young women. Thousands of them never get married because they are "bitterly opposed to housework," he opined.[849] Later he seemed to go beyond the usual griping with an article from a biologist arguing that because college-educated women produce fewer children than immigrant women, America has more ugly female children that become ugly women.[850] No doubt some readers, many of them immigrants themselves, took offence.

In November, William K. Esling was back in the *News*. Premier John Oliver's government had allowed the Conservative MLA from Rossland to examine the books regarding the Pacific Great Eastern Railway and the Northern Construction Company.[851] Soon enough, Premier Oliver was "after W.K. Esling" regarding an apparent botch job in reviewing the government's PGE files.[852] Also, Esling's "conservative opposition, as well as some of the independent and labor members, caused no end of trouble" during the debate of an eight-hour day bill. It was passed despite employer claims that industry "would practically be shattered if an eight-hour bill were passed."[853]

In December, the *News* was a fat fourteen pages and "we are not ashamed.... Few communities can boast of a bigger or better newspaper."[854] Earlier he had penned this thought. "To produce a newspaper that would gratify the whims and desires of every individual would be a difficult job and would probably result in a newsless journal," he stated. Newspapers "are not responsible for court trials, arrests, bootleg raids, labor conventions, political activities and the other happenings in daily life. It is their duty to publish what has happened, colorless and free from editorial opinion."[855]

Much as it began, 1923's *News* ended with another feature on ancient Egyptians. A few days before Christmas, it was announced that Syd Desireau would not be able to play amateur hockey until a review was completed. An article doubted that the semi-professional hockey player would be allowed back into amateur hockey. The issue had simmered for the season, pitting two old rivals, Trail and Nelson, against each other. The problem would continue long after the New Year's revelry had ended. It would bring more conflict on and off the ice and the *News* would be there to cover it as best a weekly could do so.

Mother Love, Fear of Feminism and Hatred of Wobblies Marked 1924

As 1924 began, the *News* promised increased prosperity for the mining industry bolstered by the reopening of the Rossland mines, once the Eldorado of early prospectors. With it came another promise: an unusually harsh cold snap would freeze water pipes. It was anyone's guess who would be victorious among the "small army of candidates" running in the January 17 local election. The voting public would soon elect Herbert Clark to replace outgoing mayor A.J. Martin. The big shock of the coming year would be the local farmers' victory in the smelter fumes war. The most unpredictable event was a young letter writer's challenge to Hall's repeated sexist editorials about young women. Hidden among the promises and the surprises was the pending arrival of a daily newspaper for the smelter city.

Now in his forties, Hall seemed to vacillate between melancholic despair and enthusiastic pride on his editorial page. "With the new year comes the resolution to make this newspaper better during 1924," he told readers. The country editor "can no longer stretch his lazy limbs on the top of his desk and blow rings of smoke from his old black pipe while his one compositor fills the columns of his paper with clippings from the exchanges," he reflected. "He is no longer fed upon fruit and vegetables from his subscribers' farms, and brought angel food cake from the wedding feast. Those good old days are past and gone."[856]

More than ever, Hall was becoming the conscience of the town. His editorials could sound like moralistic sermons from the likes of local Methodist Reverend W. Lashley Hall. He repeatedly passed along advice to young girls. Articles warned of kidnappings, white slave rings and late-night dances at Swartz Hall. The editor recommended that girls read newspapers but added this proviso: "Don't read descriptions of awful murders; don't read details of vile intrigues, and don't read silly personalities. The girl who reads a daily newspaper properly is very apt to be the girl quick of wit and fully informed of what the world is doing."[857]

Hall was emphatically not a feminist. "There are women who maintain that their domestic career does not give full scope to their powers!" he complained. "In the name of the great Goddess Common Sense, what more do they want?" He added that "the young men that gadding girls 'catch' are not worth catching."[858] In "Listen, Lady" he offered another homily on motherhood, suggesting that the good daughter should "get up tomorrow morning and get breakfast, and when our mother comes and begins to express surprise, go right up to her and kiss her."[859] Young men also got lectured: "You cannot loaf around the street corners, smoke, tell stories and sponge on someone else without making a failure in life."[860] He later demanded that city council establish a curfew.

The IWW lingered in Hall's mind in early January when he ran a story about striking Wobblies at Camp 2 of the BC Spruce Company of Lumberton. The strikers wanted a minimum wage of $4 and an eight-hour day.[861] As long as the IWW was a presence, however distant, the *News* covered it. The One Big Union, with a previous following on smelter hill, again felt the slap of Hall's editorials: "The town has again been plastered with the red labels of the OBU. About every so often this red cloud casts its austere influence over Trail and despite the fact it has had its fling in this section and failed, it bobs up periodically to remind us that someone is trying to build up a job for himself at the expense of misguided workers." His conclusion, as constant as ever, was that "labor has had enough of these red label men and the sooner they realize this fact and go to work and earn an honest living, the better off they will be."[862]

The radical unions were communist and thus were even more wide open to Hall's angry assaults. In an editorial defending free enterprise capitalism, he complained about "these days when reds and radical and mangy politicians are engaged in making war on every man who has saved and accumulated a competency, or enough to enable him to engage in business for himself." He stressed that "capitalism enables the thrifty one who saves to enjoy the fruit of his industry." He allowed that "there are phases of capitalism that require correction," but "communism or common ownership which would efface capitalism would destroy thrift and industry, and in the end would compel the prudent, industrious toiler under the reign of tyranny, to support a vast brood of indolent and worthless creatures who would not be productive under any system."[863]

The social calendar in the smelter city was as lively as ever. Zane Grey's western sagas made it to the Liberty screen and stayed show after show. Sherlock Holmes thrilled Trail's amateur sleuths. *Enemies of Women*, starring Lionel Barrymore, was set in Russia just prior to the Revolution. Bill Hart was Wild Bill Hickock. *Nanook of the North* showed audiences the lives of the Inuit people of northern Quebec. Buck, the faithful dog in Jack London's *The Call of the Wild*, would pave the way for other Hollywood animal stars like Rin Tin Tin and Lassie. Later, *The Hunchback of Notre Dame* would scare audiences. Theatre manager Allan E. Morris may have died, but nothing could stop the endless flow of silent Hollywood thrillers, comedies and love stories.

The Caledonians again honoured Scottish bard Robbie Burns, and Hall supplied space for a long poem by "Mr. H.J. Hogg, whose poems are not new to Trail." The editor hailed "The poet's complete command of the Scotch dialect, as used by Burns."[864] Readers would hear again from Harry Hogg. Activities of local service clubs like the Odd Fellows and the Rebekahs, and the Daughters of the American Revolution and those of the Empire were still often covered on the front page, as were church ladies' auxiliaries.

The year produced new miracle drugs to join the plethora already there. For example, "Deafness Can Be Cured," promised an ad for Larmalene. Miss America lauded the curative properties of Tanlac. The Mammoth Remedy Company was to set up shop in Trail to produce its Moore's Mammoth Rheumatic Preparation. Dreco, a stomach tonic, was just entering the market of over-the-counter remedies. And there was concern over the quality of mental health therapy employed at the Essondale Hospital at the coast.

Early in the year, the paper introduced "Sport News," offering a full page of local, national and international sports coverage. Boxing fans would now get weekly reports on heavyweights Gene Tunney, Jack Dempsey and Luis Firpo. Hockey games were well covered and rightly so since they could attract crowds of 800 or more. Curling, too, had a following, and the CM&S added to the excitement by donating silver curling stones. One of these went to company manager Blaylock, whose rink won in Schedule A competition that winter.

No sport seemed insignificant, although coverage of women's participation was always limited. Hall offered them this advice: "Running and Jumping Not Good For Women."[865] The page listed "Bouquets and Brickbats" for sports readers, featuring tidbits on heavyweight and flyweight boxing, swimming and hunting. The latter, along with fishing, was a popular pastime in Trail. Dog team mushing and dog derby competitions found a corner, as did the US dirigible *Shenandoah* that was set for its flight over the North Pole. Sports knew no bounds and was promoted even in poetry:

> They are packed into the bleachers,
>   And the band's begun to play,
> And the howling "ball fan" screechers
>   Are "on deck" in full array.
> Our old friend, the vendor's copping
>   Of the coin—his goodly share,
> And the hot peanuts are popping,
>   And there's popcorn everywhere![866]

Letters to the editor were welcome, Hall told readers, but he would not be held responsible for the views expressed. Early in the year, a letter writer complained that nearby Tadanac elected a person to the school board that was related to one of the teachers. Another letter complained about inaccuracies in church history. Still another was bothered about the "tax burden."[867] It was a short-lived exercise in participatory journalism that would soon be tested by a young person who was offended by Hall's pompous attitude toward youth.

Some innovations were strictly on the business end. For example, Hall proudly introduced a new nine-route delivery system in which "twenty to twenty-five newsboys of all sizes and all ages" would get more than 1,000 copies of the *News* to readers in Trail and Rossland.[868] By late February, though, flush from Hall's high praise, the newsboys were on strike for higher pay. The trouble began when Hall fired all but nine of the twenty-five, upsetting some of them and leading to a short strike "for double pay." Hall made no apologies: "While we are willing to admit their services are more or less valuable, yet we could hardly reconcile a boy's time at $2.00 per hour with our subscription price at $2.40 per year, so we decided to dispense with their services."[869]

Marriages, traffic and workplace accidents, drownings, train schedules, stage departures and veterans' smokers regularly appeared in columns like "Here and There," "Heard and Seen," "In and Around Trail" and "Trail in Brief." Terry Gilkison's "Home Sweet Home" cartoon strip was back. Historical features, such as Charles Conway's column on British landmarks and personalities, added a patina of sophistication to the paper.

"This Week" was a new column by Arthur Brisbane, a "US newspaper editor and writer, known as the master of the big, blaring headline and of the atrocity story."[870] Hall introduced Brisbane, the editor of the *New York Journal*, a top circulation Hearst paper, as "one of the world's foremost writers."[871] A "Homemakers' Corner" gave good advice to parents as in "Do Not Leave Babies Alone." Edited by Miss Alice L. Webb, of the State College at Pullman, Washington, readers could find not only advice on successful marriage, love and a regular dollop of poetry, but a huge collection of recipes such as the one for baked roly-poly pudding. A rather silly column called "This Is Pat" also found space later in the year.

Measles, Modern Youth, Beheading Editors, "Scotch" Humour, and Jed the Dog

As stated, local businessmen were a main audience for the *News*. Without their patronage the paper would cease to exist. In addition to its regular ad, the CM&S was assured of favourable coverage. "Smelter Output Nearly 12 Million [dollars] for Year Company Employs About 2500 Men," crowed one headline.[872] The CM&S annual report for 1923 showed a net profit of $2,401,346.71. Many more profitable years would follow. Even when the company was clearly in the wrong, as it would be in the eyes of the courts regarding smelter pollution, Hall defended it. Upset at a court decision fining the CM&S $60,000 and ordering them to buy four affected properties, Hall had supported the company against the farmers. Despite the finding, he continued to blame the farmers for "insufficient water for irrigation and ignorance as to the adaptability of the soil."[873] A reader, Eva H. Cross, complained about inaccurate coverage of the pollution arbitration award.

Measles afflicted the city in March, resurrecting fears of another epidemic even though the 1918–19 killer flu had long past. A court report identified four people who had failed to alert authorities to the outbreak of an infectious disease.[874] To come was the even greater threat of smallpox. Some residents would later choose to refuse the available vaccine and would mount a vigorous campaign against it. Editor Hall would take the lead.

The good news that spring was that Trail smelter workers were the "Highest Paid of Any Smelter Employees on the Continent."[875] The social scene picked up as well, with the Nelson Operatic Society performing Gilbert and Sullivan's *The Gondoliers* in Trail. Not to be undone by rival Nelson, the Trail Musical Society later produced *The Country Girl*. It won plaudits from the *News* for being the "best show ever seen in this city."[876] Hall hailed the production skills of Mr. and Mrs. Tregoning and credited Mr. Blaylock with funding the production.

In another innovation, the *News* provided weekly space for a new section called "Features, Fiction and Illustrated World Events." The first feature was chapter 1 of *The Inverted Pyramid*, Bertrand Sinclair's serialized novel about BC. Hall boasted that the *News* "is the first paper in British Columbia to obtain the serial rights."[877] The book ran for many weeks without comment from the reading public.

From February onwards, Hall gave readers a steady supply of his views on newspapers, journalism and naysayers. He demanded that local business patronize the "home newspaper" by helping to make it profitable. Singing his own praises,

Hall said the home newspaper "has the entire public to deal with. It is criticized on all occasions. It has to deal with all the cranks in the community." Seeking to loosen business advertising dollars, he added that the paper "has power, and that power is, to the credit of journalism, nearly always wielded for public good."[878]

He moved on to the *News*'s critics: "Newspaper work is done in a hurry. The field to be covered is large. Very few newspapers have forces big enough to cover the field with ideal thoroughness." Hall then blamed the public, saying they are "careless in their ways of giving information." He pressed his point with a quote from the *Cranbrook Courier* in the East Kootenay district: "Running a country newspaper is not all cream and honey."[879]

The *Rossland Miner*, one of the West Kootenay's oldest newspapers, also took a beating. "The Trail News has been chastised and we feel humble and penitent," Hall began. "We have been caught red handed trying to 'slur' Rossland's hockey team by calling some of their players 'birds of passage,' [three players had left town] and have received a severe reprimand. Who do you suppose caught us? Why, the Rossland Miner, that grand old guardian of the people's rights and purveyor of quack ads." The old rivalry continued, with Hall arguing "It is not the hockey question that is agitating the Rossland Miner, but it is the fact that the Trail News is putting on a carrier system in Rossland with a 12-page paper—that's the fly in the ointment."[880] Disgruntled readers were next. Hall's chosen weapon to fend off their negative comments was a poem, one he had used before to make the same point:

> He reads about the weddin's and he
> snorts like all get out;
> He reads the social doin's with a most
> derisive shout,
> He says they make the papers for the
> women folks alone;
> He reads about the parties and he'll
> fume and fret and groan;
> He says of information it doesn't have
> a crumb—
> But you ought to hear him holler when
> the paper doesn't come.[881]

Clearly, critical views of the *News* were met with a sharp rejoinder. If a reader didn't like what he or she read, it was their own fault. "A newspaper is a peculiar thing in the public's eye. The news-gatherer is stormed at because he gets hold of one item and is abused because he does not get another," Hall fumed. "Young men and young women, as well as older persons, perform acts… and then rush to the newspaper office and beg the editor not to notice their escapades. The very next week they condemn the same paper for not having written up another party doing the same thing." He gloried in the discretion of a country editor, telling readers to "be thankful that he has a heart and is not as indifferent to your feelings as the cold and calculating circulation builder who sits at the desk on the big city papers."[882]

Nothing better illustrated Hall's inability to accept criticism gracefully than a letter exchange with a "Modern Youth" who took issue with Hall's complaint about girls not being able to cook and sew. "You question whether any of the modern youths ever go around the house to peep in the kitchen window. Please permit me to ask you the same question," the youth had the audacity to write. "If you would take the trouble to [do] so before writing such editorials… you would find these 'dolls, flappers and empty-headed models for style shows' playing the same part as the 'sensible girls' of your day, frying chicken, making biscuits and washing dishes with possibly a few modern utensils instead of the old tin pan."[883]

Hall penned this angry rebuttal: "Ridicule under the guise of criticism may temporarily befog an issue but it has never changed facts. Less than three per cent of our high schools teach girls to cook,… and a goodly percentage couldn't boil water with-

Many dignitaries visited Trail. Here, Governor General Lord Willingdon and Lady Willingdon are met by smelter president S.G. Blaylock. Courtesy Trail Historical Society

out burning it." Hall was palpably upset: "The present time will go down in history as the 'jam and toast age' and 'Modern Youth' ten years hence can with complacency look back to 1924 with its multitude of gastronomical burlesques and marvel at the stamina and recuperative powers of the human anatomy."[884]

Reader Mary C. Ledoux, in a long and rambling agreement with Hall's insensitive rebuttal of the "Modern Youth," suggested that the editor "displayed that fullness of moral and spiritual freedom in your editorial.… I endorse every one of your sentiments." She added that the "callow youth… has much to learn, before he can allow his able pen to run away with his wits." Whether the Modern Youth was male or female is left unstated, but the writer could well have been either. Also questionable is Ledoux's motive in supporting the editor. She signed her letter "Yours in comradely appreciation and esteem."[885] A few weeks later, "The Glory of Womanhood" appeared in the paper under the byline M. Catherine Ledoux.

That exchange occurred in May. In June, Hall seemed to argue that he was not a liar. It was not clear what provoked the statement, but Hall felt it necessary to explain that "the editor isn't a liar from choice. The truth struggles in his manly breast the same as it does in the village preacher, but the pride of his community makes him a trembling rabbit—and he lies to save the local pride of the town."[886] Earlier he published an article that mysteriously stated "I am the country newspaper.… I am the friend of the family, the bringer of tidings from other friends. I speak to the home in the evening light of summer's vine clad porch or the glow of winter's lamp.... I speak the language of the common man; my words are fitted to his understanding."

Was he experiencing a crisis of confidence? It seemed so when the article boasted that "my congregation is larger than that of any church in my town; my readers are more than those in the school. Young and old alike find in me stimulation, instruction, entertainment, inspiration, solace, comfort. I am the chronicler of birth, and love and death—the great facts of man's existence.... I am the word of the week, the history of the year, the record of my community in the archive of state and nation. I am the exponent of the lives of my readers. I am the country newspaper."[887]

Among Hall's various causes, he approached none so passionately as prohibition. The enemies were many, but leading the pack was the Moderation League of BC with its "Beer Plebiscite—Vote and Work for Beer by the Glass." An election ad accorded with Hall's view on the issue. Addressed to women voters, the ad asked them not to vote for beer being sold by the glass. "Who Will Suffer?" it asked. "The Women and Children in the Homes, but the men also."[888]

At mid-year as usual, the *News* learned from a "reliably informed" source that the CM&S would announce a 3 per cent dividend for the first six months ending June 30.[889] MLA James Schofield would again represent the Trail riding in Victoria. Premier John Oliver lost his seat, but the Liberal government stayed in power. Oliver would later run in a by-election and become the MLA for Nelson after what the *News* called "one of the bitterest campaigns ever waged in the interior."[890] Governor General Lord and Lady Byng visited Trail that summer, and "Mr. Blaylock took charge of the party and conducted them through the shops."[891] Byng was soon to be embroiled in a fight with Prime Minister William Lyon Mackenzie King over King's request to dissolve Parliament. Byng refused and the King government fell momentarily in 1925.

By the start of summer, Hall's editorial page was increasingly a platform for dictating public morality. Displaying a cranky attitude, he rejected the notion of the "good old days," saying they weren't so good. Baseball did not escape a lecture on recruiting better players. "Last Sunday's debacle before the largest crowd of the season was not only pitiable but disgusting," he wrote.[892] With school a month away, girls once again got some marriage counselling: "She may be intelligent, educated and beautiful, but if she speaks in a loud voice, we instinctively feel that there is a lack of natural refinement or thorough good breeding."[893] Girls and women got some relief when Hall trained his guns on "wildcatting, 'kiteing,' bootlegging, gambling, moonshining, and the several and devious ways some have of acquiring a few dollars."[894] Hall also commented on the Leopold and Loeb trial, arguing that the judge resigned before passing sentence because the two young men, charged with murder, were rich and had rich people's backing.[895]

Summertime was bathing beauty contest time and the *News* seldom failed to run a bathing suit photo. In the fall, the *News* would report that "Peter Veregin [*sic*], 'King of the Douks,' was dead."[896] The killer who blew up the Kettle Valley train would never be found. Not long after the explosion, eight Doukhobor schools were burned to the ground. The weekly also reported that smelter worker Donald Smith had died in the smelter lead furnaces. Another CM&S fatality was narrowly avoided when a company farm employee was "nearly killed by [a] horse."[897] The following month, a "young Italian musician [was] found with [his] body cut into three sections," noted the headline announcing another grisly death.[898] A member of the Moose Orchestra, he was found next to the CPR track. "There was a time in the history of Trail when she enjoyed a reputation for being a good clean town," Hall later commented. "Those were the days when the law was enforced and gambling and bootlegging were frowned upon. But it seems we have fallen into evil ways."[899]

Still, it was also a cheerful time full of promise at the *News*, for Hall had acquired a new press to mark "another epoch in the history of the local paper." More changes were to come in the way of "general news feature attractions."[900] In a poetic attempt to anthropomorphize the paper, the writer offered this: "Where men have gathered together I am. And until the last man has gone to the great beyond, I shall be. I am the papyrus of time. I am the newspaper."[901]

In October, the paper celebrated its twenty-ninth birthday with the publication of "a facsimile (as nearly as possible with our modern plant) of the first page of the Trail Creek News of 29 years ago."[902] He added a brief history of the paper, noting that he had worked with its founder, "W.F. Thompson, one of the best 'boom' newspaper men in the west in his day."[903]

For some reason, Hall chose to include an item about beheading editors in a fall edition. "Down in China they are cutting off the heads of newspaper editors," he explained. "While this method is considered by Europeans as being drastic, it has made the press amenable to the opinion of the government and has put a stop to criticism." He acknowledged that he didn't agree with this course of action. However, "there are several publications in BC where this rule should be invoked." Calling the critics of government "soreheads," he suggested that in those cases "the headsman" should proceed with his work.[904]

In mid-October, letter writer Max Meimann of the Moose Orchestra called for dancing restrictions at Swartz Hall. Apparently, a "degenerating element" had stepped onto the dance floor, and Meimann wasn't having it. Neither was Hall. He agreed that "the majority desire good clean dancing, and those who cannot or do not wish to conduct themselves accordingly, are advised to discretely keep away."[905] With November came the good clean entertainment of the Baldy Strang Concert Party with baritone Baldy Strang, a "Scotch humorist and character artist," at the KP Hall.[906] The Rhondda Welsh Male Glee Singers were also in town.

Late in the year, Hall told readers about a bill to "prevent the employment of Orientals and white girls together."[907] He noted that the CM&S had financed fifty new homes. Canadians were to assist Armenians. General manager Blaylock dedicated the Memorial Hall in a "short address" in which he suggested hiring an athletic instructor for the children.[908] Following his debut at the Caledonian Society, Trail poet Harry Hogg was back with a long poem called "The Trail Football

Team." That was followed by his Armistice Day poem, stating "They died that we might live. What e'er betide/We now must live to prove how well they died."[909] A few editions later, "The Roarin' Game" appeared, making him probably the most frequently published poet in the weekly's history and thus solidifying his status as Trail's poet laureate.

In mid-November, Hall offered this aphorism: "Blessed are the righteous for they do not litter up the front pages."[910] The following month, he appealed to editors to quit cluttering up their front pages with criticisms of the country. He also had words for the striking Fernie coal miners, "who have been on strike for many months and who were on the verge of starvation." They "have repudiated their union and voted to return to work." He allowed the anti-union *Fernie Free Press* to add "when men refuse to listen to reason and common sense, they must pay the penalty."[911] In December, he returned to the issue of mental health, publishing the views of Dr. E.J. Rothwell, a New Westminster Liberal MLA. The doctor wanted to "weed out mentally defective children and place them in special classes by themselves."[912] Apparently, if mental illness could not be treated effectively, it should be hidden.

The year's closing CM&S news was that workers would receive a total payout of $321,000 for the six months ending December 31.[913] "Jed, the Shepherd's Dog," a short story by poet Hogg, appeared the last week of December, telling the sad tale of a sheepdog's love for its deceased master. On the same page, a poem by an unnamed poetaster seemed appropriate for a working-class town during the festive season:

> 'Twas the night before pay-day
> And all through my jeans
> I was searching in vain
> For the price of some beans.
> But nothing was doing.
> The milled edge had quit—
> Not a copper was showing,
> Not even a "jit."
> Forward! Turn forward!
> Oh time in your flight,
> Make it tomorrow just for tonight.[914]

In the final edition of 1924, another hint surfaced to suggest that Hall was seriously considering a switch to daily publication: "Last Friday's issue of the Trail News was the largest weekly printed in British Columbia among all the extra Christmas numbers. The issue contained twenty pages and over 1300 inches of advertising, nearly all of which was local."[915] The numbers were definitely looking good. It had, indeed, been the prosperous year the editor had predicted back in January.

Trail Gets Heaping Doses of Big-City Murder and Mayhem

As we've seen, for two years or more, Elmer D. Hall had been preparing to launch the first-ever daily in the smelter city. He had been quietly growing the readership for its arrival on their doorsteps by subscription or newsboy delivery. Changes were afoot, he had told them the previous autumn, when "the great multiple magazine linotype machine" took "the place of the old hand-set cases" that founding editor "Wrong Font" Thompson "took so much pride in." New promises came with the installation of "the automatic job press[,] which took the place of the little foot-treadle press of his time." The "only one outside Vancouver," Hall boasted.[916]

Hall was technically equipped to launch the daily, but were he and his staff ready to step into the more intense world of daily journalism? No one really knew, but Hall was clear that he did not want his daily to emulate other dailies. "When will the editors of big city newspapers learn the difference between news and history?" he asked.[917] Still, as 1925 pressed on, several big-city stories emerged. A former Trail Hospital nurse was murdered in February, providing an opportunity for the little weekly to test its reportorial mettle. The smallpox scare also lent itself to some energetic newsgathering, with Hall using his editorial page to expose what he called the vaccine profiteers. When the CM&S offered to give the town a hospital, another opportunity knocked. Big-city dailies might have plastered their front pages with lurid headlines on such stories, and Hall was revealing that the *News* could emulate the big press with Hall's editorial biases solidly in evidence.

Instead of reportage, the weekly favoured argument as it pursued its trademark coverage of local events, personalities and political battles. The city had suffered from "petty shoplifting" that Christmas. City council meetings were always fair game. Another old-timer died in January, and another was celebrated with the placing of a memorial window. Mayor Herb Clark was re-elected by acclamation. The Trail Public Library had 500 books in its stacks at their Memorial Hall location.

For several years the *News* had included numerous historical articles especially focused on Egyptian antiquity. It would continue this emphasis in 1925. So would annual coverage of Robbie Burns Day. In

The *Trail Daily Bulletin* building, ca. 1928.
Courtesy Trail Historical Society

late January, Trail's Scots celebrated the 166th anniversary of Burns's birth, and Hall devoted two columns to the Scottish bard's work. Hall reignited his crusade against whisky smuggling, but his pro-prohibition stance was being hindered by liquor profits from government-controlled sales that were filling local coffers. Trail's share was $3,211.38. Still, the crusade called for another poem:

> Jack and Jill went up the hill
> To buy some bootleg liquor.
> Jack went blind,
> And lost his mind,
> And Jill was even siquor.[918]

No one could claim that poetry was the weekly's strong suit, but there was always plenty of it.

His complaint about gambling stayed on target, but he let himself get distracted by a new concern, asking Trailites to "leave your dog outside." Trail women got no respite in the New Year: "The creator intended every woman to be a mother," he advised, "and those who evade this supreme edict must sometime pay the penalty."[919] In his self-appointed role as the city's moral compass, he advocated "the youth of today would be infinitely better off if things did not come so easy for them. Success is attained by going after things, not having them handed to you."[920]

Shockingly, the *Nelson Daily News*, arch-rival of the Trail weekly, praised the *News*'s twenty-pager at Christmastime. Praise also came in poetic form from a reader who wrote gleefully,

> Today is Friday!
> Everybody happy?
> Well, I should say!
> Work done early,
> House all tidy.
> What's the big idea?
> Trail News Day!![921]

Past syndicated columns made space for new ones like Cowichan Lake newspaper editor Hugh Savage's travel articles about Britain. With so many British, Scottish and Irish smelter workers, no Trail newspaper could afford to neglect the old-country traditions. So it was that Charles Conway's "Shrines of Britain's Glory" would be welcomed. Later, "Pick's Paragrams" joined the *News*. Written by "Thos. E. Pickerill," it was to be "A Live Wire Resume of Things in General and Nothing in Particular." American transplants to the smelter workforce still got "This Week" by Arthur Brisbane. "This Is Pat" also continued puzzling some readers. "The Night Shift," a poem by "FAO" was perhaps more appropriate to the setting than usual.

Big silent men that one sees
They work while others sleep.
They're on the job, rain, snow or
freeze,
They climb the hillside steep
And toil on through the darkest night
There's work that must be done.
Ere morning comes they're out of sight
Unnoticed praised by none.[922]

"Old-country football" held its place on the new "Sport News" page. Hockey dominated, with the Trail Tigers intermediate team beating Kimberley to win the Larson Cup and preparing to tackle Endersby for the Coy Cup. But curling nosed onto the page with the thirteenth annual BC bonspiel under way. Trail ski jumper Nels Nelson broke his own world record of 202 feet in Revelstoke, jumping 212 feet. Another Trail man won the seven-mile ski race at the Revelstoke competition. The Churchmen's Football Club was also warming up. Bowling, badminton and basketball seasons opened to much applause. Motoring was classified as a sport, and Trail drivers were warned not to place stickers on their windshields. Also new that spring was a tennis court.

Tom Mix, Buck Jones, House Peters and Rudolph Valentino were constants on the Liberty Theatre marquee, as were Lillian Gish, Mary Pickford, Pola Negri, Gloria Swanson and Norma Talmadge. Thomas Meighan, Richard Barthelmess, Buster Keaton and Harry Carey also joined the Hollywood crowd. Some would survive when the talkies arrived at the Liberty, some would soon be forgotten. In between movies, locally produced shows were available, such as *The Runaway Girl,* with a cast of sixty-six. The Nelson Operatic Society visited town with its light operas. Victor, the champion piano-accordion player, continued to thrill audiences. A column on how to play "Auction Bridge" would arrive in the fall to stimulate the mind.

In February, hospital staff nurse Mildred Neilson, twenty-seven, was murdered, shot to death at the Aldridge Hotel. Her assailant, Patrick Hanley, a First World War veteran, was possibly suffering from a mental illness. The hotel was named after the first CM&S company general manager, Walter H. Aldridge. The owner was former *News* editor W.K. Esling. Local historian Elsie G. Turnbull provided a brief but colourful account of the incident. "Carrying a box of cookies from her mother as an excuse," she noted, "Hanley took out a gun and shot her through the heart, then turned the gun on himself."[923]

The Workmen's Co-operative Committee called on smelter workers and the public to donate to a monument in honour of the nurse.[924] By the end of the month, $1,300 had been collected, with the funds eventually going to purchase a monument and a microscope in her name for the hospital. The Aldridge had been converted to an auxiliary medical ward during the 1918–19 flu pandemic, with an adjoining nurses' residence where Neilson lived. It would eventually become the long-running C.S. Williams Clinic.[925]

Murder could now be added to the police chief's annual report of indecent acts, crimes by "weak minds," liquor offences and loitering by night with intent. The *News* was on top of the story, reporting that the "self-confessed slayer of Mildred Neilson" was improving.[926] In March, the paper reported that the nurse's "slayer [was] bound over." It was an ideal story for a weekly that aspired to become a daily. More was to come in the fall, but the story dropped out of sight for a time, and Hall shifted to other issues.

He returned, for example, to voicing concern about drunkenness in Trail, tracked "Chinamen who have lately joined the illicit traffickers,"[927] and campaigned for an end to the inhumane use of "crippled horses... employed on our streets." He explained that "every day a horse is seen in Trail making his torturous journeys (trotting, generally) attached to a bakery wagon."[928] Of his many civic worries, Hall's most important had to be the quality of local education. A poem expressed his concern:

> You may lead a horse to water,
>   But you cannot make him drink;
> You may send a boy to college,
>   But you cannot make him think.[929]

Hall praised CM&S general manager S.G. Blaylock's non-union Workmen's Co-operative Committee for asking city council to stop the influx of unemployed workers because it has "the resultant effects of drinking, fighting, and begging."[930] He always dutifully reported workplace fatalities. Edward Cartwright, for example, had died after falling from a scaffold. The *News* was still a weekly country newspaper, after all.

Another favourite cause was wayward youth. Hall wondered what parents would say "if they knew what the young people are reading."[931] The plight of young girls was also fertile ground. An article from the *Yeoman Shield* offered Hall some support. "There are upwards of 20,000,000 girls in our country (the US) between the ages of 12 and 21 years," the article said, and "one out of three is alien born—or reared under alien influence."[932] Hall's intent was unclear. Could this be another of his outcries against immigrants?

Back in February, the *News* published an ad promoting "chiropractic adjustments" as "your best armor" against the flu.[933] By early April, Hall had added health to his ever-expanding list of editorial issues. This time it revolved around smallpox and chicken pox. Vaccines had been developed, but critics argued that the vaccine producers were in it for profit. In a letter to the weekly, a "Conscientious Objector" said the health authorities were only "interested in the sale of vaccines."[934] "Small Pox Scaremongers" ran the headline above the letter. It was followed in the same edition by an article with the heading: "Government Acts Too Hastily." The article declared that "the chicken pox scare in Vancouver has done what it has been doing at other places for twenty years—scared people into being vaccinated." For added emphasis, the article described it as being "inoculated with the pus of cow pox."[935]

The campaign escalated when another unsigned article in that edition concluded that "unquestionably an attack of chicken pox is indefinitely preferable to an attack of bovine syphilis artificially induced through vaccination." Hall supported the letters and articles, arguing that "some time the real truth regarding vaccination records of the German army will be given to the world, and when that time comes the pus of cow pox will cease to be the magic wand for extracting elusive dollars from the pockets of the credulous."[936]

On April 10, the health department issued a ruling that appeared on the front page of the *News*. Headlined "Exemption from Vaccination," it assured the public that children would not be vaccinated without parental consent.[937] It also gave objectors an option; they could seek exemption through a magistrate. Hall did not relent in his public campaign. The same day, the *News* published "Is Vaccination a Preventive?", another article against smallpox vaccine.[938] On the editorial page, an Australian doctor argued against vaccination with a confusing array of points.[939]

Then, on April 17, Hall blasted vaccines again, questioning "'vaccination' as a disease preventive."[940] Later in the same edition, this headline spelled out his objection in graphically clear terms: "The Pathological Nature of Vaccine Creates Problem for Thinking Citizens—Origin of Smallpox Vaccine From Bovine Pus Virus Causes Repugnance to Inoculation—England and America Discard Compulsory Vaccination in Light of Results."[941]

The battle returned two weeks later with Hall warning of a "scheme to force compulsory vaccination." His comment was in response to "that recent 'dash to Nome' by dog teams with anti-toxin." Allegedly, it was part of "a big publicity stunt organized by the Vaccine Trust." Hall was quoting from "a startling discovery made by the *New York Evening Graphic*," reprinted in the *News*. Hall claimed that "according to the big-city daily, the Nome 'epidemic' was deliberately engineered, just as the Vancouver 'epidemic' seems to have been engineered for business purposes of the vaccine trust."[942] The anti-vaccination fight had still not abated in early May when the *News* reported that Esquimalt residents faced fines of $100 or six months in prison for refusing to comply with the law regarding smallpox vaccinations.[943] A Seattle daily also struck a blow against vaccines that week.

In mid-May, Hall reported that a counteroffensive had begun: "Since the Trail News commenced its campaign of education against the practice of vaccination as a smallpox preventive the medical trust, one of the strongest combinations, either business or social in the world today, has started a counter propaganda in the Nelson Daily News." He warned readers that "this body of men will not loose its strangle hold on the public without a fight to the death." The bold accusation was followed by some editorial hyperbole: "Sorcery witchcraft, and the supreme authority of the ancient priesthood never ruled with more tyrannical authority than that exercised by the present day medical trust."[944] The smallpox scare was briefly set aside for scarlet fever, which was forcing the continual quarantining of schoolchildren. Hall estimated that the failure to obtain a public health nurse had cost the city $10,000 over four years.

Murder Trial Continued, Vaccination Revolt and "That Chicken Dinner Episode"

The new Sport News section was brimming with items that spring, including a poem by Trail poet laureate H.J.G. Hogg recounting a hockey game between the Trail seniors and intermediates. In what was perhaps the longest poem ever to appear in the weekly, Hogg told the story of how the latter team won. It began this way:

> I don't know who suggested it;
> It was a deep-laid scheme
> To have somebody wine and dine
> The Senior Hockey Team.
> Hank had a craving, so I'm told,
> For hot mashed spuds and chickens,
> And viewed the Intermediates
> With thoughts of easy pickins.[945]

Things ended badly for Hank, as Hogg describes below:

> The Intermediates had the lead,
> And there they meant to camp.
> Poor Harris in the scorer's seat
> Had almost writer's cramp.
> Try as they would the seniors lost;
> The Intermediates beat 'em,
> And now it's up to Hank, et al.
> To buy the chicks and treat 'em.

In a playful mood, the editor inserted a shorter poem on the sports page: "Ashes to ashes,/Dust to dust,/Get away from that parking space/I saw it fust!"[946] Sport News also reported on the "unbeatable" Ernie Arthur, Trail's own professional wrestler, who "has returned to us with notches a-plenty on his hatchet-handle."[947]

A flippant item informed readers that "Adam Did Not Eat An Apple." Hall shared some historical facts about Mongolia, where "discoveries of tombs 2,000 years old have revealed a hoard of valuables exhibiting a high degree of luxury."[948] A Trail man was fined $15 and court costs for a total of $19.50 for "spitting in a lady's face."[949] Another man committed suicide by jumping off the Trail Bridge. An Austro-Hungarian man's decomposed body was found on a sand heap in East Trail. Local gossip suggested that mechanic Donald Martin had run over a boy. In fact, Martin was a Good Samaritan who took the boy, injured in a bike accident, to hospital.

The "Swat the Fly" campaign was underway again with the provincial Department of Agriculture "girding its loins for a terrific battle in the near future.... Thousands will die!"[950] The News also seemed to be winning its long-fought battle for cleaner streets. "No longer will citizens of Trail have to tramp their way through the dust in their nifty two-colored sport shoes;" the *News* affirmed, "no longer will its fair sex mess their skirts with flying particles of terra firma."[951]

More seriously, Ypres Day was sparsely attended, prompting Hall to explain that it was one of "the blackest dates in Canadian military history but to be popular it must be deprived of some of its morbidness."[952] CM&S base wages remained at $3.50 per day for miners and $3.00 per day for muckers. "The cost of living bonus of 50c and the metal bonus, which averaged 87c, were continued and increased the daily wage accordingly."[953]

The courtroom was busy again in May. In one case, a James McEwan was fined $20 for assaulting a young women. He "gets off lightly," the weekly reported.[954] In another case before acting magistrate R.E. Plewman, "although only twelve years of age, Seto How escaped with an admonition and cost of medical attention required by Elsie Stone, a young girl, as a result of his having scratched her, causing blood poisoning." But the big case, the nurse murder trial, also returned to the docket and the front page when Patrick Hanley pleaded not guilty. He had sufficiently recovered to stand trial for murder after shooting himself immediately after killing nurse Mildred Neilson.

Among the trial exhibits placed before Mr. Justice Murphy were "a pair of corsets stained with blood, pierced through with a bullet, the lead from the bullet fired through the nurse's body, and interior photographs of the nurse's home in which the killing took place."[955] For the first time in years, the weekly had a real live story of a crime of passion to report. But it was short-lived, for the trial was remanded to the fall when it would be re-heard due to a "mistake."[956] Readers would have to wait for the final outcome.

The vaccination fight was revived by another anti-vaccination letter from "An Outsider," who was against the "medical men who want to get the public under their thumb."[957] Another article cited "the perils of vaccination."[958] The fight seemed to generate *News* interest in other aspects of health care. Fitting well with Hall's moralistic crusades, a doctor said too much tobacco and liquor would make you go blind. A Chicago doctor declared that "Americanitis"—the hustle and bustle of life—has caused 240,000 deaths.[959] Still another claimed "crossworditis, an ultra-modern ill, is fast taking the place of society's pet ailment, appendicitis."[960] It could get silly at times.

The jocularity ended when an article by "J. Bates, BA," added more ferocity to the vaccine debate: "It is repugnant to our idea of God, and of nature, to think that the only way we can render ourselves immune to disease is to resort to such a despicable practice as torturing one of the lower animals and injecting into our blood the filth from its diseased body."[961]

In June, another reprint from the *Vancouver Tribune* suggested more foul play by the medical trust. In July, a letter from Bernard MacFadden expressed fear that vaccination meant going back "to the time of witchcraft." He added, "at the same time[,] people were burned at the stake, and the authorities were just as sure that they were public enemies as the vaccination fanatics are now sure that people should be vaccinated at so much per head for the financial benefit of the vaccine trust."[962]

Still another article warned about serum and vaccine manufacturers who were unreliable.[963] In late August, another anti-vaccinationist wrote "if the departments and the Press persist in ignoring and suppressing the case against vaccination until there is another explosion, the result may possibly be that vaccination will be made a crime."[964]

Not since the nurse murder trial had the *News* been sent such a scintillating news story, one with legs. It took another health issue to move an angry public off its concerns about vaccination. It had to do with a new hospital. Apparently, the $75,000 building was to be a CM&S company gift to the city to be built on CM&S land. Then things changed. Blaylock had decided that the new hospital should be built in Tadanac, the newly created municipality situated on company land. Trail as the location was off the table.[965]

Apparently several citizens were unhappy with the original choice of CM&S property, fearing higher noise levels, and they complained. Mayor Herb Clark was not pleased: "I sincerely trust that those who have been making so much ado about the noises, etc., which makes the site chosen by the council so undesirable, will have ample time (when climbing the golden stairs on their way to visit some sick friend) to consider the wisdom of looking a gift horse in the mouth."[966]

Hall jumped on the bandwagon. First they lost the federal building. Now the hospital had been lost: "Why? Because interested parties, backed by a small coterie of knockers, have made life a burden to the donors, and in all likelihood the hospital will be constructed at Tadanac." Then he opened up both barrels: "It seems a pity that the decent people of Trail should be deprived of this fine building because of the greed, avarice, and petty jealousy, of a set of individuals who have outlived their usefulness to this community and who seem determined, at whatever cost, to turn even this charitable offer into one of profit to themselves."[967] Who were these knockers? Hall never told his readers. Of course, they knew who they were. Perhaps most readers did as well.

The workers' committee, in an action that had rarely if ever happened, seemed to go against Blaylock when it endorsed a city council proposal to build the hospital in a downtown location. The resolution read as follows: "Now, therefore, be it resolved that Mr. Blaylock be asked to reconsider the matter and have the hospital built on the site chosen by the city council where, it is believed, it would best serve the interests of the smelter employees and public."[968] The motion carried and the hospital was built in Trail as the Trail-Tadanac Hospital.

Hall may have been feeling the need to pump up his courage for the creation of a daily when the *News* carried several items on newspaper editors. He wrote that "the fearless newspaper is admired and respected by the man who stops to think, but with many even a slight jolt through the local press causes a wound that creates a thirst for vengeance, and a desire to punish the editor." He was so emboldened as to remark that "when a local paper takes a firm stand on a question of public concern men will admire and applaud as long as the other fellow gets hit, but when it does not agree with their pet theories they are ready to fight and are soon after the editor's scalp."[969]

Later, an item appeared that praised the country weekly. Writer Edward N. Teall wrote that the local paper was "an institution, the mouthpiece of democracy, the moulder and reflection of public opinion, the educator of the masses, the scripture searched by the multitudes, the guiding star of the provinces, the articulation of the yearnings of the non[-]effete, the Bible of the commonality, the wellspring of the great silent vote."[970] It was a tall order for a daily, never mind a weekly.

Columnist Thomas Pickerill chimed in with his view of the value of "The Home Newspaper," calling it "the echo of the community's voice, a spokesman of the community's mind, a reflection of the community's vision, a champion of the community's rights, and a direct avenue for the community's progress."[971] Hall added his two bits worth with this humorous account: "An editor once kept track of his profits and losses during the year, and gives an invoice of his business diary at the end of 12 months of ups and downs in the following manner: Been broke 361 times, praised the public 89 times, told lies 720 times, missed prayer meeting 52 times, been roasted 431 times, roasted others 52 times, washed office towel 3 times, missed meals 0, mistaken for preacher 11 times, mistaken for capitalist 0, got whipped 8 times, whipped others 0, cash on hand at beginning $1.47, cash on hand at ending 15c."[972]

Boasting a circulation of 1,250 "bona fide paid subscribers," Hall must have assumed he was doing something right.[973] Certainly he could claim he had been covering local affairs thoroughly. One example was the front-page obituary for "Trail's oldest prospector," Edward Negent, also known as Johnny Troy.[974] After all, Trail's roots were buried with those pioneer prospectors. The source of the town's wealth, the CM&S, was featured that summer when the Sullivan Mine was listed as "the world's premier lead-zinc-silver producer."[975] Three more teachers resigned before the fall term began, and Hall showed the concern he often did for the cause of developing a better education system.

The weekly never strayed far from its moral quest. Hall paid tribute to William Jennings Bryan, one of the great US moralizers, who died suddenly. In keeping with another favourite lecturing topic, the editor lamented that "women are coming more and more to rebel against the drudgery of the kitchen sink." He wanted them to stay at home, "for, after all, there is 'no place like home,' and being queen in your own kitchen and mother to your own babies beats all the careers ever mapped out."[976] However, there was one place that some women could not enter. New liquor restrictions stressed that "undesirable women must not be allowed to patronize beer parlors."[977] Hall saluted the measure. A case of failed child support also won coverage when a man was ordered to pay $35 a month under the Deserted Wives Maintenance Act.[978]

Perhaps Hall was pondering the future when he wrote, "if you think publishing a newspaper is an independent profession remember that the results of a newspaper's efforts are placed squarely before its readers and in a larger sense before the world. There is nothing a newspaper can hide.... Its work is an open book. It is here in black and white for your approval."[979] A month later, Hall was elected to the executive of the BC Press Association, perhaps another sign of his future intent.[980]

Also in September, the *News* reported that Canada had more than a million phones in 1924, the Boy Scouts were organizing a Trail troop, the annual Fruit Fair was "one of the best in local history," and a "popular" woman drowned in the Columbia.[981] Perhaps the latter was partly what stirred Hall to agitate for a public swimming pool. Like the weekly, Hall's daily would no doubt continue to bring readers news of the ancient world. Rome and Egypt were a regular focus. In one report, readers learned that a mastodon tooth weighed four pounds.[982] Other news continued to cover the anti-vaccination movement, although Malta Fever, infantile paralysis (polio) and sleeping sickness were also local health concerns. One item advised readers not to squeeze blackheads, but to dissolve them in peroxide.

Hall continued his anti-Asian campaign with an angry editorial following the release of seventeen Chinese at Vancouver. Apparently they had been charged with drug peddling. "Steal a loaf of bread and get five years and the lash," he chided, "but rich Oriental criminals can despoil the youth of the land with impunity, simply by hiring a smart lawyer to provide a convenient technicality."[983] The city dailies had long catered to anti-Asian racism, so Hall probably saw it as part of the editorial mandate of his new daily.

October was carnival time in the smelter city, and "Conklin & Garrett's All Canadian Shows" featured "Fremmini's Temple of Mystery," giving the kids the time of their lives. Trail got a new funeral parlour that fall. CM&S opened a new zinc plant with a big stack. Election time was around the corner, and Hall took a shot at "the party press" for its attempts to stampede the voters. "Some of our hair-brained editors" offered "cheap mouthings and wild antics" that reminded Hall of "a medicine man taking a fall out of an evil spirit."[984] Such rants might not have pleased his fellow executive members at the press association.

Readers also got a hint of what was to come. "The News has always endeavoured to be frank and fair in its dealing with the public," Hall wrote. "The very name 'newspaper' suggests at once a sort of 'open diplomacy' with its friends, its enemies and its neutrals. No newspaper can expect to reach its highest destiny and at the same time sidetrack, white-wash, back slide, or sideswipe an issue that needs pressing or a cause that deserves to be championed."[985] Hall then called on the public to show co-operation and understanding. On the eve of the federal election campaign, Hall noted that W.K. Esling was in the running. Then he offered a poem to stimulate readers.

> Since Mr. Meighan and Mr. King
> > Have joined in verbal battle,
> Talking of almost everything
> > Like children in their prattle—
> 'Tis time that we who have the vote
> > Should of our country's ills take note
> Before we use 'em.[986]

He also informed readers that the weekly would appear Thursday instead of Friday "to better serve merchants and the public." To the astute reader, it was a subtle hint that bigger changes were afoot. To advertisers, it meant a rate increase to 30 cents per column inch. Hall apologized, "but with 1550 circulation we find we can no longer carry the overhead expense at the old rate."[987]

Over on the editorial page, Hall celebrated the *News*'s thirtieth birthday, "making it one of the oldest continuously published weeklies in the province."[988] On the news pages that autumn, another big-city story occupied Hall when the Dominion, St. Elmo and Wellington Hotels on Victoria Street went up in flames. These were some of Trail's oldest buildings—the Wellington had been built in 1896—and the *News* hastened to report the loss. "Prospectors and miners, capitalists and smeltermen have come and gone, sharing shelter in the Dominion Hotel, studying its menu and wine lists," the *News* writer lamented. "In its passing went one of the landmarks of Trail."[989]

In late October, Patrick Hanley's second trial for the murder of nurse Neilson began in Nelson. Earlier, some observers had claimed Hanley, the district manager of the Monarch Life Insurance Company, had been gassed during the war, resulting in mental illness. The *Rossland Miner* described him as "a deranged war veteran."[990] Two jurists stated that he was insane, the *News* reported. But that fall he seemed "in better health."

The twelve-person jury heard new evidence from the prosecution to suggest that Hanley felt he "had been deeply wronged by a woman."[991] Surprisingly, Hall never wrote an editorial about the trial nor did the paper cover the end result, which it predicted would be of short duration. It was a curious editorial decision, given the news value of such a story. Historian Frances Welwood, who described the murder and subsequent trials in detail, noted that the *News* covered the story as best it could, but "citizens of the Kootenay relied on the *Nelson Daily News* for up-to-date coverage of the trial."[992]

Decades later, the *Trail Daily Times*, the daily that would grow from the weekly *News*, provided a flashback that focused on the details of both the murder and the trials. "There were no eye witnesses," the story said, "so no one will ever really know what transpired between the two of them that Friday morning before Hanley shot the nurse, then himself."[993] Again, it was surprising that the paper's weekly predecessor had chosen not to give readers an explanation for what was clearly an attempted murder-suicide.

As it happened, Hanley survived, recovered, was subsequently tried a third time, found guilty and sentenced to hang. His sentence was commuted to life imprisonment even though "the town was shocked by this cold-hearted act and such a sudden and brutal demise of a caring young nurse," as the modern-day account noted. The nurse's body was shipped to the coast where it was interred at the Ocean View Burial Park in Burnaby. The monument Trail citizens had purchased in her memory stands there today.

Finally, in the third week of October, Hall told readers to look for a small service sheet called *The Daily Bulletin* from November 2 on. "It has been openly stated that Trail needs a daily paper," he explained. "By starting small we can determine just what is meant be a daily newspaper.... If it should, perchance, grow, well and good. If it does not, it can be credited with establishing the fact that there is no need for any other paper than the 12-page weekly you now have."[994] Only 700 copies would be distributed free each day to subscribers. Hall alerted merchants that "an advertising solicitor will probably call upon you sometime within the next few days. He will not be a very persistent individual, as the launching of this sheet is purely experimental."[995]

A week after the announcement, Hall again puzzled readers when he issued a stinging critique of the daily press: "Turning from the city newspapers to the small town exchanges that come to the editor's desk is like stepping from the slums, full of vile, into an old-fashioned garden sweet with lavender and thyme and the scent of perennial flowers." But surely the *Bulletin* was heading in that same direction? If so, would its pages be any different from those of "many of the big dailies [whose pages] are so full of murder, thievery, immorality and selfishness that the better news is obscured by these glaring, shatterings of the decalogue."[996]

Hall's readers might agree that "one puts the papers aside with a feeling of depression and heartache that the world is so full of terrible and unhappy things. Then picking up the papers that record the happenings of the little cities around Trail one gains renewed faith in life."[997] And yet there was reason to suspect that the *Bulletin* might offer some of those same terrible and unhappy things.

By November, the Ku Klux Klan was developing a following in BC and the provincial government had declared war on "this seditious movement."[998] American columnist Arthur Brisbane used his space to challenge the "alleged authority of the grand wizard... to fight Catholic organizations, the Knights of Columbus, making friends of negroes and Jews, hitherto included among the enemies of the Klan, to strengthen their anti-Catholic fight."[999] Hall had also declared war, but it was not on the KKK. His enemy was the *Nelson Daily News*, which, he argued, had a "mad desire to create campaign thunder in the interests of its party owner."[1000]

Late in the month and into December, the *News* reported three executions, three deaths by fire, the death of the king of Siam, a sick-crazed Spaniard cutting the throat of a Vancouver nurse with a razor, a Prince Rupert man killed by an accidental gunshot and a Trail police raid on the Palace Hotel acting on a gambling tip. It seemed to smack of yellow journalism, but Hall had earlier expressed another view: "The newspaper that lives for itself alone has not reached the highest aim of living," he wrote. "It should go forth each week bringing joy and gladness to every home."[1001]

On December 3, the paper changed to a larger column width for its main news items and headlines gravitated toward the more sensational. Hall also hired a new circulation director, so there was clear evidence that the paper was moving forward on a sound business footing. Although Hall stated "it is our intention to make the Trail Daily Bulletin one of the best daily papers in the district," there was no new evidence to reveal that editorial improvements were forthcoming.

On December 10, the new front-page banner read "The Trail Daily Bulletin and The Trail News." Murder and mayhem graced the first front page. It would seem that the editor was about to steer the *News* into the world of sensational journalism under the *Trail Daily Bulletin* banner. "Five Men Killed, Twelve Injured in Coal Gas Explosion in Mine Near Birmingham, Alabama," read one headline. "Sheriff and Deputy Wounded and Beaten by Desperate Prisoners" read another. Two others screamed of crime and war: "Aged Latharios [*sic*] Stage Mortal Combat Over Girl of 34—One Succumbs" and "Session of League of Nations Hears of Various Atrocities Committed by Turkish Soldiers on Mosul Frontier." Flipping to page 8, readers could learn that northern China was on the eve of two major battles and "Five Convicts Escape from Prison Farm at Houston—Take Guards."

The rest of that day's paper offered much of the same news as did the weekly. The guest columns did not change nor did the sports coverage. The ads were as thick as ever. Clearly the business community liked what it saw and would continue to support the Trail paper as a daily. Hall, and presumably J.J. Clarke, his original co-owner, renamed the *News* the *Trail Daily Bulletin* on December 11, 1925.

After thirty years of serving the smelter city, Trail's pioneer weekly had gone to the newspaper "boneyard." Eventually, the "Trail Bull," as some called it, would be replaced by the *Trail Daily Times*, which was still publishing, although only twice weekly, in 2022. Trail never did grow to be a big city, but it can boast that its newspaper is one of the oldest continuously published in the province. "Wrong Font" Thompson and all the printer's devils that succeeded him would have been proud.

9–What Became of Trail's Pioneer Printer's Devils?

"Where men have gathered together I am. And until the last man has gone to the great beyond, I shall be. I am the papyrus of time. I am the newspaper."[1002]

Trail's pioneer printer's devils may not have seen themselves as the "papyrus of time," but they all endured and moved on to other newspapers. Each of the preceding chapters ends when the specific editor either sells the Trail newspaper or assigns the editing to others. But the newspaper careers of each editor-publisher helped them to find new soil for their fertile minds and the business acumen acquired from working on the *Trail Creek News* and *Trail News*.

Many of them went on to edit other country weeklies. Some went to dailies. One became a politician. They all continued to influence their communities in significant ways, getting elected to school boards, press associations, service clubs and other local organizations. Parts of their post-*News* lives are covered below.

William Fentress Thompson

Toward the end of the 1890s, "Wrong Font" Thompson, spouse Martha and stepson Loss Bernard, had come and gone from Glenora, BC, where they started the *Glenora News*. After that, the three of them seem to have gone their separate ways. In 1902, Thompson, who migrated and stayed in Alaska, married Maude Stone, a young woman from a successful Alaskan mining family.[1003] The marriage lasted until at least 1906. In 1911, "he married Nell Mulrooney, sister of Belinda Mulrooney, the Klondike hotel proprietress who made a fortune through lucky investments," Thompson biographer Paul Solka Jr. writes. She was known as "The Countess," Bernard told Solka, and she eventually entered the banking business. Thompson had three children with Nell and was "completely devoted to his wife and his children."[1004]

When the *Glenora News* soon folded, Thompson helped set up the *Dawson Daily News*. He then established the *Yukon Sun* and bragged that the poet Robert Service "sent his first poems outside for review, through *The Sun* office."[1005] By 1904, perhaps reminiscent of his earlier run-ins with the law, he was caught up in a libel suit over a political cartoon. He apparently won the case, but left Dawson City for Fairbanks in 1905.

With financial backing from a group of Fairbanks investors, he started the *Tanana Miner* in a "roughneck camp... where is gathered the flotsam of the Sea of Chance, things are just what they seem—or the majority of the population is wise to the fact that they are not."[1006] It was Thompson's first editorial in his new surroundings far from Trail Creek and yet perhaps the towns were not so dissimilar. In 1909, he would begin editing the *Fairbanks Daily News-Miner*, founded as a weekly in 1903. It was the only daily in the Alaskan interior and he continued in that role for the next seventeen years.[1007]

By one account, Thompson had a reputation as "likable, attractive to both men and women."[1008] The account added that "he liked to drink, and he never worried about money.... He was dapper, with a Vandyke beard, and was always immaculately dressed, head back and shoulders squared. He limped and carried a cane because of a poorly healed broken leg from a train accident. He had a world of friends, and few enemies."[1009]

On January 4, 1926, Trail's first newspaper editor died of pneumonia in Fairbanks at sixty-two years old.[1010] Obituary notices hailed him as a "pioneer Alaska newspaperman."[1011] He was "a fighter, a soldier of fortune with a pen in his hand," wrote *News-Miner* colleague A.H. Nordale. "He had no fear and he knew no quarter—his battlefields were wherever chance or fate landed him."[1012] Judge Cecil Clegg remembered him as a "frontiersman" who had "the faith, the hope, the energy and persistence of the true pioneer."[1013]

W.F. Thompson in Alaska where he edited newspapers until he retired, ca. 1920s. Courtesy Paul Solka Jr., *Adventures in Alaskan Journalism Since 1903*

Martha Lavinia Thompson

Perhaps Martha Thompson had finally had enough of "Wandering Foot" Thompson, as he once called himself, for she apparently divorced him while they were in the North. Two years after Billy Esling bought the *Trail Creek News* in 1898, Martha Thompson was back in Rossland permanently. She lived with her stepson and her father, Judge Caton.[1014] She worked as a printer at the *Rossland Evening Record* and married Alfred Thomas Collis, also a *Record* printer. Collis was a member of the Spokane Typographical Union and later became publisher of the *Rossland Evening World*, the daily owned by the Western Federation of Miners.

Her Trail friends remember Martha as "quite capable of editing two newspapers herself," wrote local historian Elsie G. Turnbull.[1015] She was an active member of the lodges of the Eastern Star, Pythian Sisters, and the

Martha Thompson with husband Robert Leete, ca. 1877. Courtesy Robbin Roots Blog

Maccabees. At her death on September 6, 1923, the *Rossland Miner* said "she was numbered among the pioneer matrons of this city, having resided here for over twenty-five years." She was fifty-nine years old.[1016] The *Trail News* also saluted her as "one of the best known residents of the district."[1017]

William Kemble Esling

After leaving the *News* managing to A.R. Babington, Billy Esling bought the daily *Rossland Miner* and struggled to keep it alive. The paper once had a reputation as pro-worker, an asset in a pro-labour town. But when the Le Roi Company, a mining conglomerate, bought the daily from copper king F. Augustus Heinze in 1901, it turned "virulently anti-union," according to local historians Rosa Jordan and Derek Choukalos. "Organized labour was portrayed as dangerous and destructive to the economy," they noted, "and union members were repeatedly referred to as 'agitators'."[1018] That included the unionized newsboys that delivered the paper.

When Esling bought the paper in 1905, he "immediately adopted a more conciliatory tone," using "humanitarian prose," said Jordan and Choukalos. As local historian Ron Shearer has suggested, it was a turn away from the "ultra-conservative" tone he had taken in late 1899 and 1900 when he owned the *Rossland Record*.[1019] Despite a kindlier editorial approach toward unions, "in the summer of 1911, the *Miner* suspended publication," Jordan and Choukalos wrote. "According to its owner, Billy Esling, 'of 78 business and professional men in the city, just 20 are represented in the Miner. Until there is sufficient advertising to meet the payroll this paper will not resume publication'."[1020] Rosslanders raised the money to save the paper, and it resumed publishing two months later, but the struggle went on interminably.

Esling finally sold the *Miner* in 1915, declaring that failing eyesight no longer permitted him to work as a journalist. For the next five years, he occupied himself with constructing several buildings in Rossland and Trail, becoming "one of the largest property owners in the two cities," including several business properties.[1021] In 1921, Esling was elected to the BC legislature as the Conservative candidate representing Rossland. In 1925, he won the Kootenay West seat and went to Ottawa, serving as the local Member of Parliament for the next twenty years.

For many, Billy Esling left a sterling legacy. Naming a local park and a street after him reveals his popularity with the public as do his multiple wins at the ballot box. During the 1930 election, W.A. Elletson, the man who had bought the *Miner* from Esling years before, noted that he had "employed more men in constructing and improving buildings in Rossland and Trail than any half dozen individuals in either city." For some, he was Rossland's "Gentleman Journalist."[1022] Others had a different view.

While he may have been "attuned to the needs of ordinary people," as Jordan and Choukalos maintain, it did not extend to the Chinese and Doukhobors, whom he wanted excluded from Canada.[1023] For all his good works, including his promotion of food sustainability, fights against the evils of deforestation, support for cleaner streets, and better roads to local mines, his vocal stance against the minorities of the district marred his legacy in later years. As John George Diefenbaker, Canada's thirteenth prime minister, put it, "Little Billy loved all mankind except Doukhobors."[1024]

For the editors of *Trail of Memories*, a compendium of family histories in Trail, "Esling was known for his courtesy, kindliness, and personal interest in people." The book's editors add "he was well known and well loved: a well respected member of the Trail-Rossland community."[1025] To others, Esling's apparent lack of interest in the region's unions and workers' institutions wrought somewhat less kindly memories, although evidence shows he urged better compensation for injured workers and pushed for an eight-hour day for all mine workers.[1026]

During his twenty years as the MP for Kootenay West, Esling delivered 113 speeches, questions, or points of order in the House of Commons, covering such topics as settlement on Crown land, old age pensions, immigration, unemployment, labour, trade, the Criminal Code, copyright law, income tax, railways, mines, national security, the Excess Profits Act, family allowances, and strawberry prices.[1027] His final victory in the House of Commons was to win low-cost hearing devices for Canadians.[1028] He maintained his membership in several fraternal lodges, including the Freemasons. He was an Anglican with a charitable bent. When his sister died, he set up the Mary Esling Davidson fund for needy children with defective vision.

Esling suffered from colorectal carcinoma, leading to his death on December 2, 1946.[1029] Herbert "Bert" Herridge of the Co-operative Commonwealth Federation (CCF) had won his vacated seat in the 1945 election. On Esling's death, the *Trail Daily Times* proposed renaming a local mountain after him. His "many unpretentious benefactions, his kindly ways, his thoughtfulness, his earnestness, his philosophies, and his courage made for true greatness," the editor wrote. "His was the kind of leadership men held dear."[1030] An Ottawa-based journalist wrote: "He's a little wisp of a man,… the smallest man in the Commons, with the biggest heart."[1031] To many in the smelter city, it was a fitting epitaph for the second editor of the *Trail Creek News*.

Arthur Richard Babington

Trail's third pioneer editor, Arthur Richard Babington, left the smelter city after serving as the *Trail News* manager from 1907 to 1914. He seems to have departed as quietly as he came, and he left a quiet imprint on the social life of the community. Mayor F.E. Dockerill saluted him at a farewell dinner at the Arlington Hotel, saying the *News* manager "had worked so amiably and conscientiously amongst them for the past ten years."[1032]

A year after he was hired to manage the *News*, Babington married British-born Ethel Mary Freeman in Nelson in 1908. The couple had two, possibly three, children during their stay in the Kootenays. A daughter was stillborn, then came a son, Dickie, who died at two years old in 1916. The birthdate of their daughter Francis is not available, so she may also have been born in the Kootenays.

In 1914, the Babingtons left Trail to live in Melfort, Saskatchewan. The *Melfort*

Moon was up for sale that year, and Babington was keen to own and edit his own weekly newspaper. After seven years of working under Esling, it must have been a dream come true to be in charge, with editorial policy, appearance, and marketing solely under his control.

The *Moon* was established in 1903 and listed in *N. W. Ayer & Son's American Newspaper Annual and Directory* for 1916. In his first edition published on July 8, 1914, he called himself "Proprietor" in the masthead, but soon listed himself as editor and publisher. The masthead stated that it was "A Progressive Independent Newspaper." An advertising rate card issued many years later claimed a gross circulation of 1,500, with 700 in Melfort itself.[1033]

Steady news coverage in the *Moon* shifted from smelter and mine concerns to farming and irrigation challenges, but much of the content was similar to that in the *Trail News*. There were the "Local Briefs" and a plethora of ads for everything from hotels, banks and building companies to Clark's Plum Pudding, Dr. Chase's Nerve Food and a compound for "women weak and nervous."[1034] Cures for terminal diseases sat beside cure-all claims from Zam-Buk, the skin food. Like the *News*, real estate advertising remained a constant. So did the boilerplate articles that filled the *News* pages.

Babington presented a clear editorial policy when he stated, "the *Moon* has no use for asinine toadying and shame, and any time it feels unequal to honest, independent opinion, this great family journal will put up the shutters and to the war."[1035] Those fighting words were never seen in Babington's *News*. Another key difference between the two papers was length; the *Moon* doubled and sometimes tripled Babington's news hole and advertising space to eight pages or more. It was also a much better looking paper and was better organized, with varying headline sizes and styles. Still another difference was the regular appearance of letters to the editor.

An initial foray into the pages of the *Moon* suggests that Babington had thrown off his editorial shackles and was eager to share his opinions with his new readership. A perusal of archival fonds further suggests that he was a serious practitioner of the newspaper trade. For example, he kept a copy of a 1928 pamphlet called *Small-Town Papers* that contained twenty-seven pages of advice in the form of a short memoir. Perhaps more important is another of his booklets called *Newspaper Is Town Building*, offering "pointers newspapers should be familiar with."[1036]

Like Esling in Trail and Rossland, Babington was eager to be part of civic life in his new city. To that end, he served several terms as a Melfort town councillor and was mayor in 1931–1932. He also served as chair of the waterworks committee when the new dam was built in 1930. He was president of the Melfort Board of Trade, and, much like in Trail, he became a member of the high school board, where he was chair for twelve years. In addition, he was a member of the Agricultural Society, a Freemason (as he had been in Trail along with Esling), and a Shriner. Unlike Esling, a life-long Conservative, he was president of the Melfort Federal Liberal Association, secretary of the provincial association, and president of the local association.[1037] In these ways Babington left his mark on Melfort. The city showed its appreciation by naming a street Babington Avenue.

Babington stayed at the helm of the *Moon* through the First World War, the Great Depression, and the onset of the Second World War and might have stayed longer but for a tragic incident. Death came unexpectedly, the *Moon* obituary reported, when Babington drove off the road and into a ravine while on the way to a family outing at a local park. He died of heart failure on August 11, 1940.[1038]

James Joseph Clarke

J.J. Clarke helped steer the *News* to daily status, but eventually left the smelter city for the coast where he worked as a compositor on several Vancouver dailies. He ended his career as a compositor with the *North Shore Press*. He lived the rest of his life in Lynn Valley where he enjoyed gardening.[1039] Clarke never gave up the saxophone, playing for seven years with the Vancouver Park Board Band. For half a century, he was a member of the International Typographical Union in Canada and Britain. He died at seventy years old on April 25, 1943.

Walter Beach Willcox

W.B. Willcox returned to Spokane to re-establish himself at the Franklin Printing Company.[1040] He soon engaged in "community affairs and tourist promotion work with the publicity touring bureau of the Chamber of Commerce."[1041] After his return, he bought the Keystone Printing Company and ran it until he retired in 1937. The year before, the *Spokane Chronicle* commemorated his role as its managing editor during the Great Spokane fire of 1889.

Willcox recalled in detail the experience of preparing an account of the fire on a makeshift table under an umbrella and issuing the paper in spite of the fire destroying the newspaper plant. A photograph of Willcox, then seventy-five, sitting at a table near a tent marked "Chronicle Office" accompanied his account.

He died in New Orleans on September 22, 1945, having suffered from a coronary obstruction. He was eighty-three years old.[1042] His short tenure at the *Trail News* was mentioned only in passing in the obituaries.

Elmer D. Hall

Some Trailites considered Elmer D. Hall a worker's friend, others did not. Those who toiled at the Trail smelter read his newspaper from front to back, but his support for their unions was not always evident in his years at the helm of the *Trail News*. In fact, as we have seen, he was a vocal critic of radical organizations such as the Industrial Workers of the World (IWW) and the One Big Union (OBU). Hall vigorously opposed the OBU at the time, but later allowed unions to hire his print shop to "communicate the feelings and ideas of the people."[1043]

On April 23, 1928, Hall sold the *Trail Daily Bulletin* to *Nelson Daily News* owner Howard Green and it became the *Trail Times*. A young *Nelson Daily News* man named William Curran became editor. On December 3, 1931, the paper was renamed the *Trail Daily Times*, with Curran serving as its editor until the early 1950s. A British editor named Dennis Williams then replaced him.

Trail Daily Times editor William Curran. Courtesy Trail Historical Society

In the late 1930s, Hall launched the *Trail Daily Ad-News* in direct competition with the *Times*. Due to an absence of extant editions—BC Archives has only two issues on microfilm: May 28 and June 4, 1940—historians have only anecdotal evidence of the role it played. We know, for example, that when smelter workers were organizing Local 480 of the International Union of Mine, Mill and Smelter Workers, an affiliate of the Congress of Industrial Unions (CIO), Hall was ready to assist the union with the *Ad-News*. He "had been blacklisted earlier by the CM&S for union organizing," recalled Local 480 president Al King, "so he was willing to help us out."[1044] But that wasn't the only thing that endeared him to the union.

First, "with the publishing of his liberal editorials he was a free thinking protagonist to Selwyn Blaylock of Cominco's hierarchy."[1045] He was also willing to challenge *Times* editor Curran. Local 480's *Commentator* viewed the *Times* as a pro-company organ and workers often agreed. One letter writer called the Hall daily a "fearless, caustic and unrelenting opposition" to the CM&S Company's "propaganda outlets."[1046]

In 1939, the Hall paper celebrated the arrival of a Mine-Mill newspaper called the *Union Bulletin* along with a direct attack on Blaylock's co-operative committee system. On September 5, 1939, the *Ad-News* noted: "The Union Bulletin... was distributed throughout the city last night. Its general tone was reminiscent of the days when men made their wage contracts unhampered by 'happy family' ideas and 'big dividends'."[1047]

Hall's son Elmer (Bunny) Hall Jr., told Craig Barnsley his father had a "free hand at the paper." On the other hand, smelter workers thought the company "had a good deal of control over the Times."[1048] In February 1939, a *Times* editorial charged that "the CIO is after its scalp." Hall disagreed: "While we hold no particular brief for the CIO, we cannot believe our contemporary's claims are made in good faith. It appears to be but a puny effort to distort public opinion and appear in the role of champion of the people's rights when, as a matter of fact, their chief concern is the welfare of big business."[1049]

The rivalry between the *Times* and *Ad-News*, never friendly, turned nasty in late 1939 when Hall was charged with libeling Curran. Hall had alleged that Curran, as Red Cross publicity manager, showed favouritism in parcelling out paid wartime advertising. Simply stated, the *Times* was allegedly getting it and the *Ad-News* was not.

The headline-grabbing court case ended in early May 1940 with Hall winning a stay of proceedings, but the trial had raised issues about his loyalties to the war effort and to the community. Not least, it indirectly sought to discredit him for his CIO connections and his union-supporting background. With the Hall libel case over, the *Times* returned to its critical stance against the CIO.

Hall remarried twice after Mabel Mrkvicka's death, first to Sarah M. Beckerton in October 1939 in Colville, Washington, and then to Pearl Mrkvicka, Mabel's younger sister, on January 18, 1959. He died February 24, 1960, in Southgate, California, at age eighty-four. Hall Printing Company, which he founded in 1920, continues to do job printing for local unions and other clients.

ε

The *Times* continues to serve Trail readers albeit as a twice-weekly paper appearing Tuesdays and Thursdays. Under owner Black Press Media, it has diminished its news and editorial content while continuing to build advertising. Editorial staffing has been minimized, with a single editor doubling as a news reporter and one sports reporter. Like many small newspapers, the owner is looking for ways to maximize profit in a marketplace filled with other reading options. Clearly, the days of the feisty printer's devils that once ran the smelter city's lively weekly newspaper are long gone.

Conclusion

The Fading Tradition of BC's Country Editors

The era of weekly country newspapers is quickly dying across North America. As the CBS program *60 Minutes* noted in February 2022, "for two decades now, owing largely to the loss of advertising revenue to Facebook and Google, fewer and fewer Americans get their news, comics and sports from all those Gazettes and Tribunes and Journals." The program pointed to a corporate "vulture, bleeding newspapers dry." The reporter then asked, "to what extent does democracy shrink with it?"[1050] *60 Minutes* was referring to small city dailies, but much of what was said applies to the country weeklies represented here by the *Trail News*.

In Canada, by the end of 2018, 189 of this tough breed of news sheets had succumbed to the trials and tribulations of the twenty-first century.[1051] From 2019–2020, dozens more fell victim to the Internet, social media, the high cost of production, and the predatory nature of the big media chains.[1052] A fast disappearing breed indeed. "More than 330 local outlets in hundreds of communities have shut since 2008, a death rapidly escalated by Covid-19," CBC reporter Haydn Watters noted in January 2022. "Each time a radio or TV station, newspaper, or online site closes, important untold stories are lost, erasing the history, current events, and local lore in small-town Canada."[1053]

Still, perhaps a lingering scent of musty old ink reminds us of how the little pioneer paper we've just met once rallied its readers to many causes and joined them as they rooted for the home team. No loss, some might say. These little ink-stained sheets had their day, bringing local stories to small-town homes and providing local businesses with an advertising vehicle that reached out to the buying public. As a reporter in the *60 Minutes* broadcast explained, these institutions "are all important elements about holding people together." As the *60 Minutes* item said, "Anyone could walk through the front door and say, 'I need to talk to a reporter. My sewer is backing up and the township isn't doing anything about it. Can you do something?'" Often the paper, including the *Trail News*, did try to do something, as illustrated in *Printer's Devils*.

For more than a century, papers called the *Nugget*, *Times*, *News*, *Record*, *Miner*, *Ledge* and many other names represented those communities. Such papers were a source of news about such things as Little League baseball scores, seniors' hockey games and raucous debates at city hall. Business and the stock market were well represented; so was the Board of Trade and the Chamber of Commerce. As we've seen, service clubs, such as the Elks, Eagles, Moose, Pythians, and Freemasons, all got plenty of news play.

As a local institution, the paper was a participant in community activities, sponsoring contests, publicizing fall fairs and local picnics, and publishing high school honour rolls. Some editors even ran for school board positions. Here also is where you would find letters, some of them scathing indictments; some full of wit and wisdom; and some even ghost written by the editors.

Reading the *Trail News* informed citizens about important decisions that affected their community. Based at least partially on the editor's advice, they agreed or disagreed with his outspoken opinion, took positions for and against issues of the day, acted for or against the proposals in the editorials, and voted for or against the paper's endorsed political candidates.

From a glance at the *Trail Daily Times* of the twenty-first century, readers may not know that it represents the legacy and the history of a pioneer weekly that helped build the smelter city. As *60 Minutes* suggested, newspaper owners "are often committed not to headlines and deadlines, but to bottom lines." The Trail daily is no exception.

Still, despite its diminishing number of pages, its smaller and smaller page size, its increasing number of advertising flyers, and its boilerplate news and opinion, it remains one of the province's oldest newspapers of record. It is the embodiment of that little four-page sheet that reported on the beginnings of Trail as a vibrant BC town. If it goes under, the loss will be felt.

The Trail weekly's editors were more business owners than journalists. They chose to cover events that mostly pleased local businesses. Regular service club and church coverage was a good example of the back-scratching approach to keeping the paper afloat. It was assumed that readers liked the coverage of events and saw the paper as guiding their civic duty. Similarly, it was assumed that they would see fit to patronize the businesses that ran advertising alongside the church and sports news. In the same vein, businesses appreciated the coverage of Board of Trade meetings, market news and city council sessions because they were often officials of all three.

Probably the closest the *News* came to actual reporting was in the world of sport. Trail was a BC sports centre. Its various teams—hockey, lacrosse, baseball, curling and so on—were major competitors for local and provincial championships. Games, especially hockey games, were given full goal-to-goal coverage. Trail's winning teams received much praise from the editors. On occasion, the editors also blasted teams that they thought were not performing up to snuff.

The CM&S was, naturally, the *News*'s most important business connection and editors devoted much space to the company's activities: new properties, new machinery, market share, and virtually every move that company officials made both for business and for pleasure. CM&S president S.G. Blaylock's travels, and those of his family members, were recorded regularly.

Another linkage of business to the editorial side was coverage of the local workforce and its unions. From the moment the Western Federation of Miners (WFM) arrived, first in Rossland in 1895 with Local 38, and later when Trail smelter workers were being organized into WFM Local 105, the editors went on the attack. The Industrial Workers of the World (IWW), which the WFM helped found, took the lion's share of editorial invective. Unions were simply bad for business, as many editors saw it. And a radical union, a striking union like the IWW or the One Big Union (OBU), was anathema to business.

It would be another ten years before the rumblings of unionism would again be felt in Trail. In the meantime, the *News* covered a company town, a company union and a company that is the main generator of the city's wealth. Our printer's devils seldom stepped out of line when it came to company business. Later critics would accuse the paper of being a company shill. Probably so, but through the decades, it helped create a sense of community, of neighbourliness, of togetherness that is cherished by many today. As one *Trail News* editor put it, "the editor who fails to realize the great opportunities he has of doing good in this way" will miss the chance "to give each week something of helpfulness and sympathy to the mass of humanity."[1054]

As we've seen, the riotous era of the weekly community newspaper in Trail lasted until 1925 with the coming of the *Trail Daily Bulletin*. The pioneer years had seen rapid development for both the smelter city and the newspaper industry in the Kootenays. As the coronavirus swept across the globe in the spring and summer of 2021 and 2022, the *Trail Times* suffered along with the afflicted population, reducing frequency to twice a week. Local historian Jamie Forbes, former president of the Trail Historical Society, suggested that the paper might never again return to its daily status.[1055] If it succumbs, it would be the final end to the legacy of the *Trail Creek News* and *Trail News*.

ACKNOWLEDGEMENTS

First, I am indebted to local historians Ron Shearer and Greg Nesteroff, who deserve much credit for guiding me through the newspaper history of the Kootenays. They are dedicated to uncovering the splendid pioneer history of the region and seldom miss a detail. Former Trail Historical Society president Jamie Forbes also provided invaluable historical insight. As always, I must thank the many workers at libraries and historical archives in Canada and the United States for supporting my efforts. These are the tireless researchers and archivists without which local historians could not survive. Research staff at the Rossland Museum & Discovery Centre, the Trail Museum & Archives and the Columbia Basin Institute of Regional History were also of much help in tracing local history. Particular thanks go to Gregg Currie, the librarian at Selkirk College in Castlegar. Thanks, too, go to the families of Elmer D. Hall and Kevin Kult, the great-grandson of *News* editor A.R. Babington. Thanks also to Vici Johnstone of Caitlin Press and her staff. Finally, and as always, my thanks and undying love and respect for Leola Jewett-Verzuh.

NOTES

Abbreviations Used in the Notes

RER   Rossland Evening Record
REW   Rossland Evening World
TCN   Trail Creek News
TDT   Trail Daily Times
TN   Trail News

Introduction

1   Allyson Kenning, "Tales and Legends of the Mountain Kingdom: A Tale of Many Papers," *Rossland Telegraph*, May 3, 2011, https://rosslandtelegraph.com/news/tales-and-legends-mountain-kingdom-tale-many-papers-11083#.XhkRFdZKi-p.

2   Kenning, "Tales and Legends."

3   See Sarah McNelis, *Copper King at War: The Biography of F. Augustus Heinze* (Missoula: University of Montana Press, 1969).

4   Elsie G. Turnbull, *Ghost Towns and Drowned Towns of West Kootenay* (Surrey, BC: Heritage House, 1988), 5.

5   Elsie G. Turnbull, *Trail... An Invitation to History* (Trail: Hall Printing Company, 1987), 10.

6   Mollie E. Cottingham, "A History of the West Kootenay District in British Columbia" (master's thesis, Unversity of British Columbia, 1947), 237.

7   Donald M. Wilson, "Trail, BC," Crowsnest Highway website (www.crowsnest-highway.ca), 2004.

8   "Trail's Progress," *Trail Creek News* (hereafter *TCN*), March 28, 1896, 1.

9   Cottingham, "History of the West Kootenay," 238.

10   Cottingham, "History of the West Kootenay," 250.

11   Jamie Forbes, "Frank Hanna: The Full Story," *Trail Journal of Local History* 4 (Winter 2011): 46–49, offers a brief biography in which he calls Hanna "Trail's co-founder."

12   John Forsyth, "The Pioneer Press of British Columbia," *British Columbia History* 45, no. 1 (Spring 2012): 5–10, 6.

13   Forsyth, "Pioneer Press," 8–9.

14   Forsyth, "Pioneer Press," 9–10.

15   William Rayner, *Images of History: Twentieth Century British Columbia Through the Front Pages* (Victoria: Orca Book Publishers, 1997), 1.

16   Jeremy Mouat, *Roaring Days: Rossland's Mines and the History of British Columbia* (Vancouver: UBC Press, 1995), 18.

17   See Art Downs, *British Columbia-Yukon Sternwheel Days* (Surrey, BC: Heritage House, 1972).

18   See Michael A. Cone, *Connecting the Kootenays: The Kootenay Lake Ferries—A Hundred Years of Service, 1921–2020* (Self-published, 2022).

19   Ronald Howard Meyer, "The Evolution of Railways in the Kootenays" (master's thesis, University of British Columbia, 1970), 11.

20   See Terry Gainer, *When Trains Ruled the Kootenays: A Short History of Railways in Southeastern British Columbia* (Victoria: Rocky Mountain Books, 2022).

21   Burt R. Campbell, "From Hand-Set Type to Linotype," *British Columbia Historical Quarterly* 10, no. 4 (October 1946): 258–70, provides detailed descriptions of the Washington press and other equipment used by tramp printers. Also, Greg Nesteroff, "Wandering Printing Presses of West Kootenay," *Kütne Reader*, April 7, 2019, explains that Thompson's celebrated Washington hand press, or those like it, had a history of use at Kootenay newspapers long before he arrived. The *Kaslo Slocan Examiner* was printed on one as early as 1892 and the *Kaslo Times* used one in 1894. New Denver's *Slocan Times* printed its debut number using such a press on August 25, 1894. The *Rosslander* probably also used one just before the *Trail Creek News* began publishing in October 1895. Nesteroff also notes that the press journeyed to the *Sandon Paystreak* on September 26, 1896, and to the *Trout Lake Topic* on October 21, 1897. In 1900, socialist Parm Pettipiece, who would later publish the *Western Clarion*, used it to publish the *Ferguson* (later *Lardeau*) *Eagle*.

22   W. Turrentine Jackson, *Treasure Hill: Portrait of a Silver Mining Camp* (Reno and Las Vegas: University of Nevada Press, 1963), no pagination.

23   Harold Kingsmill, *First History of Rossland, BC* (Rossland: Stunden & Perine, 1897), 4.

24   Depending on how you interpret Kootenay geography, the first paper could have been the *Kootenay Star* of Revelstoke (first published in 1889). That distinction could also fall to the *Donald Truth*, first published in 1888.

25   Sean Arthur Joyce, Foreword, in Cole Harris, *Newspapers & the Slocan in the 1890s* (New Denver, BC: Chameleon Fire Editions, 2016), 2.

26   "Turned Out Wrong: He Tried to Whip the Editor and Failed," *TCN*, February 29, 1896, 4.

27   See Greg Nesteroff, *Kootenay News: The History of Nelson's Newspapers* (Nelson: Touchstones Nelson: Museum of Art and History, 2019).

28   Kingsmill, *First History of Rossland*, 6.

29   "Our First Issue," *Rossland Evening World* (hereafter *REW*), May 1, 1901, 1. For more on the *World*, see Ron Verzuh, "The *Rossland Evening World*: A Workers' Voice for the Kootenays," *British Columbia History* 54, no. 4 (Winter 2021): 5–10.

30   John R. Bone, and Arthur H. Urquart Colquhoun, *A History of Canadian Journalism in the Several Portions of the Dominion* (Toronto: Canadian Press Association, 1908), 2.

31   John Adcock, "Kootenay Newspaper Pioneer—'Colonel' R.T. Lowery," *Yesterday's Papers*, January 7, 2016, https://john-adcock.blogspot.com/2016/01/kootenay-newspaper-pioneer-colonel-rt.html.

32   Elsie G. Turnbull, "Trail's Pioneer Newspaperman," in *Pioneer Days in British Columbia*, vol. 3, ed. Art Downs, (Victoria: Heritage House, 1977), 118–23.

33   "Noted in Passing," *Trail News* (hereafter *TN*), August 23, 1918, 5.

34   "Plain, Interesting Talk About the Local Paper," *TN*, June 14, 1918, 5.

35   "Phone the Editor," *TN*, June 28, 1918, 5.

36   "Noted in Passing," *TN*, December 13, 1918, 6.

37   "Editors Never Strike," *TN*, July 26, 1918, 2.

38   "News for A Newspaper—Suggestions for Those Who Are Uninitiated," *TN*, March 21, 1919, 3.

39   "From the Observatory," *TN*, February 14, 1919, 2.

40   "From the Observatory," *TN*, August 16, 1918, 2.

41 "Noted in Passing," *TN*, August 8, 1918, 3.

42 "From the Observatory," *TN*, August 16, 1918, 2.

43 "Heavy Casualties," *TN*, August 30, 1918, 2.

44 Frank Parker Stockbridge, "Small-Town Papers," *Saturday Evening Post*, 1928, re-printed in booklet form by the Toronto Type Foundry Co. Ltd., 4.

45 Stockbridge, "Small-Town Papers," 25.

46 "Some Truths," *TCN*, April 23, 1897, 4.

47 *TN*, November 25, 1905, 1.

48 *TN*, January 14, 1911, 4.

49 "How It Is Done," *TN*, September 17, 1911, 2.

50 "Trail, BC—Keep It Dark," *TN*, September 24, 1915, 2.

51 "Note and Comment," *TN*, April 14, 1916, 2.

52 "Four Cents Worth of News," *TN*, February 11, 1921, 2.

53 "When the Paper Doesn't Come," *TN*, September 2, 1921, 5.

54 *TN*, November 18, 1921, 2.

55 See W.L. Carr, *Newspaper Is Town Builder* (Salt Lake City: Porte Publishing Company, 1938).

56 See "History of Canadian Newspapers, Printers and Publishers," Wikipedia, the Free Encyclopedia, https://en.wikipedia.org/wiki/History_of_Canadian_newspapers#Printers_and_publishers.

57 "History of Canadian Newspapers."

58 Joyce, Foreword, Harris, *Newspapers & the Slocan*, 2–3.

59 Cole Harris, *Newspapers & the Slocan in the 1890s* (New Denver, BC: Chameleon Fire Editions, 2016), 6.

60 Bone, et al., only note Kootenay pioneer editors and journalists if they graduated to the bigger city dailies. David B. Bogle of the *Rossland Miner* is one example.

61 Editor W.B. Willcox used this slogan in his newspaper's banner during the First World War.

Trail Creek News (1895–1898)
"Wrong Font" Thompson Meets the Montana Copper King

62 "Wrong Font" was not a nickname that Thompson liked. Apparently, he preferred "Wandering Foot." For more, see Paul Solka Jr. and Art Bremer, "Introducing 'W.F.'," in *Adventures in Alaskan Journalism Since 1903* (Fairbanks: Commercial Printing Co., 1980), 67. Also see Jim Rearden, "Wrong Font Thompson" in *Alaska's First Bush Pilots, 1923–30* (Portland: Graphic Arts Books, 2009).

63 Elsie G. Turnbull, *Topping's Trail: The First Years of a Now Famous Smelter City* (Vancouver: Mitchell Press, 1964), 12.

64 Turnbull, *Topping's Trail*.

65 Garnet Basque, *West Kootenay: The Pioneer Years* (Surrey, BC: Heritage House, 1990), 41, describes Topping's early years at Nelson.

66 See E.S. Topping, *Chronicles of the Yellowstone* (St. Paul: Pioneer Press Company, 1888).

67 *TCN*, October 19, 1895, 1.

68 Turnbull, *Topping's Trail*, 40.

69 "Notes on the Thompsons," Elsie G. Turnbull fonds, Selkirk College Regional Archives, shows that Loss Bernard, usually listed as R.L. for Raleigh Lawson Bernard, "had a special relationship with the editor." He "had been taken into Thompson's home and treated like a son" and "went with the family to Trail." Turnbull adds that Bernard went to Alaska with Thompson and would be associated with him until Thompson died.

70 Loss Bernard, as quoted by Paul Solka Jr., "Wrong Font Thompson," *Alaska Journal* 4, no. 2 (Spring 1974):75.

71 Loss Bernard, as quoted by Solka Jr., "Wrong Font Thompson," 74.

72 *Aberdeen Herald*, March 31, 1892.

73 *TCN*, October 19, 1895, 1.

74 *Seattle Post-Intelligencer*, March 5, 1889, no page number.

75 "What T'ell, Billy," *TCN*, September 4, 1896, 2, tells us that "The editor has a 'game' foot and can't run." Solka Jr., *Adventures in Alaska Journalism*, 68, explains the "secret" of W.F.'s lame foot. Apparently the injury occurred while he was playing baseball at Westport-on-the-Sea, Washington, where Thompson was editor of the local newspaper. The injury and subsequent amateur medical treatment left him permanently disabled. Solka, *Alaska Journal*, 68, contradicts this version of events, saying that "he acquired a permanent limp when a leg, broken in a train accident, failed to heal properly."

76 Jamie Forbes, "Trail Times," in *Trail of Memories: Trail, BC, 1895–1945* (Trail: Trail History and Heritage Committee, 1997), 36.

77 A Thompson family tree on ancestry.com shows that W.F. was born in Colton, New York, on June 11, 1865. However, chroniclers of his career cite the birth year as 1863 at Reed City, Michigan. See Solka Jr., "Wrong Font Thompson," for details of Thompson's early life.

78 Turnbull, *Topping's Trail*, 17.

79 "A New Year," *TCN*, October 9, 1896, 2.

80 Turnbull, *Topping's Trail*, 17.

81 The Washington hand press, also known as the iron hand press was a type of letterpress introduced in the early nineteenth century to rival the wooden press. It "used moveable type set in a frame, along with pre-cut graphic images such as woodblocks." For more, see Eleanor Boba, "A Machine for the 19th Century: The Iron Hand Press," American Bookbinders Museum, https://bookbindersmuseum.org/a-machine-for-the-19th-century-the-iron-hand-press/, San Francisco, July 24, 2014.

82 Turnbull, *Topping's Trail*, 17.

83 *Victoria Daily Colonist*, November 3, 1895, 5.

84 *The Washington Newspaper: A Publication Dedicated to the Study and Improvement of Journalism in Washington* 8, no. 1 (October 1922), 27.

85 The temperance-minded rejected claims that Dr. Leslie E. Keeley's cure, developed during the Civil War as he studied afflicted soldiers, could successfully combat alcoholism. See *The Keeley Cure* (Mason, OH: Digger Odell Publications, 2009), www.bottle-books.com.

86 *TCN*, October 19, 1895, 1.

87 *Cominco Magazine*, January 1952.

88 *TCN*, December 25, 1896, 4, first names Esling on the *News* staff.

89 Thompson's promotion of the "Holiday Number" apparently was so successful that not a single copy remains even for historical research purposes.

90   "Why We Blush," *TCN*, February 29, 1896, 1.

91   "Why We Blush."

92   *TCN*, February 29, 1896, 1.

93   *TCN*, February 29, 1896, 1.

94   *TCN*, February 22, 1896, 4.

95   *TCN*, February 22, 1896, 4.

96   *TCN*, February 22, 1896, 4.

97   "News of the Week," *TCN*, February 22, 1896, 3.

98   "News of the Week," 3.

99   "Turned Out Wrong—He Tried to Whip the Editor, and Failed," *TCN*, February 29, 1896, 4.

100   Editorial, *TCN*, February 29, 1896, 2.

101   *Spokane Falls Review*, December 6, 1888.

102   *Review.*

103   *TCN*, March 7, 1896, 1–2.

104   *TCN*, March 7, 1896, 3.

105   Ron Shearer, "Eber Clark Smith, Biographical Notes, Version 6," draft manuscript, June 2018, author's copy. See also "Ron Shearer: The Early Days of the Rossland Miner," *Rossland News*, April 27, 2017, https://www.rosslandnews.com/opinion/ron-shearer-the-early-days-of-the-rossland-miner/.

106   "Peace vs. War," *TCN*, March 14, 1896, 2.

107   "News of the Week," *TCN*, May 16, 1896, 3. Note that the reference to "family" may have included Martha's stepson from her first marriage. Claude Leete grew close to Judge Caton and moved to Rossland with Martha after she left Thompson.

108   "Goodbye, Old Stage!," *TCN*, May 16, 1896, 1.

109   *TCN*, May 29, 1896, 2.

110   "Sensationalism," *TCN*, June 5, 1896, 2.

111   Shearer, "Smith, Biographical Notes."

112   Shearer, "Smith, Biographical Notes."

113   Shearer, "Smith, Biographical Notes."

114   "What T'ell, Billy," *TCN*, September 4, 1896, 2.

115   See Downs, *British Columbia-Yukon Sternwheel Days.*

116   "Improvements," *TCN*, September 11, 1896, 2.

117   "It's a Fine Hotel," *TCN*, September 18, 1896, 3.

118   "A Prominent Citizen," *TCN*, October 2, 1896, 1.

119   "A New Year," *TCN*, October 9, 1896, 2.

120   "They Can't Boom Trail," *TCN*, October 30, 1896, 4.

121   "Leadville Strike Still On," *TCN*, November 13, 1896, 1. "Leadville History," *Western Mining History*, details the history of the strike of Local 33 of the Western Federation of Miners (WFM), the same union that represented miners in Rossland. https://westernmininghistory.com/towns/colorado/leadville/.

122   "75,000 Are Dead," *TCN*, November 13, 1896, 6.

123 "A New Year," *TCN*, October 9, 1896, 2.

124 *TCN*, June 12, 1896.

125 "He's a Hustler," *TCN*, November 13, 1896, 5.

126 "The Finest in Our District," *TCN*, February 12, 1897, 1, names the other three female staff members as "Miss Rouse," "Miss Poole" and "stenographer and bookkeeper Miss L.R. Rigney."

127 "A Happy New Year," *TCN*, January 1, 1897, 4.

128 "A Happy New Year."

129 "Back from the East," *TCN*, January 1, 1897, 5.

130 "Trail Is the Hub," *TCN*, February 5, 1897, 1.

131 "Doings in and around Trail," *TCN*, March 5, 1897, 5.

132 The history appeared as a "Third Special Number" of the *TCN*, March 1, 1897.

133 *TCN*, February 26, 1897, 4. See also Greg Nesteroff, "Conner Malott and the *Trail Creek Miner*," *Trail Journal of Local History* 5 (Winter 2014): 48–50, for a brief history of the weekly.

134 *TCN*, April 2, 1897, 1.

135 "Petition Signing," *TCN*, March 5, 1897, 4.

136 "Sunday Closing," *TCN*, March 19, 1897, 4.

137 "Who Is to Blame?" *TCN*, April 9, 1897, 4.

138 "Advertising," *TCN*, April 16, 1897, 6.

139 "Some Truths," *TCN*, April 23, 1897, 4.

140 "Some Truths," *TCN*, April 23, 1897, 4. For a brief profile of John Houston, see Greg Nesteroff, *Kootenay News: The History of Nelson's Newspapers* (Nelson: Touchstones Nelson: Museum of Art and History, 2019), 1.

141 "A Disappointment," *TCN*, June 4, 1897, 4.

142 "Local Notes," *TCN*, June 18, 1897, 1.

143 "In Re. Heinze," *TCN*, June 25, 1897, 4.

144 "Local Mention," *TCN*, February 1, 1896, 3.

145 "Better Times Are Here," *TCN*, July 9, 1897, 4.

146 "Coxeyites" referred to unemployed workers that marched on Washington, DC, as Coxey's Army, a group led by Jacob S. Coxey, a populist agitator. See Benjamin F. Alexander, *Coxey's Army: Popular Protest in the Gilded Age* (Baltimore: Johns Hopkins University Press, 2015).

147 *TCN*, July 9, 1897, 4.

148 "The Smelter Question," *TCN*, July 23, 1897, 1.

149 "The Klondyke, the People, and the Festive Nugget," *TCN*, July 30, 1897, 1.

150 "On to Klondyke," *TCN*, July 30, 1897, 4.

151 "Mr. Heinze's Scheme," *TCN*, August 20, 1897, 2.

152 "A Questionable 'Benefit'," *TCN*, August 20, 1897, 2.

153 Shearer, "Smith, Biographical Notes."

154 "Bargain and Sale," *TCN*, September 3, 1897, 2.

155 "Oh, Dave!" *TCN*, September 24, 1897, 2.

156 "Oh, Dave!"

157 Shearer, "Smith, Biographical Notes," offers a full account of the dispute.

158 "The Last Attempt," *TCN*, October 16, 1897, 4.

159 "The Outlook for Trail," *TCN*, October 22, 1897, 2.

160 "What Is the Object?" *TCN*, November 5, 1897, 2.

161 Shearer, "Smith, Biographical Notes," offers this speculation about Heinze's possible plan to buy the *News*.

162 "Rumors of a Sale," *TCN*, December 10, 1897, 1.

163 "Rumors," *TCN*, December 17, 1897, 2.

164 "Rush to Klondyke," *TCN*, December 24, 1897, 2.

165 "Rush to Klondyke."

166 "A Merry Christmas," *TCN*, December 24, 1897, 2.

167 "Heinze and the CPR," *TCN*, January 15, 1898, 2.

168 Supplement to the issue of January 29, 1898, *TCN*, January 29, 1898.

169 "Not Forgotten," *TCN*, February 5, 1898, 2.

170 "Rossland and the CPR," *TCN*, April 2, 1898, 2.

171 Turnbull, *Trail: An Invitation*, 40, quoting a friend of Heinze.

172 *TCN*, April 16, 1898, 4.

173 *Nelson Miner*, April 17, 1897. The story of the *Miner* is in Nesteroff, *Kootenay News*, 1–2.

174 *Nelson Miner*, April 2, 1898.

175 "Local Mentions," *TCN*, September 4, 1896, 3, notes that Jowett "of the Nelson Miner," had visited Trail Creek.

176 *Vancouver Daily World*, August 27, 1897.

177 "The Daily Miner," *TCN*, December 4, 1896, 4.

178 *Victoria Daily Times*, June 17, 1897.

179 *TCN*, May 20, 1898, 2.

180 *Nelson Tribune*, July 24, 1901.

181 *Nelson Tribune*.

182 *Nelson Daily Miner*, December 1, 1898, 2.

183 Nesteroff, *Kootenay News*, provides a chronological chart showing the *Miner*'s history and states that December 1, 1898, was the first daily edition.

184 *The Washington Newspaper* 8, no. 1 (October 1922): 27.

185 Solka, "Wrong Font Thompson," 69.

186 "New Publishers," *TCN*, May 6, 1898, 2.

Trail Creek News/Trail News (1898–1907)
Billy Esling, Future Politician, Takes the Helm

187 "He's a Hustler," *TCN*, November 13, 1896, 5.

188 1892 Thurston County Territorial Census, https://digitalarchives.wa.gov/DigitalObject/Download/53d7028e-ae2c-48bc-b2b9-7d1e15e13d33, states that she was fifty-three in 1892. The *News* noted her death at eighty-eight years old. She had been in

Rossland for eighteen years living with her son and a daughter, Mrs. M.E. Davidson. See "Jane Catherine Esling," *TN*, March 12, 1915, 2. She is buried in Philadelphia with her husband and seven of her children.

189   Thomas J. DeFilippo, *Stephen Girard, The Man, His College and Estate*, 2nd ed., 1999, http://www.girardweb.com/girard/download.htm, includes a chapter on the Girard will, 23.

190   John Keats, "Legacy of Stephen Girard," *American Heritage* 29, no. 4 (1978), https://www.americanheritage.com/legacy-stephen-girard#4.

191   "'Billy' Esling Dies This Morning," *Trail Daily Times* (hereafter *TDT*) December 2, 1946, 1.

192   "Personal Mention," *Morning Olympian*, September 1, 1891, 1, specifies that Esling became "the *Tribune*'s editorial chair, under the 'syndicate' management."

193   The following biographical sources were consulted: National Guard Enlistment Register, https://digitalarchives.wa.gov/DigitalObject/Download/df39e80d-3db5-4ccc-80c8-7809daab98931; 1892 Thurston County Territorial Census, https://digitalarchives.wa.gov/DigitalObject/Download/53d7028e-ae2c-48bc-b2b9-7d1e15e13d33; Find a Grave, https://www.findagrave.com/memorial/109068876/william-kemble-esling/photo#view-photo=183705245; and *Olympia Tribune* Souvenir Issue 1891, https://olympia-history.org/tag/transcriptions/.

194   *TCN*, April 16, 1898, 1.

195   See ancestry.com. Jane Esling appears to have travelled west from Philadelphia to join her son in Washington. Billy had two older siblings, Lemuel Jr., born 1856, and Mary, born 1865. Lemuel Jr., disappeared from the records after 1870. Jane Esling had been a widow for forty-seven years when she died in Rossland in 1915.

196   *TCN*, April 16, 1898, 2.

197   "W.F. Thompson Retires," *TCN*, April 30, 1898.

198   "Thompson Retires."

199   See Anne Mercier, *Father Pat: A Hero of the Far West* (Gloucester: Michin and Gibbs, 1909).

200   "Brooklyn Is the Town," *TCN*, June 17, 1898, 1.

201   "Pell Mell to Brooklyn," *TCN*, June 24, 1898, 1.

202   Elsie G. Turnbull, *Ghost Towns and Drowned Towns of West Kootenay* (Surrey, BC: Heritage House, 1988), 37–39, offers a colourful description of Brooklyn.

203   "A Novel Newspaper," *TCN*, June 24, 1898, 2.

204   *Rossland Miner*, June 23, 1898.

205   *TCN*, June 17, 1898, 2.

206   *TCN*, June 17, 1898, 2.

207   "John McKane," *TCN*, June 24, 1898, 2.

208   *TCN*, July 1, 1898, 2.

209   *TCN*, July 1, 1898, 2.

210   *TCN*, July 1, 1898, 2.

211   *TCN*, July 8, 1898, 1.

212   Jeremy Mouat, *Roaring Days: Rossland's Mines and the History of British Columbia* (Vancouver: UBC Press, 1995), 45.

213   *TCN*, July 15, 1898, 2.

214 "'Welcome, Aberdeen'," *TCN*, July 22, 1898, 1.

215 "Rev. Mr. Glassford Home," *TCN*, July 29, 1898, 1.

216 "The Fires Are Lighted," *TCN*, August 5, 1898, 3.

217 *Cominco Magazine*, January 1952.

218 "The Dog Poisoner," *TCN*, August 12, 1898, 2.

219 "Where Women Vote," *TCN*, September 16, 1898, 1.

220 *Vancouver Sun*, April 15, 1919, citing an item in the *News-Advertiser* of April 15, 1899.

221 *TCN*, September 30, 1898, 2.

222 *TCN*, October 7, 1898, 1.

223 See Gerald Anglin, "The Strangest Insurance Company in the World," *Maclean's*, February 1, 1951, https://archive.macleans.ca/article/1951/2/1/the-strangest-insurance-company-in-the-world.

224 "Burley Skips the Town," *TCN*, October 21, 1898, 1.

225 "Ancient Order of United Workman," *Encyclopedia of Arkansas*, Little Rock, AR, https://encyclopediaofarkansas.net/entries/ancient-order-of-united-workmen-2160/, notes that the AOUW was formed in Pennsylvania in 1868 as one of many "friendly societies" that provided life insurance to workers.

226 *TCN*, December 2, 1898, 2.

227 "It Is Not True," *TCN*, December 9, 1898, 1. A highbinder describes an unscrupulous person, corrupt politician, or an assassin belonging to a Chinese criminal organization.

228 *TCN*, December 23, 1898, 2.

229 *TCN*, January 28, 1899, 1.

230 *TCN*, March 18, 1899, 1.

231 "An Object Lesson," *TCN*, April 1, 1899, 2.

232 Mollie E. Cottingham, "A History of the West Kootenay District in British Columbia" (master's thesis, University of British Columbia, 1947), 241–43.

233 "Boundary Smelters," *TCN*, April 1, 1899, 2.

234 "Those Lumber Rates," *TCN*, April 15, 1899, 2.

235 "Another Comparison," *TCN*, April 22, 1899, 2.

236 "A Newspaper Plant for Sale," *TCN*, April 15, 1899, 2.

237 *TCN*, April 22, 1899, 1.

238 *TCN*, April 29, 1899, 1.

239 "The Eight-Hour Law," *TCN*, May 20, 1899, 2.

240 "The Trail Boys Win" and other news items, *TCN*, May 27, 1899, 1.

241 Gerald R. Boucher, "The 1901 Rossland Miners' Strike: The Western Federation of Miners Responds to Industrial Capitalism" (master's thesis, University of Victoria, 1986), 25. Boucher gives a detailed account of the strike activity surrounding the eight-hour law.

242 *TCN*, August 5, 1899, 1.

243 *TCN*, August 12, 1899, 2.

244 *TCN*, August 26, 1899, 3.

245   Ron Shearer, email correspondence with the author, December 28, 2019.

246   "Rossland Record Change," *Nelson Daily Miner*, August 25, 1899.

247   *The Ledge*, August 31, 1899.

248   "Salutory," *Rossland Evening Record* (hereafter *RER*), September 1, 1899, 4.

249   "The Record's Position," *RER*, October 10, 1899, 1.

250   "Announcement," *TCN*, September 16, 1899, 1.

251   *TCN*, December 30, 1899, 1.

252   "Gone to the Boneyard," *Nelson Tribune*, December 8, 1900, 2.

253   "Corruption," *RER*, November 3, 1900, 2.

254   Elsie G. Turnbull, *Trail: A Smelter City* (Langley, BC: Sunfire Publications, 1964), 57.

255   "A Co-operative Laundry," *RER*, December 12, 1899, 4.

256   *RER*, September 15, 1899, 4.

257   The *Industrial World* had published weekly since September 1899, then switched to twice a week the following year under the ownership of the Rossland Trades and Labor Council and WFM District No. 6. See Ron Verzuh, "The *Rossland Evening World:* A Workers' Voice for the Kootenays," *BC History* 54, no. 4 (Winter 2021): 5–10.

258   *REW*, July 15, 1901.

259   Boucher, "The 1901 Rossland Miners' Strike," citing the *REW*, June 10 and July 19, 1901.

260   Turnbull, *Trail: An Invitation*, 9.

261   Turnbull, *Trail: An Invitation*, 5.

262   Turnbull, *Trail: An Invitation*, 6.

263   Turnbull, *Trail: An Invitation*, 34.

264   *Vancouver Province*, February 12, 1901.

265   *TCN*, February 2, 1901.

266   Turnbull, *Trail: An Invitation*, 7.

267   Art Downs, *Pioneer Days in British Columbia* (Surrey, BC: Heritage House, 1979), 35, notes that "calithumpian was a slang word used in England that means a parade that was noisy and boisterous, a description that fitted many of Trail's celebrations."

268   Turnbull, *Trail: An Invitation*, 71.

269   *Vancouver Daily World*, February 2, 1903.

270   "Trail," *TCN*, January 23, 1904, 2. Dowieites were followers of John Alexander Dowie, founder of a religious cult, who styled himself a modern-day Elijah.

271   *TCN*, February 13, 1904, 1.

272   "The Opera House," *TCN*, March 19, 1904, 2.

273   "Rifle League Match," *TCN*, June 11, 1904, 1.

274   "Trail Ball Players," *TCN*, October 1, 1904, 1.

275   "Trouble at Salmo," *TN*, April 15, 1905, 4.

276   "Hockey Match," *TN*, January 21, 1905, 1.

277   "Reminiscences of Ten Years Ago," *TN*, May 6, 1905, 1.

278   "Murdered for His Money," *TN*, June 3, 1905, 1.

279   "Heinze May Sell Out," *TN*, July 22, 1905, 1.

280   "Coughed Up a Lizard," *TN*, August 12, 1905, 1.

281   "Nelson Tribune on Fernie Strike," *TN*, August 26, 1905, 1.

282   "Facts and Figures about the War," *TN*, September 2, 1905, 1.

283   "Nanaimo Strike Settled," *TN*, October 7, 1905, 1.

284   John Kalmakov provides a brief history of the operation in "Granby Smelter," http://kalmakov.com/historical/boundary%20country%20smelters.html.

285   *TN*, November 25, 1905, 1.

286   "The Trail Smelter," *TN*, January 6, 1906, 1.

287   "The Hockey Arena," *TN*, January 13, 1906, 1.

288   "News of the Week," *TN*, March 3, 1906, 4. See J. Anthony Lukas, *Big Trouble: A Murder in a Small Western Town Sets Off a Struggle for the Soul of America* (New York: Simon & Schuster, 1997) for a full account of the events involving the WFM leaders.

289   *TN*, March 17, 1906, no page available.

290   *TN*, March 31, 1906, no page available.

291   Martin Robin, *The Rush for Spoils: The Company Province, 1871–1933* (Toronto: McClelland & Stewart, 1972), 101–03, offers an account of the scandal.

292   "News of the Week," *TN*, March 24, 1906, 4.

293   Heinze would be covered in the big dailies the following October when he and his brother Otto brought about the Panic of 1907 on Wall Street through a stock manipulation scheme designed to corner the copper market.

294   "News of the Week," *TN*, May 26, 1906, 4.

295   "News of the Week."

296   "The Jungle," *TN*, June 24, 1906, 1.

297   "Woman's Suffrage," *TN*, June 30, 1906, 1.

298   "Topping–Hanna," *TN*, September 22, 1906, 4. Turnbull notes in *Trail: An Invitation to History*, 26, that Hanna deserted his family and had affairs with other women.

299   "News of the Week," *TN*, September 22, 1906, 4.

300   "Nine Hours a Day," *TN*, November 17, 1906, 4.

301   "Conservatives Win Victory," *TN*, February 2, 1907, 1.

302   "'Douks Rebel'," *TN*, March 2, 1907, 3.

Trail News (1907–1914)
A Canadian Steers the *News* as the Great War Begins

303   Mayor F.E. Dockerill noted at his farewell dinner on June 22, 1914, that Babington "had worked so amiably and conscientiously amongst them for the past ten years." See "Farewell Presentation," *TN*, June 27, 1914, 1.

304   Tara's top favourite son was hockey star Fred "Cyclone" Taylor. Although Cyclone was six years younger, Babington would have heard of him. Perhaps this helped him encourage fans of Trail's favourite winter sport while he was there.

305   https://www.findagrave.com/memorial/139119912/arthur-richard-babington. BC marriage certificate #48597 has his birthplace as Invermay.

306   C.F. Campbell to J.A. Bellamy, June 27, 1902. Author's copy.

307 Great-grandson Kevin Kult to author, email correspondence, February 2, 2020.

308 Kult to author.

309 *TN*, April 22, 1911, 4.

310 See Julie Gilmour, "Interpreting Social Disorder: The Case of the 1907 Vancouver Riots," *International Journal* 67, no. 2 (Spring 2012): 483–95.

311 "Death of the Modern Elijah," *TN*, March 16, 1907, 2.

312 "Future of Canada," *TN*, March 23, 1907, 2.

313 "Let Well Enough Alone," *TN*, March 30, 1907, 2.

314 "Ore Production and Better Labor," *TN*, May 4, 1907, 2.

315 "Chinese Paying Head Tax," *TN*, May 11, 1907, 1.

316 "Successful Smoker," *TN*, July 20, 1907, 4.

317 "Successful Smoker."

318 "Trades and Labor Congress," *TN*, August 3, 1907, 3.

319 *TN*, July 6, 1907, 1.

320 "The Country Press," *TN*, July 6, 1907, 2.

321 "Influence of the Press," *TN*, July 13, 1907, 1.

322 "Labor Day Celebration A Big Success," *TN*, September 27, 1907, 1.

323 Robert F. Bruner and Sean D. Carr, *The Panic of 1907: Lessons Learned from the Markets' Perfect Storm* (Hoboken, NJ: John Wiley & Sons, 2007), in particular, the chapter "Copper King."

324 "Heinze's Downfall," *TN*, November 16, 1907, 1.

325 *TN*, November 2, 1907, 4.

326 Ravi Malhotra and Benjamin Issit, *Able to Lead: Disablement, Radicalism, and the Political Life of E.T. Kingsley* (Vancouver: UBC Press, 2021) offers a detailed account of Pettipiece's journalistic activities.

327 *TN*, November 2, 1907, 1.

328 See Adam Hochschild, *To End All Wars: A Story of Loyalty and Rebellion, 1914–1918* (New York: Houghlin Mifflin Harcourt, 2012) for a probing examination of conscientious objectors during the First World War.

329 "Back to the Old Scale," *TN*, November 30, 1907, 1.

330 "Industrial Peace," *TN*, November 30, 1907, 3.

331 "Notes from Labor World," *TN*, April 25, 1908, 3.

332 "Problem Is Solved," *TN*, May 16, 1908, 2.

333 Black Hand was a Chinese extortion racket that started in about 1900 in North American locations.

334 "Doukhobors at Waterloo," *TN*, April 18, 1908, 4.

335 "Are Getting There," *TN*, July 18, 1908, 1.

336 "Money in Gases," *TN*, July 25, 1908, 1.

337 "Should Be Abolished," *TN*, August 1, 1908, 1.

338 *TN*, August 1, 1908, 4.

339 *TN*, September 19, 1908, 4.

340 *TN*, October 31, 1908, 4.

341   "A New Aspect of the 'Yellow Peril'," *TN*, December 26, 1908, 2.

342   "Exchanging Populations," *TN*, January 2, 1909, 2

343   "Rossland A Theory," *TN*, February 6, 1909, 2.

344   "Civic Topics," *TN*, February 13, 1909, 4.

345   "Editorial Notes," *TN*, May 29, 1909, 2.

346   "Evangelistic Services," *TN*, May 15, 1909, 4.

347   "Smith vs. Consolidated," *TN*, June 5, 1909, 1.

348   *TN*, June 5, 1909, 4.

349   "Visit to the Doukhobors," *TN*, June 19, 1909, 1.

350   "F. Augustus Heinze," *TN*, June 26, 1909, 3.

351   "The Increase of Divorces," *TN*, August 14, 1909, 2.

352   "Haywood Talks," *TN*, August 21, 1909, 1.

353   "Mitchell Speaks," *TN*, September 18, 1909, 1.

354   "Heinze's Lesson," *TN*, October 2, 1909, 1.

355   "Provincial News," *TN*, October 16, 1909, 1.

356   "A White Man's Country," *TN*, November 13, 1909, 2.

357   *TN*, July 2, 1910, 4.

358   "Jules Labarthe Leaves Trail," *TN*, July 16, 1910, 1.

359   "Suppose!," *TN*, August 6, 1910, 2.

360   "Not Without Cost," *TN*, August 6, 1910, 3.

361   "A New Way," *TN*, August 27, 1910, 2.

362   "Trail Labor Day Celebrations," *TN*, September 10, 1910, 1.

363   "How It Is Done," *TN*, September 17, 1910, 1.

364   "Memorial Church to Father Pat," *TN*, October 15, 1910, 2.

365   Turnbull, *Invitation to History*, 34.

366   "The Wily Chinee," *TN*, November 26, 1910, 2.

367   "Whom to Patronize," *TN*, January 14, 1911, 2.

368   "Young Men Who Seized Opportunities," *TN*, January 14, 1911, 4.

369   *TN*, January 14, 1911, 4.

370   "Robert Burns," *New World Encyclopedia*, https://www.newworldencyclopedia.org/entry/Robert_Burns.

371   *TN*, January 28, 1911, 4.

372   *TN*, January 28, 1911, 4.

373   "The Call to Arms," *TN*, June 17, 1911, 1.

374   "WFM After Boy Scouts," *TN*, August 5, 1911, 6.

375   "Facing Famine in Labor Wars," *TN*, August 19, 1911, 1.

376   "A Prosperous Year," *TN*, January 6, 1912, 1.

377   *TN*, March 16, 1912, 1.

378   "Enjoyable Smoker," *TN*, September 14, 1912, 1.

379   "Doukhobors Report," *TN*, January 4, 1913, 2.

380   William Blakemore, "Sect of Doukhobors," *Report of Royal Commission on Matters Related to the Sect of Doukhobors in the Province of British Columbia* (Victoria: King's Printer, 1913).

381   "Communication," *TN*, January 11, 1913, 1.

382   "Union Label League," *TN*, February 8, 1913, 4.

383   "Enforcing the Law," *TN*, March 15, 1913, 4.

384   "Labor Commission," *TN*, May 24, 1913, 1.

385   "Labor Commission."

386   "Local News," *TN*, May 31, 1913, 4.

387   "An Editor's Pleasantries," *TN*, August 16, 1913, 1.

388   Rod Mickleburgh, *On the Line: A History of the British Columbia Labour Movement* (Vancouver: BC Labour Heritage Centre, 2018) discusses the strike. See also John Hinde, *When Coal Was King: Ladysmith and the Coal-Mining Industry on Vancouver Island* (Vancouver: UBC Press, 2003).

389   "Labor Day a Great Success," *TN*, September 6, 1913, 1.

390   "The Unemployed," *TN*, October 18, 1913, 2.

391   "Notice to Union Men," *TN*, January 10, 1914, 4.

392   "The Doukhobor Legislation," *TN*, March 7, 1914, 2.

393   "Prejudice Unjust," *TN*, April 18, 1914, 1.

394   "The Colorado Strike," *TN*, May 16, 1914, 2.

395   "James Clarke, Pioneer Printer, Publisher Dies on North Shore," *Vancouver Province*, April 26, 1943. Trail's Maple Leaf Band was founded in 1917, so Clarke may also have played with them.

396   Hugh Johnston gives a brief account of the incident in "Komagata Maru," *The Canadian Encyclopedia*, Historica Canada, article published February 7, 2006; last edited October 12, 2021.

397   "The People Should Say," *TN*, July 18, 1914, 2.

398   "Latest News of the War," *TN*, August 8, 1914, 1.

399   "Still Paying Dividends," *TN*, September 26, 1914, 2.

400   "Civic Elections, Butler Mayor," *TN*, January 15, 1915, 1. Note that Butler Park in East Trail was named after the mayor who was replaced in 1917.

401   *TN*, March 26, 1915, 3.

402   "Local News," *TN*, February 5, 1915, 4.

403   "Local News," *TN*, August 6, 1915, 2.

404   "Kootenay Boys Splendid Fighters," *TN*, August 20, 1915, 1.

405   "Trail Smelter to Produce Zinc," *TN*, August 20, 1915, 1.

406   "The People Will Decide," *TN*, September 17, 1915, 2.

407   "The Spokane Street Grade," *TN*, October 15, 1915, 1.

408   "So Reckless," *TN*, October 15, 1915, 2.

409   "Must Restore Rates," *TN*, October 15, 1915, 2.

410   "Commendable," *TN*, October 15, 1915, 2.

Trail News (1915–1919)
A Spokane Man Migrates to the Smelter City

411   "The New Publisher," *TN*, December 3, 1915, 4.

412   "Change in Management," *TN*, December 3, 1915, 4.

413   *TN*, December 3, 1915, 4.

414   Certificate of Death No. 1372, Washington State Department of Health, September 25, 1945.

415   A.J. Medlock, senior archivist, St. Louis Archives, State Historical Society of Missouri, email correspondence with the author.

416   "Education Spelled Freedom," Marie Updegraff, in *Stamford Past & Present, 1641–1976* (Stamford, CT: Stamford Historical Society, 1976), http://www.stamford-history.org/pp_ed.htm.

417   "Pioneer Trail Publisher, W.B. Willcox, Dies Sunday," *TDT*, September 25, 1945, 3.

418   "Editor 50 Years Ago Was Undismayed by Situation," *Spokane Chronicle*, August 4, 1939.

419   "Willcox Described Publication of Chronicle After City Fire," *Spokane Chronicle*, May 23, 1936, 3.

420   *TCN*, November 18, 1898.

421   "Future of the News," *Brooklyn News*, August 6, 1898, 2.

422   Gainer, *When Trains Ruled the Kootenays*, provides information on various railways in the region.

423   Shearer, "Smith, Biographical Notes," quoting from "Again in Hot Water," *Boundary Creek Times*, December 16, 1899.

424   Basque, *Ghost Towns*, 87.

425   *Greenwood Ledge*, October 29, 1908, no page available.

426   *Phoenix Pioneer*, January 29, 1910, 1.

427   Obituary, *Spokane Spokesman Review*, September 28, 1945.

428   "POS of America," *Spokane Review*, July 5, 1891, 3.

429   Lorraine Boissoneault, "How the 19th-Century Know Nothing Party Reshaped American Politics," *Smithsonian Magazine*, January 26, 2017, https://www.smithsonian-mag.com/history/immigrants-conspiracies-and-secret-society-launched-american-nativism-180961915/.

430   "The New Publisher," *TN*, December 3, 1915, 2.

431   "News and Comment," *TN*, December 3, 1915, 2.

432   "Boxing Contest a Draw," *TN*, December 17, 1915, 1.

433   "Local Paper Should Be Recognized as Such," *TN*, December 10, 1915, 6.

434   "Hockey Team Now Complete," *TN*, December 24, 1915, 1.

435   "Note and Comment," *TN*, December 24, 1915, 2.

436   *TN*, January 7, 1916, 1.

437   "Let's Resolute for 1916," *TN*, January 7, 1916, 2.

438   "Soldiers for Trail," *TN*, January 21, 1916, 1.

439   "Prohibition Campaign First Shot in Trail," *TN*, January 28, 1916, 1.

440   *TN*, January 28, 1916, 2.

441   "Note and Comment," *TN*, February 11, 1916, 2.

442   "Building Prospects Are Bright in Trail," *TN*, March 17, 1916, 4.

443   "Building Prospects."

444   "Note and Comment," *TN*, March 3, 1916, 2.

445   "Note and Comment."

446   "The Home Newspaper," *TN*, March 17, 1916, 4.

447   "Pure Glory Was Their Chief Reward," *TN*, March 24, 1916, 6.

448   *TN*, March 24, 1916, 2.

449   "Local Matters," *TN*, March 17, 1916, 6.

450   "Note and Comment," *TN*, March 24, 1916, 2.

451   *TN*, April 7, 1916, 2.

452   "Mother's Day Next Sunday," *TN*, May 12, 1916, 2.

453   "Running a Newspaper—An Easy Matter?" *TN*, May 12, 1916, 7.

454   *TN*, March 31, 1916, 2.

455   *TN*, May 26, 1916, 2.

456   "Note and Comment," *TN*, June 2, 1916, 2.

457   "Note and Comment." For more on Lowery, see R.J. Welwood, "Lowery, Robert Thornton," in *Dictionary of Canadian Biography*, vol. 15, University of Toronto/Université Laval, 2003–, accessed December 21, 2021, http://www.biographi.ca/en/bio/lowery_robert_thornton_15E.html.

458   "Grits Talk Plain About Government," *TN*, August 18, 1916, 1.

459   "Grits Talk."

460   "(Adv.) Labor Condemned the Prohibition Act," *TN*, August 4, 1916, 7.

461   Yves Tremblay, "Blaylock, Harry Woodburn," in *Dictionary of Canadian Biography*, vol. 15, University of Toronto/Université Laval, 2003, http://www.biographi.ca/009004-119.01-e.php?&id_nbr=8037&&PHPSESSID=ychzfqkvzape.

462   *TN*, September 1, 1916, 2.

463   "Note and Comment," *TN*, September 8, 1916, 2.

464   "Note and Comment," *TN*, September 22, 1916, 2. Small-town banker and horse trader David Harum is a fictional character in an 1898 novel by American writer Alfred Noyes Westcott.

465   "Crying Need in Trail," *TN*, October 6, 1916, 2.

466   "Note and Comment," *TN*, October 6, 1916, 2.

467   "Note and Comment," *TN*, November 3, 1916, 2.

468   "Night School Assured for Trail," *TN*, November 17, 1916, 1.

469   *TN*, November 17, 1916, 2.

470   "Note and Comment," *TN*, November 17, 1916, 2.

471   "Note and Comment," *TN*, January 19, 1917, 2.

472   "Brief News Notes of Trail," *TN*, March 30, 1917, 1.

473   *TN*, March 30, 1917, 2.

474   Ron Verzuh, "Oregon Doukhobors: The Hidden History of a Russian Religious

Sect's Attempts to Found Colonies in the Beaver State," *BC Studies* 180 (Winter 2013–2014): 43–81.

475   "Try This on Your Piano," *TN*, April 6, 1917, 6.

476   "Editors Do Not Lack Copy," *TN*, April 13, 1917, 4.

477   *TN*, April 20, 1917, 2.

478   "Consolidated Co. Issues Statement to 3,000 Employees," *TN*, April 20, 1917, 6.

479   *TN*, May 4, 1917, 2.

480   "Line-o-Type Or Two," *TN*, May 11, 1917, 2.

481   *TN*, May 25, 1917, 2.

482   *TN*, June 8, 1917, 2.

483   "In and Around Trail," *TN*, June 22, 1917, 4.

484   "Rocking the Boat," *TN*, June 29, 1917, 2.

485   "From the Observatory," *TN*, June 29, 1917, 2.

486   "To Members of Trail Unions and Citizens," *TN*, July 6, 1917, 1.

487   "Time to Revive It," *TN*, July 6, 1917, 3.

488   *TN*, July 13, 1917, 2.

489   *TN*, July 20, 1917, 2.

490   "Trail's Baptism of Fire," *TN*, August 10, 1917, 1.

491   Garnet Basque, *Ghost Towns and Mining Camps of the Boundary Country* (Langley, BC: Sunfire Publications, 1992).

492   "Labor Day Was One of Pleasure for Thousands," *TN*, September 7, 1917, 8.

493   "'Win-the-War' Movement Is Growing," *TN*, September 14, 1917, 2.

494   "Treat All Alike," *TN*, September 28, 1917, 2.

495   "Cons. Co. to Ask for Exemption for Employees," *TN*, October 12, 1917, 9.

496   "Smeltermen Now Paying Patriotic Fund to Bank," *TN*, November 8, 1917, 1.

497   "1,500 Men Quit at Consolidated Smelter," *TN*, November 16, 1917, 1.

498   Much has been written about the 1917 strike. Possibly the most often quoted is Stanley Scott, "A Profusion of Issues: Immigrant Labour, the World War, and the Cominco Strike of 1917," *Labour/Le Travail* 2 (1977): 54–78.

499   *TN*, November 16, 1917, 2.

500   "Statement by S.G. Blaylock," *TN*, November 23, 1917, 1.

501   "Proceedings to Be Taken Against the Daily Province," *TN*, November 23, 1917, 5.

502   "Resent Libel on Trail Workmen from Victoria," *TN*, November 23, 1917, 9.

503   "Smeltermen Issue Statement re Strike to Press," *TN*, November 23, 1917, 9.

504   *TN*, November 30, 1917, 2.

505   "Federal Officer Arrives to Investigate Strike," *TN*, December 7, 1917, 1.

506   "Premature Peace Negotiations," *TN*, December 7, 1917, 2.

507   "From the Observatory," *TN*, December 7, 1917, 2. Billy Sunday was a promising baseball player turned conservative evangelist. For more, see "Billy Sunday," *New World Encyclopedia*, https://www.newworldencyclopedia.org/entry/Billy_Sunday.

508   "To Mothers, Wives and Sisters," *TN*, December 7, 1917, 5.

509   For a full account of the strike, see Scott, "A Profusion of Issues: Immigrant Labour, the World War, and the Cominco Strike of 1917."

510   "Smeltermen Decide to Resume Their Work at Trail Plant," *TN*, December 21, 1917, 1.

511   "Smeltermen Decide."

512   "Smeltermen Decide."

513   "Smeltermen Return to Work," *TN*, December 21, 1917, 2.

514   "Union Government Sweep," *TN*, December 21, 1917, 2.

515   "One Blast Furnace in Operation at the Trail Smelter," *TN*, December 28, 1917, 1.

Trail News (1918–1919)
War's End, Global Flu and Labour Martyrdom

516   "From the Observatory," *TN*, January 25, 1918, 2. For more, see Ron Shearer, "Patrick O'Farrell: Pen for Hire," in *Chicanery, Civility & Celebrations: Tales of Early Rossland* (Rossland: Rossland Heritage Commission, 2019), 48.

517   "Gone Are the Good Old Days," *TN*, January 25, 1918, 3.

518   "From the Observatory," *TN*, February 8, 1918, 2.

519   "From the Observatory," *TN*, March 22, 1918, 2.

520   "Notes in Passing," *TN*, March 22, 1918, 5.

521   *TN*, January 18, 1918, 1.

522   *TN*, January 4, 1918, 1.

523   *TN*, February 15, 1918, 1.

524   "Trail Has Given $98,747.61 to the Pat. Fund to Date," *TN*, March 29, 1918, 3.

525   *TN*, February 15, 1918, 1.

526   "Germany Financed Russian Bolsheviki: Lenine [*sic*], Trotsky and Other Leaders Had Unlimited Credit," *TN*, March 1, 1918, 3.

527   "Walter Truswell Writes," *TN*, March 22, 1918, 3.

528   "Trail Man in the Thick of the Air Raids in London," *TN*, March 29, 1918, 1.

529   "47 Enemy Aliens Now Reporting to Trail's Police Chief," *TN*, March 15, 1918, 6.

530   *TN*, March 15, 1918, 7.

531   *TN*, March 22, 1918, 6.

532   *TN*, March 22, 1918, 7.

533   "Ten Good War Commandments," *TN*, January 4, 1918, 3.

534   *TN*, January 4, 1918, 3.

535   "From the Observatory," *TN*, January 4, 1918, 2.

536   *TN*, January 11, 1918.

537   *TN*, January 4, 1918, 4.

538   Ad, *TN*, April 26, 1918, 3.

539   *TN*, February 15, 1918, 1.

540   *TN*, January 4, 1918, 8.

541   "Encouraging the Yellow Peril," *TN*, January 25, 1918, 2.

542   "Extra Mining Tax Is Not Liked, Nor Is Coolie Labor," *TN*, February 1, 1918, 1.

543   "Douks May Return to Their Native Land—Free Russia," *TN*, February 22, 1918, 5.

544   "Notes in Passing," *TN*, March 22, 1918, 5.

545   *TN*, March 29, 1918, 2.

546   *TN*, February 22, 1918, 8.

547   *TN*, March 22, 1918, 9.

548   "Millions Starving to Death," *TN*, May 31, 1918, 5.

549   "Pte. Harold Weller Was in Prison Camp for 29 Months," *TN*, April 5, 1918, 1.

550   "Payne Met By the Band," *TN*, April 12, 1918, 1.

551   "From the Observatory," *TN*, April 12, 1918, 2.

552   "Fags," *TN*, August 30, 1918, 3.

553   "Taken in Their Own Trap—Huns Gassed," *TN*, May 10, 1918, 7.

554   "A Lin-O-Type or Two," *TN*, May 24, 1918, 2.

555   "Bullet Proof Verses," *TN*, December 13, 1918.

556   "Noted in Passing," *TN*, December 6, 1918, 6.

557   "Canadian Battle Song," *TN*, April 26, 1918, 4.

558   "The Road to France," *TN*, May 3, 1918, 3.

559   "Knitting Song," *TN*, April 26, 1918, 6.

560   "Swat the Fly," *TN*, April 26, 1918, 2.

561   "Must Omit Icing," *TN*, May 31, 1918, 6.

562   "Many Trail Men Are Being Called to Defend the Empire," *TN*, April 26, 1918, 1.

563   "Warrant Made Out for the Arrest of Albert Goodwin," *TN*, May 17, 1918, 1.

564   "Hunt for Goodwin on Vancouver Island," *TN*, June 7, 1918, 8.

565   "A. Goodwin, of Trail, Draft Evader, Shot and Killed," *TN*, August 2, 1918, 1.

566   "Case of Albert Goodwin," *TN*, August 9, 1918, 2.

567   See Roger Stonebanks, *Fighting for Dignity: The Ginger Goodwin Story* (St. John's, NL: Canadian Committee on Labour History, 2004); and Susan Mayse, *Ginger: The Life and Death of Albert Goodwin* (Madeira Park, BC: Harbour Publishing, 1990).

568   "Miss Newman Hurt," *TN*, April 26, 1918, 1.

569   "Noted in Passing," *TN*, April 26, 1918, 5.

570   "Fakir Gets the Coin," *TN*, April 26, 1918, 2.

571   "From the Observatory," *TN*, May 10, 1918, 2.

572   "Noted in Passing," *TN*, May 31, 1918, 5.

573   "To Hear 'Em Click," *TN*, June 7, 1918, 6.

574   "TNT—Travel, Niggah, Travel," *TN*, May 30, 1919, 3.

575   "BC Sidelights," *TN*, May 23, 1919, 7.

576   "Green Handled Alien Labor Matter Without Gloves," *TN*, May 10, 1918, 5.

577   Editorial, *TN*, May 17, 1918, 2.

578   "Endersby was Given Damages, $2,170 Vs. Consolidated," *TN*, May 24, 1918, 1.

579   *TN*, July 12, 1918, 1.

580   "Practical Advice on Arrest and Control of Influenza," *TN*, October 11, 1918, 5.

581   "The Late M.R. McQuarrie—An Appreciation—By the Editor," *TN*, November 29, 1918, 4.

582   "Rossland and Nelson Hard Hit," *TN*, October 25, 1918, 1.

583   "Noted in Passing," *TN*, November 22, 1918, 4.

584   "200 Flu Cases—One Death in this City," *TN*, November 1, 1918, 1.

585   "Through Our Periscope," *TN*, November 1, 1918, 2.

586   *TN*, November 1, 1918, 2.

587   "Dr. Hunt at Arlington Hotel," *TN*, November 1, 1918, 12.

588   "Hundreds of Influenza Cases in Trail, 15 Deaths," *TN*, November 8, 1918, 1.

589   *TN*, November 8, 1918, 2.

590   "Flu Epidemic Still Serious in Trail," *TN*, November 15, 1918, 1.

591   "Lid Not Ready for Lifting," *TN*, November 29, 1918, 2.

592   "Douks Buy 10,000 Acres," *TN*, May 24, 1918, 5.

593   "In and Around Trail," *TN*, May 24, 1918, 8.

594   "Board of Trade Held Largely Attended Gathering," *TN*, June 14, 1918, 1.

595   "From the Observatory," *TN*, June 28, 1918, 2.

596   "From the Observatory," *TN*, June 28, 1918, 2.

597   "Jailed 16 Doukhobors," *TN*, August 2, 1918, 1.

598   "Provincial Sidelights," *TN*, August 9, 1918, 7.

599   "Douks Not Wanted in Canada by Veterans," *TN*, April 11, 1919, 1.

600   "Would Work the Papers," *TN*, March 7, 1919, 2.

601   *TN*, June 21, 1918, 6.

602   *TN*, July 19, 1918, 2.

603   *TN*, July 12, 1918, 4.

604   "Clipped and Censored," *TN*, July 12, 1918, 1.

605   "Trail Smelter in War," *TN*, July 26, 1918, 3.

606   "Mining Notes," *TN*, July 26, 1918, 5.

607   "Noted in Passing," *TN*, August 8, 1918, 3.

608   "Editor Explains," *TN*, August 9, 1918, 4.

609   "Noted in Passing," *TN*, October 11, 1918, 2.

610   CM&S ad, *TN*, November 15, 1918, 8.

611   Ad, *TN*, January 10, 1919, 3.

612   *TN*, December 6, 1918, 5.

613   "Made in Germany," *TN*, December 13, 1918, 4.

614   "What of the New Year," *TN*, December 27, 1918, 2.

615   "Co-operative Efficiency," *TN*, December 27, 1918, 2.

616   "The Mystery of the Flu," *TN*, January 24, 1919, 5.

617   "That Flu Stuff," *TN*, January 24, 1919, 5.

618   "Good Year for Consolidated," *TN*, January 10, 1919, 1.

619   "Remarkable Record," *TN*, January 10, 1919, 2.

620   "Mr. Blaylock's Report," *TN*, January 10, 1919, 4.

621   "Star Theatre Reopened," *TN*, January 3, 1919, 7.

622   "In and Around Trail," *TN*, January 3, 1919, 8.

623   "Dancing Ban to Be Raised," *TN*, March 2, 1919, 1.

624   "Need for Level Heads," *TN*, January 31, 1919, 1.

625   "Be Builders, Not Wreckers," *TN*, January 31, 1919, 2.

626   "Russia's Example Should Be a Clear Warning to Other Nations," *TN*, June 28, 1918, 7.

627   Gregory S. Kealey, "The Canadian Labour Revolt," in *Canadian Labour History Selected Readings*, ed. David Jay Bercuson and David Bright (Toronto: Copp Clark Longmans, 1994), 193–222, discusses the conference and subsequent creation of the OBU.

628   *TN*, January 17, 1919, 2.

629   See Robert Friedheim, *The Seattle General Strike, Centennial Edition* (Seattle: University of Washington Press, 2018).

630   "Through Our Periscope," *TN*, February 14, 1919, 2.

631   "Sympathetic Strike Failed," *TN*, February 14, 1919, 1.

632   "The General Strike," *TN*, February 21, 1919, 6.

633   "Bolshevism and Spartacanism Turned Down Hard in Trail," *TN*, April 4, 1919, 1.

634   "Scotching Bolshevism," *TN*, April 4, 1919, 2.

635   "Bol-she-veek!" *TN*, February 28, 1919, 3.

636   "OBU Man Talked at Meeting Last Night," *TN*, May 16, 1919, 1.

637   "Safety Rules," *TN*, April 18, 1919, 4.

638   "Not Good for Prohibition," *TN,* January 10, 1919, 2.

639   "The Doukhobor and His Status in This Country," *TN*, March 28, 1919, 6.

640   "Douks and Other Sects Scored by Robinson," *TN*, April 25, 1919, 7.

641   "27,000 Strike at Winnipeg," *TN*, May 16, 1919, 1.

642   See Donald Campbell Masters, *The Winnipeg General Strike* (Toronto: University of Toronto Press, 1950), and Michael Dupuis, *The Reporter and the Winnipeg General Strike* (Vancouver: Granville Island Publishing, 2020).

643   "Time For Level Heads," *TN*, May 23, 1919, 2.

644   "Trail Charter Revoked," *TN*, May 23, 1919, 1.

645   "Fallacy of One Big Union," *TN*, May 2, 1919, 6.

646   "Problems Confronting BC Publishers," *TN*, May 23, 1919, 2.

647   "Noted in Passing," *TN*, May 8, 1919, 2.

648   "Remember Russia," *TN*, May 30, 1919, 2.

649   "Announcement," *TN*, May 30, 1918, 2.

650   "Pioneer Trail Publisher, W.B. Willcox, Dies Sunday," *TDT*, September 25, 1945, 3.

651   *New Denver Ledge*, June 5, 1919.

Trail News (1919–1921)
From Printer's Devil to Editor-in-Chief

652 Paul Bowles, "A History in Print—Hall Printing," a seventy-fifth anniversary booklet published by the Hall Printing Co. Ltd., Trail, BC, April 1995, 1.

653 Pam Lavoie, a Hall family member, in email correspondence with the author, provided biographical details, June 5, 2012. The "D" in Hall's name designated D'Nettis or De Nettis, after his maternal grandfather, Preston Nettis Baker. The "D" might have been an affectation added by his father or even Hall himself to suggest high birth.

654 "Minor Mentions," *REW*, December 30, 1901, 2, said her name was Mabel Edwin.

655 Lavoie, correspondence with the author.

656 *Cascade Record*, November 25, 1899.

657 Editorial, *TN*, October 24, 1925, 2.

658 "News and Comment," *REW*, August 6, 1901, 2.

659 *New Denver Ledge*, January 20, 1910, and *Nelson Daily News*, October 19, 1912. "Fire Wipes Out Bossburg Merchants," *Bossburg Herald*, May 14, 1910, 1, reported that an incendiary was the cause of the blaze.

660 "From Print Shop to Farm," *TN*, April 10, 1909, 3.

661 "From the Observatory," *TN*, September 7, 1917, 4, quoting the *Orient Journal* in Washington State.

662 Editorial, *TN*, December 7, 1917, 2.

663 *Northport News*, May 10, 1918.

664 *Northport News*.

665 Bowles, "History in Print," 1.

666 Editorial, *TN*, June 6, 1919, 2.

667 "Labor Meeting Brings Out a Large Crowd," *TN*, June 6, 1919, 1.

668 "Notice," *TN*, June 6, 1919, 10.

669 Rachel Holmes, *Sylvia Pankhurst: Natural Born Rebel* (London: Bloomsbury Publishing, 2020) provides a 1,000-page biography of the "brat."

670 "Clipped and Censored," *TN*, June 6, 1919, 2.

671 "Local Happenings," *TN*, June 13, 1919, 1.

672 "Safety Rules" (from the *Safety Engineering Journal*), *TN*, June 13, 1919, 3.

673 "Beetles and Buttons," *TN*, June 13, 1919, 2.

674 Editorial, *TN*, June 13, 1919, 2.

675 "Colored Minstrels Are the Best," *TN*, July 18, 1919, 4.

676 "In and Around Trail," *TN*, June 13, 1919, 8.

677 Editorial, *TN*, July 25, 1919, 2.

678 "Granby Sings Swan Song," *TN*, June 27, 1919, 2.

679 "Smelter City Celebrates in Royal Manner," *TN*, July 25, 1919, 1.

680 Editorial, *TN*, July 4, 1919, 2.

681 Editorial, *TN*, July 4, 1919, 2.

682 "Provincial Sidelights," *TN*, July 4, 1919, 3.

683 Editorial, *TN*, August 15, 1919, 2.

684   *TN*, September 5, 1919, 4.

685   "They Tell the Truth," *TN*, August 1, 1919, 4.

686   Stephen Hume, "A Deadly Fight for Labour Rights," *Vancouver Sun*, August 31, 2012.

687   Editorial, *TN*, July 18, 1919, 2.

688   "M'Kim Latest Directory Shows Many Changes," *TN*, July 25, 1919, 4.

689   "Consolidated Will Establish Up-to-Date Experimental Farm," *TN*, August 1, 1919, 1.

690   Editorial, *TN*, August 1, 1919, 2.

691   Editorial, *TN*, August 22, 1919, 2.

692   Editorial, *TN*, August 29, 1919, 2.

693   "S.G. Blaylock Is Made General Manager of Consolidated," *TN*, August 15, 1919, 1.

694   Editorial, *TN*, August 22, 1919, 2.

695   "Fears 'Flu' No More Than a Boil on Neck," *TN*, August 22, 1919, 5.

696   Editorial, *TN*, August 22, 1919, 2.

697   Editorial, *TN*, October 3, 1919, 2.

698   "Country Papers," *TN*, September 12, 1919, 4.

699   "Heart to Heart Talk," *TN*, September 12, 1919, 3.

700   "Kimberley Miners Ask for Increase," *TN*, September 26, 1919, 4.

701   Report of the Department of Labour for the year ending December 31, 1919.

702   *TN*, October 17, 1919, 5.

703   "Duke of Devonshire and Party Visit City," *TN*, October 17, 1919, 1.

704   "Big Football Game Ends in a Draw," *TN*, October 17, 1919, 1.

705   "Endersby Wins Appeal," *TN*, October 17, 1919, 2.

706   Editorial, *TN*, December 5, 1919, 2.

707   Editorial, *TN*, October 31, 1919, 2, quoting John R. Sovereign of the *San Poil Eagle*.

708   "Provincial News Notes," *TN*, October 24, 1919, 10.

709   Editorial, *TN*, November 21, 1919, 2.

710   "Trotsky," *TN*, December 12, 1919, 2.

711   Editorial, *TN*, December 26, 1919, 2.

712   "Fernie, 'the Calamity City'," *TN*, December 26, 1919, 2.

713   "Local Happenings," *TN*, January 9, 1920, 1.

714   Editorial, *TN*, January 9, 1920, 2.

715   "Good Riddance," *TN*, January 16, 1920, 2.

716   "'Songs of Hate' in IWW Hymnal," *TN*, January 23, 1920, 4.

717   "Strike Game Petering Out," *TN*, January 30, 1920, 5.

718   "Local Happenings," *TN*, March 5, 1920, 1.

719   Editorial, *TN*, February 20, 1920, 2.

720   "Consolidated Mining and Smelting Co. Grants Wage Increase," *TN*, February 13, 1920, 1.

721 Editorial, *TN*, February 20, 1920, 2.

722 "Father Pat," *TN*, February 13, 1920, 4.

723 "Strategy," *TN*, February 27, 1920, 2.

724 "Don't Grumble," *TN*, February 27, 1920, 6.

725 Editorial, *TN*, March 19, 1920, 2.

726 "In and Around Trail," *TN*, March 19, 1920, 4.

727 Editorial, *TN*, March 26, 1920, 2.

728 Editorial, *TN*, April 23, 1920, 2.

729 "He Broke the Strike…," *TN*, March 26, 1920, 4.

730 Editorial, *TN*, April 23, 1920, 2.

731 "They'll Get Tired Digging Up," *TN*, May 14, 1920, 6.

732 "Smoke Eaters Defeat Nelson," *TN*, June 4, 1920, 1.

733 For a full account of Phoenix's demise, see Garnet Basque, *Ghosts Town and Mining Camps of the Boundary Country* (Langley, BC: Sunfire Publications, 1992).

734 "Smelter Committee Gives Explanations," *TN*, June 18, 1920, 1.

735 "The Regulars and the One Big Union," *TN*, September 10, 1920, 4.

736 "Strike at Bluebell," *TN*, July 30, 1920, 5.

737 "Capitalism," *TN*, June 11, 1920, 5.

738 Editorial, *TN*, July 9, 1920, 2. For more on the Moderation League, see Robert A. Campbell, "Liquor and Liberals: Patronage and Government Control in British Columbia, 1920–1928," *BC Studies* 77 (Spring 1988): 30–53.

739 "'Dokey' Parade Was Best Ever," *TN*, September 10, 1920, 1.

740 "Phoenix Sings Her Swan Song," *TN*, August 27, 1920, 2.

741 Editorial, *TN*, September 3, 1920, 2.

742 "'30' for Lowery," *TN*, May 27, 1921, 2. For more on Lowery, see John Adcock, "Kootenay Newspaper Pioneer—'Colonel' R.T. Lowery," Yesterday's Papers, January 7, 2016, http://john-adcock.blogspot.com/2016/01/kootenay-newspaper-pioneer-colonel-rt.html.

743 Editorial, *TN*, October 1, 1920, 2.

744 "To Our Advertisers," *TN*, October 9, 1920, 2.

745 Editorial, *TN*, November 26, 1920, 2.

746 Editorial, *TN*, October 22, 1920, 2.

747 "Local Athletes Hold Successful Meet," *TN*, October 29, 1920, 1.

748 Editorial, *TN*, January 7, 1921, 2.

749 Editorial, *TN*, January 28, 1921, 2.

750 Ad, *TN*, February 4, 1921, 5.

751 "Trail Narrowly Escapes Destruction by Fire," *TN*, July 29, 1921, 1.

752 CM&S annual report, *TN*, April 22, 1921, 1.

753 "OBU Dying Out at Copper Mountain," *TN*, January 28, 1921, 3.

754 "Labor Troubles Cripple Brittain [sic]," *TN*, February 11, 1921, 1; Editorial, *TN*, January 28, 1921, 2.

755 Editorial, *TN*, May 27, 1921, 2.

756   *TN*, January 28, 1921, 7.

757   Editorial, *TN*, May 27, 1921, 2.

758   Editorial, *TN*, July 8, 1921, 2.

759   Editorial, *TN*, June 17, 1921, 2.

760   *TN*, February 4, 1921, 1.

761   See Nancy McGregor and Patricia Wardrop, "Chautauqua," *The Canadian Encyclopedia*, Historica Canada. Article published February 7, 2006; last edited December 16, 2013.

762   "What We Need," *TN*, November 11, 1921, 6.

763   "An Impression of Socialism," *TN*, January 28, 1921, 2.

764   *TN*, May 6, 1921, 1.

765   "Four Cents Worth of News," *TN*, February 11, 1921, 2.

766   Editorial, *TN*, July 22, 1921, 2.

767   "Communications," *TN*, August 12, 1921, 6.

768   "Tom Is Still Striking," *TN*, August 26, 1921, 2.

769   Editorial, *TN*, October 14, 1921, 2.

770   Editorial, *TN*, October 14, 1921, 2.

771   "When the Paper Doesn't Come," *TN*, September 2, 1921, 5.

772   *TN*, November 18, 1921, 1.

773   Editorial, *TN*, September 23, 1921, 2.

774   Editorial, *TN*, December 30, 1921, 2.

775   Editorial, *TN*, December 30, 1921, 2.

Trail News (1922–1924)
The *News* Advances Toward an Elusive Goal

776   Editorial, *TN*, January 27, 1922, 2.

777   *TN*, March 17, 1922, 6.

778   Editorial, *TN*, February 10, 1922, 2.

779   "Trail Beats Nelson in Exciting Game," *TN*, January 6, 1922, 1.

780   See Jamie Forbes, "The Daily News Cup," *Trail Journal of Local History* (Winter 2011): 30.

781   "Men! Girls! Don't Be 'Lonesome'," *TN*, March 24, 1922, 6.

782   *TN*, February 24, 1922, 3.

783   Editorial, *TN*, January 27, 1922, 2.

784   *TN*, March 10, 1922, 1.

785   *TN*, April 28, 1922, 1.

786   Editorial, *TN*, January 27, 1922, 2.

787   Editorial, *TN*, March 3, 1922, 2.

788   "Annual Report Continued," *TN*, April 21, 1922, 7.

789   "Trail News Installs Modern Linotype," *TN*, May 12, 1922, 1.

790   Editorial, *TN*, May 12, 1922, 2.

791 Editorial, *TN*, May 19, 1922, 2.

792 Editorial, *TN*, June 9, 1922, 2.

793 "Grants Bonuses For Efficiency," *TN*, June 23, 1922, 1.

794 Editorial, *TN*, July 14, 1922, 2.

795 Editorial, *TN*, July 21, 1922, 2.

796 Editorial, *TN*, December 1, 1922, 2.

797 Editorial, *TN*, July 28, 1922, 2.

798 "The Knockers," *TN*, July 28, 1922, 7.

799 Editorial, *TN*, August 4, 1922, 2.

800 Editorial, *TN*, September 1, 1922, 2.

801 "Should Ask Road of Government," *TN*, November 3, 1922, 1.

802 Editorial, *TN*, November 24, 1922, 2.

803 Editorial, *TN*, September 29, 1922, 2.

804 Editorial, *TN*, December 1, 1922, 2.

805 Editorial, *TN*, December 8, 1922, 2.

806 "Premier Oliver Exonerated," *TN*, December 15, 1922, 5.

807 Editorial, *TN*, December 22, 1922, 2.

808 Editorial, *TN*, December 29, 1922, 2.

809 "Trail Tigers Get Their Claws Cut," *TN*, December 22, 1922, 11.

810 Editorial, *TN*, January 12, 1923, 2.

811 Editorial, *TN*, January 5, 1923, 2.

812 Editorial, *TN*, March 2, 1923, 2.

813 "City Team Scores Victory," *TN*, June 22, 1923, 1.

814 "Happenings," *TN*, February 16, 1923, 3.

815 Ad, *TN*, June 8, 1923, 2.

816 Editorial, *TN*, January 5, 1923, 2.

817 Editorial, *TN*, February 16, 1923, 2.

818 Editorial, *TN*, February 23, 1923, 2.

819 Editorial, *TN*, June 8, 1923, 2.

820 Editorial, *TN*, March 16, 1923, 2.

821 "Education and Monuments," *TN*, April 6, 1923, 2.

822 American writer Ross Farquhar was the author of Slats' Diary, a newspaper serial that originally began in the *Iroquois Chief* newspaper during the Great Depression. The *Chief* was published in Iroquois, South Dakota, from 1888 to 1953.

823 *TN*, April 20, 1923, 7.

824 "Are You Guilty?," *TN*, April 20, 1923, 2.

825 "Old Graves," *TN*, April 20, 1923, 2.

826 "No Wonder We're Sick," *TN*, May 11, 1923, 2.

827 "All Dairy Herds to Be Inspected," *TN*, June 29, 1923, 1.

828 "The Strength of Small," *TN*, May 18, 1923, 5. See the *Dictionary of Unitarian and*

Universalist Biography, General Assembly of Unitarian and Free Christian Churches, website of the Unitarian Universalist History & Heritage Society, https://uudb.org/articles/richardlloydjones.html, for an account of columnist Richard Lloyd Jones (April 14, 1873–December 4, 1963). The dictionary describes him as "an outspoken and influential journalist" and "the longtime owner and editor of the Tulsa Tribune." The description continues: "He used his newspaper as a pulpit, regularly preaching to his readers in editorials printed under the banner, 'Saturday Sermonette.' His reputation is tainted however, by an editorial, the alleged content of which some hold responsible for helping to incite the 1921 Tulsa Race Riot, an act of violence directed against Blacks, unparalleled in American history."

829   Editorial, *TN*, April 13, 1923, 2.

830   "Over the Back Fence," *TN*, April 27, 1923, 2.

831   "Take Your Pick," *TN*, May 11, 1923, 2.

832   "Tell Him Now," *TN*, August 17, 1923, 2.

833   "We Worry Too Much," *TN*, May 4, 1923, 2.

834   "To the Flapper," *TN*, May 4, 1923, 2.

835   "Tell It To Jane," *TN*, May 25, 1923, 2.

836   "The Sweet Girl Graduate," *TN*, June 1, 1923, 2.

837   "Oleo Banned at Great Cost," *TN*, July 6, 1923, 7.

838   Editorial, *TN*, July 20, 1923, 2.

839   *TN*, June 22, 1923, 11.

840   "Is Home Life Passing," *TN*, August 3, 1923, 2.

841   Editorial, *TN*, October 19, 1923, 2.

842   "My City and I," *TN*, July 13, 1923, 1.

843   Editorial, *TN*, June 8, 1923, 2.

844   "Why We Boost the Schools," *TN*, July 27, 1923, 2.

845   "Send It In," *TN*, August 10, 1923, 8.

846   "Only a Few Exceptions," *TN*, September 21, 1923, 2.

847   *TN*, August 24, 1923, 4.

848   *TN*, August 24, 1923, 4.

849   "The Good Housewife," *TN*, September 7, 1923, 2.

850   "Are American Women Growing Ugly?" *TN*, November 16, 1923, 2.

851   "Will Audit Government Accounts," *TN*, November 23, 1923, 5.

852   "Premier Oliver Is After W.K. Esling," *TN*, December 7, 1923, 4.

853   "Legislative Session Ends," *TN*, December 28, 1923, 5.

854   *TN*, December 21, 1923, 4.

855   "Publishing the News," *TN*, November 16, 1923, 2.

856   "The Editor Talks," *TN*, January 19, 1924, 2.

857   Editorial, *TN*, January 19, 1924, 2.

858   "What Do They Want," *TN*, January 25, 1924, 2.

859   "Listen, Lady," *TN*, February 1, 1924, 2.

860   Editorial, *TN*, February 1, 1924, 2.

861   "IWW Call Out Lumber Workers," *TN*, January 19, 1924, 5.

862   Editorial, *TN*, February 29, 1924, 2.

863   "Capitalism," *TN*, May 8, 1924, 2.

864   "Local Bard Sings of Bobbie Burns," *TN*, February 1, 1924, 9.

865   *TN*, February 22, 1924, 6.

866   "Play Ball," *TN*, May 9, 1924, 4.

867   "Communication," *TN*, January 25, 1924, 6.

868   "Our New Carrier System," *TN*, February 1, 1924, 1.

869   "Our Carrier Troubles," *TN*, February 22, 1924, 1.

870   "Arthur Brisbane, American Editor," https://www.britannica.com/biography/arthur-brisbane.

871   Editorial, *TN*, February 8, 1924, 2.

872   "CM&S Made Progress in 1924," *TN*, February 1, 1924, 7.

873   "Judge [J.A.] Forin Renders Decision in Famous Smoke Controversy," *TN*, May 2, 1924, 1.

874   "Health Regulation Violators Arrested," *TN*, March 7, 1924, 9.

875   "Trail Workmen Reaping Reward," *TN*, March 21, 1924, 1.

876   "The Country Girl," *TN*, May 2, 1924, 1.

877   "The Inverted Pyramid," *TN*, March 21, 1924, 1.

878   "A Little Straight-from-the-shoulder Talk," *TN*, February 1, 1924, 2.

879   "Journalistic Accuracy," *TN*, February 15, 1924, 2.

880   "An Editor's Discretion," *TN*, March 28, 1924, 2.

881   "This Might Be Any of Our Trail Fathers," *TN*, March 15, 1924, 4.

882   "Keep It Out of the Paper," *TN*, March 28, 1924, 2.

883   "Communication," *TN*, May 16, 1924, 3.

884   "Communication," *TN*, May 16, 1924, 3.

885   "Communication," *TN*, May 30, 1924, 8.

886   "Is the Newspaper Man a Liar?," *TN*, June 13, 1924, 2.

887   "I Am the Country Newspaper," *TN*, May 16, 1924, 2.

888   "A Women's Appeal," *TN*, June 13, 1924, 5.

889   "Consolidated Company Will Declare Dividend," *TN*, June 20, 1924, 1.

890   *TN*, August 29, 1924, 1.

891   "Vice-Regal Party Visits Trail," *TN*, August 8, 1924, 1.

892   "Let's Do Something," *TN*, June 18, 1924, 2.

893   "The Loud Girl," *TN*, August 1, 1924, 2.

894   Editorial, *TN*, August 29, 1924, 2.

895   Jeremy Lybarger, "Reopening the Case Files of Leopold and Loeb," *Paris Review*, July 26, 2018, offers a new view of the trial of two rich Chicago boys who murdered young Bobby Franks for no apparent reason, https://www.theparisreview.org/blog/2018/07/26/reopening-the-case-files-of-leopold-and-loeb/.

896   "Peter Veregin [*sic*]," *TN*, October 31, 1924, 2.

897   *TN*, September 12, 1924, 10.

898 "Eugene Bargo Meets Death," *TN*, October 17, 1924, 11.

899 Editorial, *TN*, October 17, 1924, 2.

900 Editorial, *TN*, August 22, 1924, 2.

901 "I Am the Newspaper," *TN*, August 22, 1924, 2.

902 Editorial, *TN*, October 10, 1924, 2.

903 Editorial, *TN*, October 10, 1924, 2.

904 Editorial, *TN*, October 10, 1924, 2.

905 "Communication," *TN*, October 17, 1924, 11.

906 Ad, *TN*, November 7, 1924, 3.

907 "Chinese Domestic Bill Introduced," *TN*, November 28, 1924, 6.

908 *TN*, November 14, 1924, 1.

909 "Armistice Day, 1924," *TN*, November 14, 1924, 8.

910 Editorial, *TN*, November 14, 1924, 2.

911 Editorial, *TN*, December 12, 1924, 2.

912 *TN*, December 5, 1924, 7.

913 "Consolidated Declared Dividend Yesterday," *TN*, December 12, 1924, 1.

914 "Pay-Day," *TN*, December 26, 1924, 6.

915 Editorial, *TN*, December 26, 1924, 2.

Trail News (1925)
The Smelter City Finally Gets Its Daily

916 "This Is Our Birthday," *TN*, October 17, 1924, 2.

917 "The Pugilist and the Martyr," *TN*, January 16, 1925, 2.

918 "In the Merry USA," *TN*, January 30, 1925, 2.

919 *TN*, January 9, 1925, 2.

920 "Buried at Twenty-Seven," *TN*, January 23, 1925, 2.

921 "Everybody Happy?," *TN*, January 23, 1925, 1.

922 "The Night Shift," *TN*, January 2, 1925, 9.

923 Elsie G. Turnbull, *Trail Between Two Wars: The Story of a Smelter City* (Victoria: Morriss Printing Co., 1980), 51.

924 "Monument for Nurse Neilson," *TN*, February 13, 1925, 1.

925 Greg Nesteroff, "8 Lesser-known Trail Hotels," *The Kütne Reader*, November 9, 2020, https://gregnesteroff.wixsite.com/kutnereader/post/8-lesser-known-trail-hotels.

926 "Pat Hanley Making Rapid Recovery," *TN*, February 13, 1925, 1.

927 Editorial, *TN*, February 13, 1925, 2.

928 Editorial, *TN*, February 13, 1925, 2.

929 "A Thought for You," *TN*, February 13, 1925, 2.

930 Editorial, *TN*, February 20, 1925, 2.

931 "In Days Gone By," *TN*, February 20, 1925, 2.

932 "Boys and Girls," *TN*, February 20, 1925, 2.

933   "Guard Against the 'Flu'," *TN*, February 20, 1925, 4.

934   Editorial, *TN*, April 3, 1925, 3.

935   "Government Acts Too Hastily," *TN*, April 3, 1925, 9.

936   Editorial, *TN*, April 3, 1925, 2

937   "Exemption from Vaccination," *TN*, April 10, 1925, 1.

938   "Is Vaccination a Preventive?," *TN*, April 10, 1925, 6.

939   "The Truth about Vaccines," *TN*, April 10, 1925, 2.

940   Editorial, *TN*, April 17, 1925, 2.

941   "The Pathological Nature of Vaccine...", *TN*, April 17, 1925, 6.

942   "Dash to Nome Press Agent Idea," *TN*, April 24, 1925, 6.

943   "Vaccine Culprits Face Prosecution," *TN*, May 8, 1925, 1.

944   Editorial, *TN*, May 15, 1924, 2.

945   "That Chicken Dinner Episode," *TN*, April 3, 1925, 4.

946   *TN*, April 3, 1925, 4.

947   "Ernie Arthur Is Unbeatable," *TN*, May 8, 1925, 1.

948   "Vanity Bags Prehistoric—Women Carried Them 2,000 Years Ago in Mongolia," *TN*, April 24, 1925, 7.

949   "Spitting Proves a Costly Habit," *TN*, May 8, 1925, 1.

950   "Has Declared War on Pests," *TN*, May 1, 1925, 7.

951   "Will Be Laid to Last Rest," *TN*, May 1, 1925, 3.

952   "Ypres Day Observed in Trail," *TN*, April 24, 1925, 1; Editorial, *TN*, April 24, 1925, 2.

953   *TN*, April 24, 1925, 8.

954   "James McEwan Pays for Assault—Gets Off Lightly with Fine of $20 and Costs for Assaulting Young Girl," *TN*, May 1, 1925, 1.

955   "First Evidence in Murder Trial," *TN*, May 15, 1925, 1.

956   "Hanley's Trial to Be Re-Heard—Mistake," *TN*, May 15, 1925, 11.

957   "Communication," *TN*, May 15, 1925, 1.

958   "Some of the Perils of Vaccination," *TN*, May 29, 1925, 6.

959   *TN*, May 15, 1925, 6.

960   "Cross-Word Puzzle Puzzles the World," *TN*, May 22, 1925, 6.

961   "Why I Am an Anti-Vaccinationist," *TN*, May 22, 1925, 6.

962   "Vaccination by Force," *TN*, July 10, 1925, 9.

963   "Vaccine Firm Sued by US for $599,936," *TN*, June 26, 1925, 1.

964   "The March of Smallpox," *TN*, August 21, 1925, 8.

965   "Communication from Mr. Blaylock," *TN*, July 24, 1925, 1.

966   "Mayor Speaks to Critics," *TN*, July 24, 1925, 1.

967   "At It Again," *TN*, July 24, 1925, 2.

968   "Workmen's Committee and City Council Endorse Resolution," *TN*, August 7, 1925, 1.

969   "After the Editor's Scalp," *TN*, May 22, 1925, 2.

970   "The Country Weekly," *TN*, June 5, 1925, 2.

971   "Pick's Paragrams," *TN*, June 19, 1925, 5.

972   "An Editor's Inventory," *TN*, July 17, 1925, 2.

973   Editorial, *TN*, July 17, 1925, 2.

974   *TN*, June 19, 1925, 1.

975   "World's Premier Lead-zinc-silver Producer," *TN*, July 31, 1925, 9.

976   "It's a Good Job, After All," *TN*, July 10, 1925, 2.

977   "Beer Saloons Must Obey the Regulations," *TN*, July 10, 1925, 3.

978   "Man Told to Support his Wife," *TN*, July 31, 1925, 5.

979   "Newspaper Can Hide No Mistakes," *TN*, August 7, 1925, 2.

980   "Newspaper Men Elect Officers," *TN*, September 4, 1925, 4.

981   "Fifteenth Annual Trail Fair One of Best in Local History," *TN*, September 18, 1925, 1.

982   "Mastodon Tooth Weighs 4 Pounds," *TN*, September 4, 1925, 7.

983   "Chinese Criminals at Vancouver," *TN*, September 25, 1925, 2.

984   "What Next?," *TN*, October 2, 1925, 2.

985   "Helping Ourselves by Helping Others," *TN*, October 9, 1925, 8.

986   "Politics, Policy and Piffle," *TN*, October 16, 1925, 8.

987   "Announcement," *TN*, October 16, 1925, 1.

988   *TN*, October 16, 1925, 2.

989   Turnbull, *Between Two Wars*, 51.

990   "Nurse Mildred Neilson," *Trail Historical Society Newsletter*, October 2005, 4.

991   "Hanley Again Faces Jury," *TN*, October 22, 1925, 1.

992   Frances Welwood, *Passing Through Missing Pages: The Intriguing Story of Annie Garland Foster* (Halfmoon Bay, BC: Caitlin Press, 2011), 175.

993   "The Story of Unrequited Love and Murder in the Kootenays," *Trail Times*, December 10, 2020, no page number.

994   "The Daily Bulletin," *TN*, October 22, 1925, 1.

995   Ad, "The Daily Bulletin," *TN*, October 22, 1925, 6.

996   Editorial, *TN*, November 5, 1925, 2.

997   Editorial, *TN*, November 5, 1925, 2.

998   "Will Make War on Klu [*sic*] Klux Klan," *TN*, November 12, 1925, 1.

999   "This Week," *TN*, November 19, 1925, 9.

1000   *TN*, October 29, 1925, 2.

1001   "The Editor's Opportunity," *TN*, November 19, 1925, 2.

What Became of Trail's Pioneer Printer's Devils?

1002   "I Am the Newspaper," *TN*, August 22, 1924, 2.

1003   Solka Jr., "Wrong Font Thompson," 71. Apparently Thompson preferred "Wandering Foot" as a nickname, writes Terence Cole in "'Wrong Font' Thompson Remembered," *Fairbanks Daily News-Miner*, January 5, 1976.

1004   Loss Bernard to Paul Solka, "Wrong Font Thompson," 74.

1005   *The Washington Newspaper.*

1006   Dermot Cole, "Fairbanks Daily News-Miner Entered 'Sea of Chance' 100 Years Ago Today," *Fairbanks Daily News-Miner*, March 22, 2009.

1007   Terrence Cole, "'Wrong Font' Thompson Remembered," *Fairbanks Daily News-Miner*, January 5, 1976.

1008   Rearden, "Wrong Font Thompson."

1009   Rearden, "Wrong Font Thompson."

1010   William Fentress Thompson, https://www.findagrave.com/memorial/88654265/william-fentress-thompson.

1011   "Pioneer Alaska Editor Succumbs to Pneumonia," *Victoria Daily Colonist*, January 5, 1926.

1012   A.H. Nordale, quoted in Solka Jr., "Wrong Font Thompson," 80.

1013   Judge Cecil Clegg, quoted in Solka Jr. and Bremer, *Adventures in Alaskan Journalism*, 85.

1014   Linda Kracke, researcher, "Descendants of George W. Caton," Frazier Farmstead Museum, Walla Walla, WA, 2007. Judge Caton and Martha are listed. Author's copy.

1015   Notes on the Thompsons, Elsie G. Turnbull fonds, Selkirk College Regional Archives.

1016   "Mrs. Lavinia Collis Died Friday Last," *Rossland Miner*, September 6, 1923.

1017   *TN*, September 7, 1923.

1018   Rosa Jordan and Derek Choukalos, *Rossland, The First 100 Years* (Rossland: Harry Lefevre, 1995), 59.

1019   Ron Shearer, email correspondence with the author, December 28, 2019.

1020   Shearer, correspondence.

1021   "A Statesman Passes," *TDT*, December 3, 1946, 4.

1022   Andrew Zwicker, "Walk This Way: Heritage Buildings Anchor Tourism Initiative," *Rossland Telegraph*, April 20, 2011, http://rosslandtelegraph.com/news/walk-way-heritage-buildings-anchor-tourism-initiative-10948#.Xgf3Y9ZKhcA.

1023   Jordan and Choukalos, *Rossland*, 96.

1024   John George Diefenbaker, *I Am Canadian* (subtitled The Right Honourable John G. Diefenbaker, PC). RCA Victor (CC-1027) issued the recording in 1965. Author's copy.

1025   Jamie Forbes, "Trail Times," in *Trail of Memories: Trail, BC, 1895–1945* (Trail: Trail History and Heritage Committee, 1997), 14.

1026   Jordan and Choukalos, *Rossland*, 95–96.

1027   Parliamentary Library, Parliament of Canada records.

1028   "'Billy' Esling Dies This Morning," *TDT*, December 2, 1946, 1.

1029   British Columbia Registration of Death No. 013112.

1030   "A Man and a Mountain," *TDT*, December 17, 1946, 4.

1031   Torchy Anderson, *Vancouver Province*, June 5, 1944, reprinted as "An Appreciation," *TDT*, December 17, 1946, 2.

1032   "Farewell Presentation," *TN*, June 27, 1914, 1.

1033   *Melfort Moon* advertising rate card, author's copy.

1034   *Melfort Moon*, July 8, 1914, 3.

1035   "Acting on Premature Procedure," *Melfort Moon*, September 16, 1914, 4.

1036   See Frank Parker Stockbridge, *Small-Town Papers* (Philadelphia: Curtis Publishing, 1928), originally published in the *Saturday Evening Post*; and W.L. Carr, *Newspaper Is Town Builder* (Salt Lake City: Porte Publishing, 1938).

1037   All biographical information was drawn from "Melfort Moon Editor Passes Suddenly Sunday," *Melfort Moon*, August 15, 1940.

1038   "Melfort Moon Editor."

1039   "James Clarke, Pioneer Printer, Publisher Dies on North Shore," *Vancouver Province*, April 26, 1943.

1040   "Pioneer Trail Publisher, W.B. Willcox, Dies Sunday," *TDT*, September 25, 1945, 3.

1041   *Spokane Chronicle*, October 5, 1937.

1042   Certificate of Death No. 1372, Washington State Department of Health, September 25, 1945.

1043   P. Bowles, "A History in Print," Hall Printing brochure, self-published, April 1995, 2.

1044   Al King, *Red Bait!: Struggles of a Mine Mill Local* (Vancouver: Kingbird Publishing, 1998), 39.

1045   Bowles, "History in Print," 1.

1046   "Letters to the Editor—Count Your Blessings," *Commentator*, May 19, 1943, 3.

1047   David Michael Roth, "A Union on the Hill" (master's thesis, Simon Fraser University, 1991), 30.

1048   Craig Barnsley, "Long Fight for Free Press," *The Arrow*, June 1973, 2.

1049   Barnsley, "Long Fight," quoting the *Ad-News*.

Conclusion

1050   "Headlines, Deadlines & Bottom Lines," *60 Minutes*, February 27, 2022.

1051   The Local News Research Project recorded 240 media closures from 2008 to 2018. The majority have been community papers. From J-Source, The Canadian Journalism Project, https://j-source.ca/over-250-canadian-news-media-outlets-have-closed-in-the-last-ten-years/.

1052   A Wikipedia entry listed "defunct newspapers of Canada" in February 2011.

1053   Haydn Watters, "This Journalist Says Canada Saved Him. Now, He's Saving a 136-year-old Ontario Newspaper," *CBC News*, January 19, 2022.

1054   "The Editor's Opportunity," *TN*, November 19, 1925, 2.

1055   Jamie Forbes, email correspondence with the author, April 7, 2020

BIBLIOGRAPHY

NEWSPAPERS

Weeklies

*Trail Creek News/Trail News**
BC Federationist
Bossburg Herald
Boundary Creek Times
Brooklyn News
Cascade Record
Cranbrook Herald
Donald Truth
Enderby Press and Walker's Weekly
Ferguson (later Lardeau) Eagle
Fernie Ledger/Fernie District Ledger
Grand Forks Gazette
Greenwood Ledge
Kaslo Kootenaian
Melfort Moon
Nelson Economist
Nelson Miner
Nelson Tribune
New Denver Ledge
Northport News
Orient Journal
Phoenix Pioneer
Rossland Miner
Rossland Weekly Record
Sandon Paystreak
San Poil Eagle
Trail Creek Miner
Victoria Gazette
Vidette, The

*1895–1925, absent editions from 1900 to 1903. Scanned editions are available on request at Selkirk College Library, Castlegar, BC. As of the writing of this book, the UBC Historical Newspapers collection (https://open.library.ubc.ca/collections/bcnewspapers) was planning to include the *News* online.

Dailies

British Colonist
Fairbanks Daily News–Miner
Morning Olympian
Nelson Daily Miner
Nelson Daily News
Rossland Evening Record
Rossland Evening World
Rossland Miner
Seattle Post–Intelligencer
Spokane Chronicle
Spokane Falls Review
Spokane Spokesman Review
Toronto Globe
Trail Daily Ad–News
Trail Daily Bulletin
Trail Daily Times (formerly Trail Times)
Vancouver Daily World
Vancouver Province
Vancouver Sun
Victoria Times–Colonist

Periodicals

Arrow, The
Cominco Magazine
Commentator, The
Saturday Evening Post
Saturday Night

ARTICLES

Adcock, John. "Kootenay Newspaper Pioneer—'Colonel' R.T. Lowery." *Yesterday's Papers*, January 7, 2016, https://john-adcock.blogspot.com/2016/01/kootenay-newspaper-pioneer-colonel-rt.html.

Anglin, Gerald. "The Strangest Insurance Company in the World." *Maclean's*, February 1, 1951, https://archive.macleans.ca/article/1951/2/1/the-strangest-insurance-company-in-the-world.

Barnsley, Craig. "Long Fight for Free Press." *The Arrow*, June 1973.

Boba, Eleanor. "A Machine for the 19th Century: The Iron Hand Press." American Bookbinders Museum, https://bookbindersmuseum.org/a-machine-for-the-19th-century-the-iron-hand-press/, San Francisco, July 24, 2014.

Boissoneault, Lorraine. "How the 19th-Century Know Nothing Party Reshaped American Politics," *Smithsonian Magazine*, January 26, 2017, https://www.smithsonianmag.com/history/immigrants-conspiracies-and-secret-society-launched-american-nativism-180961915/.

Campbell, Robert A. "Liquor and Liberals: Patronage and Government Control in British Columbia, 1920–1928." *BC Studies* 77 (Spring 1988): 30–53.

Campbell, Burt R. "From Hand-Set Type to Linotype." *British Columbia Historical Quarterly* 10, no. 4 (October 1946): 258–70.

Cole, Dermot. "Fairbanks Daily News-Miner Entered 'Sea of Chance' 100 Years Ago Today." *Fairbanks Daily News-Miner*, March 22, 2009.

Cole, Terrence. "'Wrong Font' Thompson Remembered." *Fairbanks Daily News-Miner*, January 5, 1976.

Fahey, John R. "Spokane Falls and Northern." *Pacific Northwesterner* 4, no. 2 (Spring 1960): 17–26.

Forbes, Jamie. "Frank Hanna: The Full Story." *Trail Journal of Local History* 4 (Winter 2011): 46–49.

Forbes, Jamie. "The Daily News Cup." *Trail Journal of Local History* (Winter 2011): 30.

Forsyth, John. "The Pioneer Press of British Columbia." *British Columbia History* 45, no. 1 (Spring 2012): 5–10.

Gilmour, Julie. "Interpreting Social Disorder: The Case of the 1907 Vancouver Riots." *International Journal* 67, no. 2 (Spring 2012): 483–95.

Godfrey, Elaine. "What We Lost When Gannet Came to Town." *The Atlantic*, October 5, 2021.

Keats, John. "Legacy of Stephen Girard." *American Heritage* 29, no. 4 (1978): 1–8, https://www.americanheritage.com/legacy-stephen-girard#4.

Kenning, Allyson. "Tales and Legends of the Mountain Kingdom: A Tale of Many Papers." *Rossland Telegraph*, May 3, 2011, https://rosslandtelegraph.com/news/tales- and-legends-mountain-kingdom-tale-many-papers-11083#.XhkRFdZKi-p.

Lybarger, Jeremy. "Reopening the Case Files of Leopold and Loeb." *Paris Review*, July 26, 2018.

McGregor, Nancy, and Patricia Wardrop. "Chautauqua." *The Canadian Encyclopedia*, Historica Canada. Article published February 7, 2006; last edited December 16, 2013.

Nesteroff, Greg. "Conner Malott and the *Trail Creek Miner*." *Trail Journal of Local History* 5 (Winter 2014): 48–50.

Nesteroff, Greg. "Wandering Printing Presses of West Kootenay." *Kütne Reader*, April 7, 2019, https://gregnesteroff.wixsite.com/kutnereader/post/wandering-printing-presses-of-west-kootenay.

Scott, Stanley. "A Profusion of Issues: Immigrant Labour, the World War, and the Cominco Strike of 1917." *Labour/Le Travail* 2 (1977): 54–78.

Solka Jr., Paul. "Wrong Font Thompson." *Alaska Journal* 4, no. 2 (Spring 1974): 66–81.

Stockbridge, Frank Parker. "Small-Town Papers." *Saturday Evening Post*, 1928, reprinted in booklet form by the Toronto Type Foundry Co. Ltd.

Tremblay, Yves. "Blaylock, Harry Woodburn." *Dictionary of Canadian Biography*, Vol. 15. University of Toronto, 2005. http://www.biographi.ca/en/bio/blaylock_harry_woodburn_15E.html.

Verzuh, Ron. "Oregon Doukhobors: The Hidden History of a Russian Religious Sect's Attempts to Found Colonies in the Beaver State." *BC Studies* 180 (Winter 2013–2014): 43–81.

Verzuh, Ron. "The *Rossland Evening World*: A Workers' Voice for the Kootenays." *British Columbia History* 54, no. 4 (Winter 2021): 5–10.

Welwood, R.J. "Lowery, Robert Thornton," in *Dictionary of Canadian Biography*, vol. 15, University of Toronto/Université Laval, 2003–, accessed December 21, 2021, http://www.biographi.ca/en/bio/lowery_robert_thornton_15E.html.

No Author. "Craig Weir: The Only Journalist on the Hill." *Trail Journal of Local History* 3 (Summer 2007): 14–19.

Books

Affleck, George Allan. *Paper Trails: A History of British Columbia and Yukon Community Newspapers.* Vancouver: Arch Communications and the Community Newspapers Association, 1999.

Alexander, Benjamin F. *Coxey's Army: Popular Protest in the Gilded Age.* Baltimore: Johns Hopkins University Press, 2015.

Basque, Garnet. *West Kootenay: The Pioneer Years.* Surrey, BC: Heritage House, 1990.

Basque, Garnet. *Ghost Towns and Mining Camps of the Boundary Country.* Langley, BC: Sunfire Publications, 1992.

Bone, John R. and Arthur H. Urquart Colquhoun. *A History of Canadian Journalism in the Several Portions of the Dominion.* Toronto: Canadian Press Association, 1908.

Brighton, Eric, and Greg Nesteroff. *Lost Kootenays: A History in Pictures.* Lunenburg, NS: MacIntyre Purcell Publishing, 2021.

Bruner, Robert F., and Sean D. Carr. *The Panic of 1907: Lessons Learned from the Market's Perfect Storm.* Hoboken, NJ: John Wiley & Sons, 2007.

Carr, W.L. *Newspaper Is Town Builder.* Salt Lake City: Porte Publishing Company, 1938.

Chow, Lily. *Hard Is the Journey: Stories of Chinese Settlement in British Columbia's Kootenay* (Qualicum Beach, BC: Caitlin Press, 2022)

Cone, Michael A. *Connecting the Kootenays: The Kootenay Lake Ferries—A Hundred Years of Service, 1921–2020.* Self-published, 2022.

DeFilippo, Thomas J. *Stephen Girard, The Man, His College and Estate,* 2nd ed., 1999, http://www.girardweb.com/girard/download.html.

Downs, Art. *British Columbia-Yukon Sternwheel Days.* Surrey, BC: Heritage House, 1972.

Downs, Art. *Pioneer Days in British Columbia.* Surrey: Heritage House, 1979.

Dupuis, Michael. *The Reporter and the Winnipeg General Strike.* Vancouver: Granville Island Publishing, 2020.

Forbes, Jamie. *Historical Portraits of Trail.* Trail: City Archives, 1980.

Forbes, Jamie. *Trail of Memories: Trail, BC, 1895–1945.* Trail: Trail History and Heritage Committee, 1997.

Friedheim, Robert. *The Seattle General Strike, Centennial Edition.* Seattle: University of Washington Press, 2018.

Gainer, Terry. *When Trains Ruled the Kootenays: A Short History of Railways in Southeastern British Columbia.* Victoria: Rocky Mountain Books, 2022.

Harris, Cole. *Newspapers & the Slocan in the 1890s.* New Denver: Chameleon Fire Editions, 2016.

Hinde, John. *When Coal Was King: Ladysmith and the Coal-Mining Industry on Vancouver Island.* Vancouver: UBC Press, 2003.

Hochschild, Adam. *American Midnight: The Great War, a Violent Peace, and Democracy's Forgotten Crisis* (New York: Mariner Books, 2022)

Hochschild, Adam. *To End All Wars: A Story of Loyalty and Rebellion, 1914–1918.* New York: Houghton Mifflin Harcourt, 2012.

Holmes, Rachel. *Sylvia Pankhurst: Natural Born Rebel.* London: Bloomsbury Publishing, 2020.

Jackson, W. Turrentine. *Treasure Hill: Portrait of a Silver Mining Camp.* Reno and Las Vegas: University of Nevada Press, 1963.

Jordan, Rosa, and Derek Choukalos. *Rossland: The First 100 Years.* Rossland: Harry Lefevre, 1995.

Kealey, Gregory S. "The Canadian Labour Revolt." In *Canadian Labour History Selected Readings,* ed. David Jay Bercuson and David Bright. Toronto: Copp Clark Longmans, 1994, 193–222.

King, Al. *Red Bait!: Struggles of a Mine Mill Local.* Vancouver: Kingbird Publishing, 1998.

Kingsmill, Harold. *First History of Rossland, BC.* Rossland: Stunden & Perine, 1897.

Lukas, J. Anthony. *Big Trouble: A Murder in a Small Western Town Sets Off a Struggle for the Soul of America.* New York: Simon & Schuster, 1997.

Malhotra, Ravi, and Benjamin Issit. *Able to Lead: Disablement, Radicalism, and the Political Life of E.T. Kingsley.* Vancouver: UBC Press, 2021.

Masters, Donald Campbell. *The Winnipeg General Strike.* Toronto: University of Toronto Press, 1950.

Mayse, Susan. *Ginger: The Life and Death of Albert Goodwin.* Madeira Park, BC: Harbour Publishing, 1990.

McDonald, J.D. *The Railroads of Rossland, British Columbia.* Rossland: Historical Museum Association, 1991.

McNelis, Sarah. *Copper King at War: The Biography of F. Augustus Heinze.* Missoula: University of Montana Press, 1969.

Mercier, Anne. *Father Pat: A Hero of the Far West.* Gloucester: Michin and Gibbs, 1909.

Mickleburgh, Rod. *On the Line: A History of the British Columbia Labour Movement.* Vancouver: BC Labour Heritage Centre, 2018.

Mouat, Jeremy. *Roaring Days: Rossland's Mines and the History of British Columbia.* Vancouver: UBC Press, 1995.

Mouat, Jeremy. *The Business of Power: Hydro-Electricity in Southeastern British Columbia, 1887–1987.* Victoria: Sono Nis Press, 1997.

Nesteroff, Greg. *Kootenay News: The History of Nelson's Newspapers.* Nelson, BC: Touchstones Nelson: Museum of Art and History, 2019.

Pryce, Paula. *Keeping the Lakes Way: Reburial and the Recreation of a Moral World among an Invisible People.* Toronto: University of Toronto Press, 1999.

Ramsay, Bruce. *Ghost Towns of British Columbia.* Vancouver: Mitchell Press, 1963.

Rayner, William. *Images of History: Twentieth Century British Columbia Through the Front Pages.* Victoria: Orca Book Publishers, 1997.

Rearden, Jim. "Wrong Font Thompson." In *Alaska's First Bush Pilots, 1923–30.* Portland: Graphic Arts Books, 2009.

Robin, Martin. *The Rush for Spoils: The Company Province, 1871–1933.* Toronto: McClelland & Stewart, 1972.

Roe, JoAnn. *Columbia River: An Historical Travel Guide.* Caldwell, ID: Caxton Press, 2013.

Shearer, Ron. *Chicanery, Civility and Celebrations: Tales of Early Rossland.* Rossland: Rossland Heritage Commission, 2019.

Solka Jr., Paul, and Art Bremer. *Adventures in Alaskan Journalism Since 1903.* Fairbanks: Commercial Printing Co., 1980.

Stonebanks, Roger. *Fighting for Dignity: The Ginger Goodwin Story.* St. John's, NL: Canadian Committee on Labour History, 2004.

Topping, E.S. *Chronicles of the Yellowstone.* St. Paul: Pioneer Press Company, 1888.

Turnbull, Elsie G. *Topping's Trail: The First Years of a Now Famous Smelter City.* Vancouver: Mitchell Press, 1964.

Turnbull, Elsie G. "Trail's Pioneer Newspaperman." In *Pioneer Days in British Columbia*, vol. 3, ed. Art Downs. Victoria: Heritage House, 1977, 118–123.

Turnbull, Elsie G. *Trail Between Two Wars: The Story of a Smelter City*. Victoria: Morriss Printing Co., 1980.

Turnbull, Elsie G. *Trail—A Smelter City*. Langley, BC: Sunfire Publications, 1964.

Turnbull, Elsie G. *Trail... An Invitation to History*. Trail: Hall Printing Company, 1987.

Turnbull, Elsie G. *Ghost Towns and Drowned Towns of West Kootenay*. Surrey, BC: Heritage House, 1988.

Welwood, Frances. *Passing Through Missing Pages: The Intriguing Story of Annie Garland Foster*. Halfmoon Bay, BC: Caitlin Press, 2011.

THESES AND DISSERTATIONS

Boucher, Gerald R. "The 1901 Rossland Miners' Strike: The Western Federation of Miners Responds to Industrial Capitalism." Master's thesis, University of Victoria, 1986.

Cottingham, Mollie E. "A History of the West Kootenay District in British Columbia." Master's thesis, University of British Columbia, 1947.

Meyer, Ronald Howard. "The Evolution of Railways in the Kootenays." Master's thesis, University of British Columbia, 1970.

Roth, David Michael. "A Union on the Hill." Master's thesis, Simon Fraser University, 1991.

OTHER SOURCES

"100 Years of Trail History: A Century of Trail's Top News Stories," published by the *Trail Daily Times*, December 12, 2000.

"Ancient Order of United Workman," *Encyclopedia of Arkansas*, Little Rock, AR, https://encyclopediaofarkansas.net/entries/ancient-order-of-united-workmen-2160/.

Blakemore, William. "Sect of Doukhobors." *Report of Royal Commission on Matters Relating to the Sect of Doukhobors in the Province of British Columbia*. Victoria: King's Printer, 1913.

Bowles, Paul. *A History in Print*, a booklet commemorating the seventy-fifth anniversary of Hall Printing, published by the Hall Printing Company, April 1995.

Dictionary of Unitarian and Universalist Biography, General Assembly of Unitarian and Free Christian Churches, website of the Unitarian Universalist History & Heritage Society, https://uudb.org/articles/richardlloydjones.html.

Griggs, Taylor. "Requiem for a Newspaper," *Eugene Weekly*, January 17, 2019.

A History of Canadian Journalism, edited by a committee of the Canadian Press Association. Toronto: Canadian Press Association, 1908.

Kütne Reader. https://gregnesteroff.wixsite.com/kutnereader.

"Leadville History." *Western Mining History*, 2020, https://westernmininghistory. com/towns/colorado/leadville/.

"Nurse Mildred Neilson," *Trail Historical Society Newsletter*, October 2005, 4.

Shearer, Ron. "Eber Clark Smith, Biographical Notes, Version 6," a draft manuscript, June 2018. Author's copy.

Storm Lake, a weekly newspaper documentary, PBS Independent Lens, Premier November 15, 2021, Directors Jerry Risius and Beth Levinson

"The Story of the Consolidated Mining and Smelting Company of Canada Ltd.," printed by the *Trail Daily Times*, 1937.

Thompson, W.F. "Commercial History of Trail, Third Special Number," *Trail Creek News*, March 1, 1897.

The Washington Newspaper: A Publication Dedicated to the Study and Improvement of Journalism in Washington 8, no. 1 (October 1922). A publication of the University of Washington Department of Journalism and Washington Press Association.

Wilson, D.M. Crowsnest Highway: Southwestern Canada's Information Resource, www.crowsnest-highway.ca/.

INDEX

ABOUT THE AUTHOR

Ron Verzuh is a writer, historian and documentary filmmaker. His most recent book is *Smelter Wars: A Rebellious Red Trade Union Fights for Its Life in Wartime Western Canada* (University of Toronto Press, 2022). His work has been published in academic journals, magazines, newspapers and on websites. He grew up in the West Kootenay district of British Columbia where the events in this book took place. He has never been a printer's devil, although he once worked for a weekly newspaper in the Northwest Territories where he learned the basics of producing a newspaper. He is married and lives in Victoria. *Printer's Devils* is his fourth book. His other books include *Radical Rag: The Pioneer Labour Press in Canada* and *Underground Times: Canada's Flower-Child Revolutionaries*. He is the producer of the award-winning short film *Joe Hill's Secret Canadian Hideout* and *Codename Project 9*, the story of a small BC city's participation in the making of the atomic bomb. His work has appeared in academic journals, magazines, newspapers and on websites. He worked at the Trail smelter in the late 1960s and early 1970s, following his grandfather, father and his father's brothers. *Printer's Devils* is his personal journey of discovery into the local environment in which his family lived and worked.